W9-BXD-858

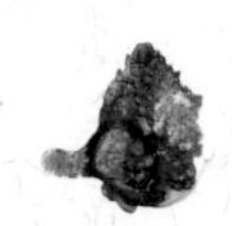

Praise for

A Government of Wolves

"John Whitehead is one of the most eloquent and knowledgeable defenders of liberty, and opponents of the growing American police state, writing today. I am pleased to recommend *A Government of Wolves* to anyone interested in learning how modern America increasingly resembles a dystopian science fiction film instead of a Constitutional Republic."

—Ron Paul

Twelve-term US Congressman and former presidential candidate

"I was privileged to have Duke Ellington as a mentor, who said of the jazz that was unsuccessfully banned in their countries by Stalin and Hitler: 'The music is so free that many people say it is the only unhampered expression of complete freedom yet produced in this country.' But only a basically free country could have produced back then such freedom of expression that has become so energizing a global presence. If we are to be again this free a nation, John Whitehead will have had a lot to do with our being able to swing again."

—Nat Hentoff

American historian and nationally syndicated columnist

"The loss of liberty doesn't begin with invading armies, but with creeping government that slowly and almost imperceptibly invades our privacy with cameras, drones, wiretaps and monitoring of email communication. We are told this is for our own good. In this book, John Whitehead sounds a warning about overreaching government we had better heed before the point of no return has been reached."

—Cal Thomas

Syndicated and *USA Today* Columnist/Fox News Contributor

"A masterfully documented chronicle of frightened citizen vassalage to a Leviathan state in a hope of a risk-free existence. An end to liberty is at hand."

—Bruce Fein

Associate Deputy Attorney General under President Reagan
Author of *American Empire Before the Fall*

"Cynical, brutal, dehumanizing. Pervasive, insidious, incremental. Any hope of getting out of this prison we've found ourselves in and in the service of—Wake up! The paramilitary junta is breaking down your door! Your Miranda rights? Where have you been? They don't need no stinking badges! Get out of the way—it's your new police state in action. We're about to be herded—digitally, of course—into some nightmarish gulag that we can't even see because it's crept up on us incrementally like a toxic fog under the insidious guise of national security and other mendacious Newspeak. How did we become the prey of capitalistic jackals, ruthless corporations and power-intoxicated lackeys of the one percent terraraptors? Where is Thomas Paine now that we need him? He's here just in the nick of time in the person of John Whitehead, an uncompromising debunker of lies, rhetoric mongers, rights-shredders and the criminal acts of our shameless, double-crossing government. Drop everything and read *A Government of Wolves* before it's too late! I loved and was horrified by this disturbing and courageous book."

—David Dalton

New York Times best-selling author
and a founding editor of *Rolling Stone Magazine*

A GOVERNMENT OF WOLVES

A GOVERNMENT OF WOLVES

THE EMERGING AMERICAN POLICE STATE

JOHN W. WHITEHEAD

SelectBooks, Inc.
New York

This edition published by SelectBooks, Inc.
For information address SelectBooks, Inc., New York, New York.

First Edition

ISBN 978-1-59079-975-8

Library of Congress Cataloging-in-Publication Data
Whitehead, John W., 1946-
A government of wolves : the emerging American police state / John W. Whitehead.
pages cm
Includes bibliographical references and index.
ISBN 978-1-59079-975-8 (hardcover : alk. paper)
1. Civil rights--United States. 2. United States--Politics and government. 3. Police power--United States. 4. Constitutional law--United States. I. Title.
JC599.U5W5245 2013
323.4'90973--dc23
2013006480

Cover art and illustrations by Christopher Combs
Interior book design and production by Janice Benight

Manufactured in the United States of America
10 9 8 7 6 5 4 3 2 1

For Nisha Whitehead, my inspiration

"A nation of sheep will beget
a government of wolves."

★

—EDWARD R. MURROW
CBS BROADCAST JOURNALIST
1908–1965

CONTENTS

Introduction

By Nat Hentoff

If James Madison or Thomas Jefferson were brought back to life, they would not recognize this country.

We have been through some troubling times before in our nation's history. There were the Alien and Sedition Acts of 1798 when newspaper editors, civilians—who criticized the government—were placed in jail. Abraham Lincoln suspended habeas corpus during the Civil War. He even arrested members of the Maryland legislature and all kinds of people around the country who objected to his policies.

We had the Red Raids in the early 1920s that started off J. Edgar Hoover's career in which hundreds of people were arrested, some of them deported without any due process at all. During the First World War, Woodrow Wilson not only practically suspended but also discarded the First Amendment. Then there were the Japanese internment camps of World War II, followed by Senator Joseph McCarthy's reign of terror, which was ended by fellow senators who realized that he had gone too far.

What we have now may be more insidious. Indeed, I believe we are in a worse state now than ever before in this country. With the surveillance state closing in on us, we are fighting to keep our country free from our own government.

Whereas we once operated under the Constitution, we are now, for example, under the USA Patriot Act, among other government dragnets, that permits pervasive electronic surveillance with minimal judicial review. The government listens in on our phone calls. It reads our mail. You have to be careful about what you do and say, and that is more dangerous than what was happening with McCarthy, since the technology the government now possesses is so much more insidious. We have no idea how much the government knows about average citizens. This is not the way the government born under the Declaration of Independence is supposed to operate.

Under the USA Patriot Act, FBI agents with a court order from a secret court, can enter people's homes and offices when they are not present, look around and take what they like. They can examine a hard drive and install in your computer the magic lantern, known less metaphorically as the keystroke jogger, which means they can record while you are not there everything you have typed on your computer, including stuff you have never sent. Then, under the USA Patriot Act, they can come back when you are not at home and download whatever information of yours they so desire. With advances in technology, they can even accomplish their clandestine objectives from a remote location.

All of this makes a prophet out of Supreme Court Justice Louis Brandeis, who, during the first wiretapping case back in 1928 *[Olmstead v. U.S.]*, said in his dissent: "Ways may some day be developed by which the government, without removing papers from secret drawers, can reproduce them in court, and by which it will be enabled to expose to a jury the most intimate occurrences of the home."

Government officials like to claim that everything they are doing is for security, to keep America safe in the so-called war against terrorism. What they are really effectuating is a weakening of why we are Americans. Unfortunately, a lot of Americans today have a very limited idea as to why they are Americans, let alone why we have a First Amendment or a Bill of Rights. People are becoming accustomed or conditioned to what's going on now with the raping of the Fourth Amendment, for example. One of the things that is taught so badly in our schools, from elementary and middle school through graduate school, including journalism schools, is the Constitution—our liberties and rights.

Too many Americans appear unconcerned about the loss of fundamental individual liberties—such as due process, the right to confront their government accusers in a courtroom, and the presumption of innocence—that are vital to being an American. Yet the reason we are vulnerable to being manipulated by the government out of fear is that most of us do not know and understand our liberties and how difficult it was to obtain them and how hard it is to keep them.

We are Americans because, under our Constitution, we are guaranteed freedom—which makes us the oldest living constitutional democracy. I think the greatest decision by the United States Supreme Court was rendered by Justice Robert Jackson in *West Virginia Board of Education v. Barnette* in the middle of the Second World War. When the children of Jehovah's Witnesses would not salute the flag, they were expelled and their parents threatened with jail for contributing to the delinquency of minors. Their religion forbade them to salute the flag, which was a graven image. Jackson said, and I am paraphrasing here, that in this country there is no orthodoxy of belief or of conscience whether political, religious or anything else. You can't say that about any other country in the world.

So that's why we are Americans: we are free to be ourselves; to believe in what we believe; to not interfere with other people's beliefs or conscience. Ronald Reagan was known for this phrase, but the first time I heard it was from William O. Douglas, who was a great Supreme Court justice in terms of liberty. Douglas used to say that the government has to be off our backs when it comes to our individual liberties: the freedom of speech, freedom of the press, and freedom to be who we are.

For more than sixty-five years as a reporter and an author (the latter beginning with *The First Freedom: The Tumultuous History of Free Speech in America*), my primary mission has been provided by James Madison: "Knowledge will forever govern ignorance; and a people who mean to be their own governors, must arm themselves with the power that knowledge gives." I have spent a lot of time studying our Founders and people like Samuel Adams. What Adams and the Sons of Liberty did in Boston was spread the word about the abuses of the British. They had Committees of Correspondence that got the word out to the colonies. We need Committees of Correspondence now.

Barring that, a good place to start is with John W. Whitehead, whose writing exemplifies George Orwell's freedom-saving advice: "If Liberty means anything at all, it means the right to tell people what they do not want to hear." If Orwell were still alive, he would be an avid reader of Whitehead's work.

As you'll find in this book, John is unequalled in revealing the removal of the Constitution's separation of powers by an executive branch that turns the Declaration of Independence upside down. At this stage of our history, with ever advancing government digital technology causing our Fourth Amendment right to privacy to hang by the thread,

I can say without exaggeration that no American guardian of the Constitution has done more continually—indeed, almost daily—than John W. Whitehead, through his writing and his legal work. Unlike any other Madisonian investigative reporter and analyst, he deploys his Rutherford Institute allied attorneys to defend—at no charge—Americans of all backgrounds whose personal constitutional liberties are being invaded by government.

The danger we now face is admittedly greater than any we have had before. If I were to judge what I do and write on the basis of optimism, I would probably go back to writing novels, but I figure you have to do what you feel you have to do and just keep hoping and trying to get people to understand why we are Americans and what we are fighting to preserve. That is why I keep writing. That is why John Whitehead continues to write and advocate for those whose rights are being trampled.

I was privileged to have Duke Ellington as a mentor, who said of the jazz that was unsuccessfully banned in their countries by Stalin and Hitler: "The music is so free that many people say it is the only unhampered expression of complete freedom yet produced in this country." But only a basically free country could have produced back then such freedom of expression that has become so energizing a global presence. If we are to be again this free a nation, John Whitehead will have had a lot to do with our being able to swing again.

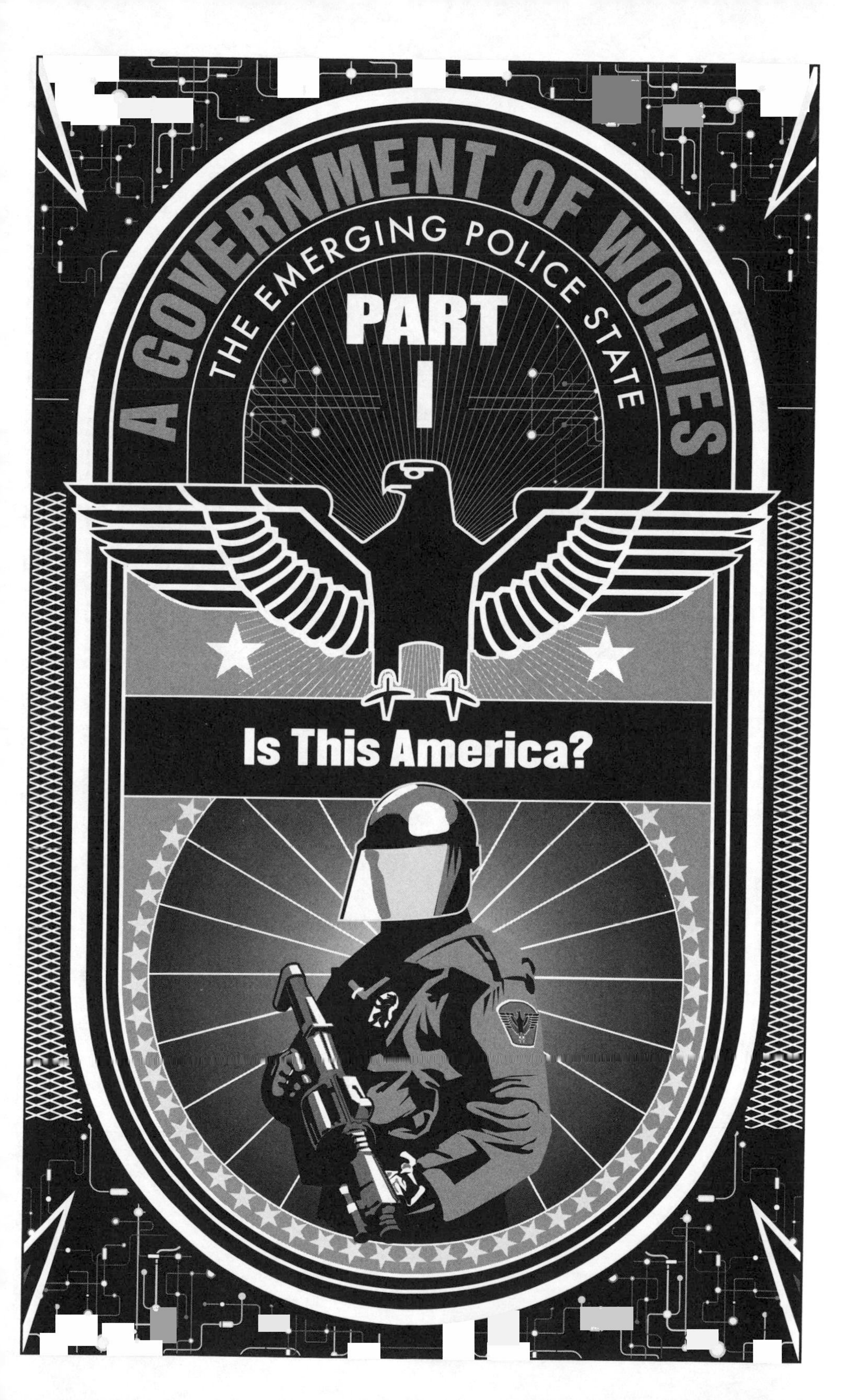
A GOVERNMENT OF WOLVES
THE EMERGING POLICE STATE
PART
I
Is This America?

"AS I LOOK AT AMERICA TODAY, I AM NOT AFRAID TO SAY THAT I AM AFRAID."[1]
—Bertram Gross,
former presidential advisor

CHAPTER 1

I Am Afraid

"America will never be destroyed from the outside. If we falter and lose our freedoms, it will be because we destroyed ourselves."[2]—ABRAHAM LINCOLN

Who can forget the television and Internet images of sinister-looking, black-garbed police officers in riot gear facing down unarmed groups of nonviolent protesters? Or the young family cowering in fear while a SWAT team crashes through their front door, killing their dog and holding them at gunpoint? Or the young Marine handcuffed, arrested, and held against his will in a hospital psych ward simply for posting song lyrics and antigovernment rhetoric on his Facebook page? Or the small farmers who had their farm raided and their equipment destroyed by armed agents of the Food and Drug Administration simply because they shared unpasteurized goat milk with friends? Or the father of six young children who was jailed for sixty days for holding religious studies in his home?

Occupy Protester Arrested by NYPD (AP Photo/John Minchillo)

While scenarios may vary, the police state response remains virtually the same—brutality, oppression, and intolerance.

The response by law enforcement to the 2011 Occupy protests in cities across America perfectly illustrates this state of affairs. Armed with pepper spray, rubber bullets, tear gas, and other instruments of compliance, the police waged war against the protesters from Oakland,

California to New York City. For example, police in Seattle pepper-sprayed an 84-year-old woman and a pregnant 19-year-old, among others, in their efforts to break up a non-violent rally.[3] The young woman allegedly suffered a miscarriage due to the pepper spray.[4] Police fired tear gas and flash grenades at peaceful protesters in Oakland in an effort to force them to disperse.[5]

Signs

With each passing day, America is inching further down the slippery slope toward a police state. And while police clashes with protesters, small farmers, and other so-called "law breakers" vividly illustrate the limits on our freedoms, the boundaries of a police state extend far beyond the actions of law enforcement. In fact, a police state is characterized by bureaucracy, secrecy, perpetual wars, a nation of suspects, militarization, surveillance, widespread police presence, and a citizenry with little recourse against police actions. In this regard, the signs of an emerging police state are all around us. In Orwellian fashion, it has infiltrated all aspects of our lives.

We were once a society that valued individual liberty and privacy. Increasingly, however, we have morphed into a culture that has quietly accepted surveillance in virtually every area of our lives—police and drug-sniffing dogs in our children's schools, national databases that track our finances and activities, sneak-and-peek searches of our homes by government agents without our knowledge or consent, and anti-terrorism laws that turn average Americans into suspected criminals. All the while, police officers dressed in black Darth Vader-like costumes have become armed militias instead of the civilian peacekeepers they were intended to be.

This is not to say that the police are inherently "bad" or "evil." However, in enforcing policies that both injure citizens and undermine freedom, the police have become part of the bureaucratic machine that neither respects citizen dignity nor freedom. Operating relatively autonomously, this machine simply moves forward in conveyor-belt fashion, utilizing the police and other government agents to establish control and dominance over the citizenry.

Gradually, but with increasing momentum, a police/surveillance state has been erected around us. This is reflected in the government's single-minded quest to acquire ever-greater powers along with the fusion of the police and the courts and the extent to which our elected representatives have sold us out to the highest bidders—namely the corporate state and military industrial complex. Even a casual glance at the daily news headlines provides a chilling glimpse of how much the snare enclosing us has tightened and how little recourse we really have.

Friendly Fascism

As anyone who has studied history knows, police states assume control with the mantra of "freedom, equality, and fraternity"—and maybe more apropos for us, "security and safety." The world, it must be remembered, has not been terrorized by despots advertising themselves as devils. As former presidential advisor Bertram Gross, who worked in both the Roosevelt and Truman administrations, explains in his book *Friendly Fascism*:

> I am afraid of those who proclaim that it can't happen here. In 1935 Sinclair Lewis wrote a popular novel in which a racist, anti-Semitic, flag-waving, army-backed demagogue wins the 1936 presidential election and proceeds to establish an Americanized version of Nazi Germany. The title, *It Can't Happen Here*, was a tongue-in-cheek warning that it might. But the "it" Lewis referred to is unlikely to happen again any place . . . Anyone looking for black shirts, mass parties, or men on horseback will miss the telltale clues of creeping fascism . . . In America, it would be supermodern and multi-ethnic—as American as Madison Avenue, executive luncheons, credit cards, and apple pie. It would be fascism with a smile. As a warning against its cosmetic façade, subtle manipulation, and velvet gloves, I call it friendly fascism. What scares me most is its subtle appeal.[6]

In this respect, what I am describing within these pages has not come about as an overnight change. Rather, the emerging American police state can be seen in subtle trends introduced by those in leadership—government, media, education—toward greater control and manipulation of the individual. With the advent of electronic media and the increasing computerization of American society, the mechanisms for manipulation have arrived. Wedded to the state and/or supportive of the statist apparatus, the corporate media (which now includes the Internet) is the one instrument more than any other that forms public opinion. In a society where the state and the media have merged, authoritarianism can and will be established even though in appearance the citizenry enjoys so-called democratic freedoms.

Years ago William L. Shirer, author of *The Rise and Fall of the Third Reich*, observed that America may be the first country in which fascism comes to power through democratic elections.[7] When and if fascism takes hold in America, the basic forms of government will remain. That, as Bertram Gross notes, is its "subtle appeal." It will appear friendly. The legislators will be in session. There will be elections and the news media will cover all the political trivia. "But consent of the governed will no longer apply," writes journalist Chris Floyd, because "actual control of the state will have passed to a small and privileged group who rule for the benefit of their wealthy peers and corporate patrons." Moreover:

> To be sure, there will be factional conflicts among the elite, and a degree of debate will be permitted; but no one outside the privileged circle will be allowed to influence state policy. Dissidents will be marginalized usually by the people themselves. Deprived of historical knowledge by a thoroughly impoverished educational system designed to produce complacent consumers, left ignorant of current events by a corporate media devoted solely to profit, many will internalize the force-fed values of the ruling elite, and act accordingly. There will be little need for overt methods of control.
>
> The rulers will act in secret, for reasons of national security, and the people will not be permitted to know what goes on in their name. Actions once unthinkable will be accepted as routine: government by executive fiat, state murder of enemies selected by the leader, undeclared wars, torture, mass detentions without charge, the looting of the national treasury, the creation of huge new security structures targeted at the populace. In time, this will be seen as normal, as the chill of autumn feels normal when summer is gone. It will all seem normal.[8]

Fear Propaganda

> It is always a simple matter to drag people along whether it is a democracy, or a fascist dictatorship, or a parliament, or a communist dictatorship. Voice or no voice, the people can always be brought to the bidding of the leaders. This is easy. All you have to do is tell them they are being attacked, and denounce the pacifists for lack of patriotism and exposing the country to danger. It works the same in every country.[9]

This was the testimony of Nazi Field Marshal Hermann Goering at the Nuremberg Trials. Goering, an expert on the propaganda of fear, knew very well how to cow and control a populace.

In like fashion, the transformation we as a society are undergoing is based on fear. In fact, one of the major forces currently shaping the psyche of the American people is fear. People are afraid of communists and socialists. People are afraid of crime. People are afraid of their neighbors. People are afraid of terrorism, and so on, ad infinitum.

Thus, as the rationale goes, to save our democracy (or republic, as it used to be called) we have to be secure and free of the onslaught of terrorism, the infiltration of immigrants, protesters, and other misfits (that is, other American citizens with whom we might disagree). That's why, we are told, we need a war on terrorism, a war on crime, a war on drugs, and other military euphemisms.

A Stop and Frisk, New York-Style
(Blend Images via AP Images)

Fear, and its perpetuation by the government, is the greatest weapon against freedom, and propaganda is the most effective tool for keeping the populace in check. Propaganda, an expertise of politicians, is in reality a fiction. But it is an effective fiction. And in an age of amusements and entertainment, the so-called masses of Americans, who often take what television's talking heads say as the gospel truth, have difficulty distinguishing between fiction and reality. As author Hannah Arendt recognized:

> The effectiveness of this kind of propaganda demonstrates one of the chief characteristics of modern masses. They do not believe in anything visible, in the reality of their own experience; they do not trust their eyes and ears but only their imaginations, which may be caught by anything that is at once universal and consistent in itself. What convinces masses are not facts, and not even invented facts, but only the consistency of the system of which they are presumably part. Repetition, somewhat overrated in importance because of the common belief in the masses' inferior capacity to grasp and remember, is important only because it convinces them of consistency in time.[10]

On the Road to a Police State

How did we allow ourselves to travel so far down the road to a police state?

American police forces are not supposed to be a branch of the military, nor are they meant to be private security forces for the reigning political faction. Instead, they should be an aggregation of the countless local police units, composed of citizens like you and me that exist for a sole purpose: to serve and protect the citizens of each and every American community.

In recent years, however, there has been an increasing militarization of the police. This has not occurred suddenly, in a single precinct. It cannot be traced back to a single leader or event—rather, the pattern is so subtle that most American citizens, distracted by entertainment and/or simply trying to make ends meet, are hardly even aware of it. Little by little, police authority has expanded, one weapon after another has been added to the police arsenal, and one exception after another has been made to the constitutional standards that have historically restrained police authority.

Already in some larger cities, the police have adopted the routine practice of stopping and frisking people who are merely walking down the street and where there is no evidence of wrongdoing (a practice that is sure to spread to smaller cities).[11] This is the mark of a police state where everyone is a suspect. Joseph Midgley of Picture the Homeless, a homeless advocacy group, explains the average experience of a person stopped and frisked:

> I have been stopped and frisked four times and each time I have been standing in public places. I've been questioned by the police and asked if I had anything illegal on me. To which I replied, "no." My pockets were still searched.

> Nothing illegal was found. I was never charged. Never even given a ticket on all four occasions. This form of discriminatory policing is outrageous and it must stop. Not tomorrow, not next year, but today.[12]

The Loss of Bodily Integrity

As journalist Herman Schwartz recognizes, "The Fourth Amendment was designed to stand between us and arbitrary governmental authority. For all practical purposes, that shield has been shattered, leaving our liberty and personal integrity subject to the whim of every cop on the beat, trooper on the highway and jail official."[13] Nowhere is this loss of Fourth Amendment protections more evident than in the practice of roadside police stops, which have devolved into government-sanctioned exercises in humiliation and degradation with a complete disregard for privacy and human dignity.

Consider, for example, what happened to 38-year-old Angel Dobbs and her 24-year-old niece, Ashley, who were pulled over by a Texas state trooper on July 13, 2012, allegedly for flicking cigarette butts out of the car window.[14] First, the trooper berated the women for littering on the highway. Then, insisting that he smelled marijuana, he proceeded to interrogate them and search the car. Despite the fact that both women denied smoking or possessing any marijuana, the police officer then called in a female trooper, who carried out a roadside cavity search, sticking her fingers into the older woman's anus and vagina, then performing the same procedure on the younger woman, wearing the same pair of gloves.[15] No marijuana was found.

Leila Tarantino was allegedly subjected to two roadside strip searches in plain view of passing traffic during a routine traffic stop, while her two children—ages one and four—waited inside her car. During the second strip search, presumably in an effort to ferret out drugs, a female officer "forcibly removed" a tampon from Tarantino's body. No contraband or anything illegal was found.[16]

Meanwhile, four Milwaukee police officers have been charged with carrying out rectal searches of suspects on the street and in police district stations over the course of several years. One of the officers is accused of conducting searches of men's anal and scrotal areas, often inserting his fingers into their rectums and leaving some of his victims with bleeding rectums.[17] Half-way across the country, the city of Oakland, California, has agreed to pay $4.6 million to 39 men who had their pants pulled down by police on city streets between 2002 and 2009.[18]

And then there's the increasingly popular practice of doing blood draws at DUI checkpoints, where drivers who refuse a breathalyzer test find themselves subjected to forcible blood extractions to test for alcohol levels. Police in Tangipahoa Parish, Louisiana, actually had a registered nurse and an assistant district attorney on hand "to help streamline the 'blood draw' warrants and collect blood samples from suspected impaired drivers" at one exercise in holiday drunk driving enforcement.[19]

It must be remembered that the Fourth Amendment to the U.S. Constitution was intended to protect the citizenry from being subjected to "unreasonable searches and seizures" by government agents. While the literal purpose of the amendment is to protect our property and our bodies from unwarranted government intrusion, the moral intention behind it is to protect our human dignity. Unfortunately, the rights supposedly guaranteed by the Fourth Amendment have been steadily eroded over the past few decades. Court rulings justifying invasive strip searches as well as Americans' continued deference to the dictates of achieving total security have left us literally stranded on the side of the road, grasping for dignity.

Emerging Technology

As utterly distasteful as stop-and-frisks and roadside strip searches may be, soon there will be no need for the police to physically stop and search Americans. Technology now makes it possible for the police to scan passersby in order to detect the contents of their pockets, purses, briefcases, and see through their clothing. In fact, thanks to the federal government's willingness to share its surplus of military weapons with law enforcement, local police agencies now have a veritable arsenal of firepower and surveillance gadgets to inflict on the American people.

For example, local police agencies are now making use of the same drone technology employed by the military to bomb and spy on people in Afghanistan, Iraq, Pakistan, Iran, Somalia, and Yemen; only this time, these drones are being used to spy on American citizens. These aerial drones, some as small as insects, can stealthily spy on unsuspecting citizens without making their presence known.

Another military weapon that has been created in partnership with domestic police agencies is Terahertz Imaging Detection, which allows police officers to see through the clothing of citizens on the street, thus

Caution: Police State (CS Muncy)

treating all passersby as if they were suspects.[20] This portable scanning technology functions by detecting the radiation emitted by a human body and highlighting any objects—such as a gun, a pocketknife, nail clippers, or any other paraphernalia in one's possession—which block that radiation.[21]

Full-body scanners, which perform virtual strip-searches of Americans traveling by plane, have gone mobile, with roving police vans that peer into vehicles and buildings alike—including homes.[22] Nowadays, police drive through parking lots, scanning the license plates of parked cars and filing the information into police databases. Even if a car isn't tied to a crime, the time that a car was in a certain location is uploaded to a police database for future reference.[23] In other words, the police can track you wherever you go—even if the places you visit are very intimate and private.

Police are also using mobile fingerprint identification scanners which instantly pull up the biographical information of those who are compelled to put their finger on it.[24] Eventually, virtually all Americans will be going through this process—a process that was once only used for criminal suspects.

Have We Become a Government of Wolves?

Whereas we once abided by a rule of law—the U.S. Constitution—which guarded our freedoms and shielded us from government abuses, we have entered a phase in our nation's life where the government largely operates above the law, while the law has become little more than another tool for compliance and control.

CHAPTER 2

Who Will Protect Us From Our Government?

"The trouble with government as it is, is that it doesn't represent the people. It controls them."[25]

—JOHN LENNON

Since the early days of the American republic, we have operated under the principle that no one is above the law. As Thomas Paine observed in 1776 in *Common Sense*, "in America, the law is king. For as in absolute governments the King is law, so in free countries the law ought to be king; and there ought to be no other."[26] Several years later, John Adams, seeking to reinforce this important principle, declared in the Massachusetts Constitution that they were seeking to establish "a government of laws and not of men."[27]

Prisoner at Abu Ghraib
(AP Photo, File)

The history of our nation over the past two hundred years has been the history of a people engaged in a constant struggle to maintain that tenuous balance between the rule of law—in our case, the United States Constitution—and the government leaders entrusted with protecting it, upholding it, and abiding by it. At various junctures, such as during the McCarthy era, when that necessary balance has been thrown off by overreaching governmental bodies or overly ambitious individuals, we have found ourselves faced with a crisis of constitutional proportions. Each time, we have taken the painful steps needed to restore our constitutional equilibrium.

Now, once again, we find ourselves in a state of crisis, skating dangerously close to becoming a nation ruled not by laws but by men—and fallible, imperfect men at that. Yet this latest crisis did not happen overnight. Its seeds were sown in the wake of the 9/11 terror attacks, when fear-addled Americans started selling their freedoms cheaply, bit by bit, for the phantom promises of security. From the hideous torture at CIA black site prisons, extraordinary renditions of Abu Ghraib abuses, and TSA body scanners to warrantless wiretaps and the USA Patriot Act, Americans have failed to be outraged by the government's repeated violations of the rule of law. In this way, as the so-called "war on terror" has unfolded beyond our wildest imaginings—from the barbaric treatment of foreign detainees at American-run prisons to the technological arsenal being used by the U.S. government to monitor and control its citizens—our rights have taken a meteoric nosedive in inverse proportion to the government's rapidly expanding powers.

USA Patriot Act

Those who founded this country knew quite well that every citizen must remain vigilant or freedom would be lost. This is the true nature of a patriot: one who sounds the alarm when freedom—in our case, the rights protected by the Constitution—comes under attack. If, on the other hand, people become fearful and sheep-like, it gives rise to a government of wolves. This is what we are faced with today, and it is epitomized by the USA Patriot Act.

Although the Fourth Amendment's protections against unreasonable searches and seizures go far beyond an actual police search of our homes, the passage of the Orwellian-named USA Patriot Act in 2001 opened the door to other kinds of invasions, especially unwarranted electronic intrusions into our most personal and private transactions, including phone, mail, computer, and medical records.

The Patriot Act drove a stake through the heart of the Bill of Rights, violating at least six of the Constitution's ten original amendments, namely, the First, Fourth, Fifth, Sixth, Seventh, and Eighth Amendments—and possibly the Thirteenth and Fourteenth Amendments, as well. The Patriot Act also redefined terrorism so broadly that anyone desiring to engage in non-terrorist political activities such as protest marches, demonstrations, and civil disobedience—all historically protected First Amendment expressive activities which are now considered potential terrorist acts—is thereby rendered a *suspect* of the police state.

The Patriot Act justified much broader domestic surveillance, the logic being that if government agents knew more about each American, they could distinguish the terrorists from law-abiding citizens—no doubt an earnest impulse shared by small-town police and federal agents alike. According to Washington Post reporter Robert O'Harrow, this was a fantasy that had "been brewing in the law enforcement world for a long time."[28] And 9/11 provided the government with the perfect excuse for conducting far-reaching surveillance and collecting mountains of information on even the most law-abiding citizen.

Suddenly, for the first time in American history, federal agents and police officers are authorized to conduct black bag "sneak-and-peek" searches of homes and offices and confiscate your personal property without first notifying you of their intent or their presence. FBI agents can come to your place of employment, demand your personal records, and question your supervisors and fellow employees, all without notifying you. And the government can access your medical records, school records, and practically every personal record about you, and secretly demand to see records of books or magazines you've checked out in any public library and Internet sites you've visited (at least 545 libraries received such demands in the first year following passage of the Patriot Act).[29]

In the name of fighting terrorism, government officials are now permitted, among other things, to monitor religious and political institutions with no suspicion of criminal wrongdoing; prosecute librarians or keepers of any other records if they told anyone that the government had subpoenaed information related to a terror investigation; monitor conversations between attorneys and clients, search and seize Americans' papers and effects without showing probable cause; and jail Americans indefinitely without a trial.

The federal government also made liberal use of its new powers, especially through the use (and abuse) of the nefarious national security letters, which allow the FBI to demand personal customer records from Internet Service Providers, banks, and other financial institutions and credit companies at the mere say-so of the government agent in charge of a local FBI office and without prior court approval.

Despite the fact that more than four hundred local, county, and state resolutions were passed in opposition to the Patriot Act, Congress, at the urging of the Bush Administration, renewed several of the Patriot Act's more controversial provisions, which were set to expire at sunset on December 31, 2005. The USA Patriot Improvement and Reauthorization Act of 2005[30] took government intrusion into the lives of average Americans to a whole new level, allowing the FBI to write and approve its own search orders—what critics termed "carte blanche for a fishing expedition"— without having to show any evidence that the citizens under investigation may be involved in criminal activities.

Barack Obama proved to be little better than George Bush in terms of civil liberties. For example, on February 27, 2010, just a little over a year after taking office, President Obama quietly signed into law three controversial provisions of the Patriot Act that were set to expire. The "roving wiretaps" provision allows the FBI to wiretap phones in multiple homes without having to provide the target's name or even phone number—merely the possibility that a suspect "might" use the phone is enough to justify the wiretap. The "lone wolf" provision allows intelligence gathering on people not suspected of being part of a foreign government or known terrorist organization. And Section 215 of the Patriot Act allows court-approved seizure of records and property in so-called antiterrorism operations.

The National Defense Authorization Act

America's so-called war on terror, which it has relentlessly pursued since 9/11, has forever altered the political and legal landscape of our country. It has chipped away at our freedoms, unraveled our Constitution and transformed our nation into a battlefield. Justifying his support of legislation allowing for the indefinite detention of Americans, Senator Lindsey Graham proclaimed, "Is the homeland the battlefield? You better believe it is the battlefield."[31]

America has indeed become the new battleground in the war on terror. In light of this, you can rest assured that there will be no restoration of the civil liberties jeopardized by the USA Patriot Act and other equally subversive legislation. Instead, those in power will continue to sanction ongoing violations of our rights, relying on bureaucratic legalese to sidestep any concerns that might be raised.

The National Defense Authorization Act of 2012 (NDAA), which was passed by the Senate with a vote of 93-7,[32] is a perfect example of this. Contained within this massive defense bill is a provision crafted by Democrat Charles Levin and Republican John McCain and signed into law by President Obama which mandates that anyone "suspected" of terrorism against the United States—which can be very loosely defined—be held in military custody indefinitely and without trial. This provision extends to American citizens on American territory.[33] The bill also revokes the citizenship of any person accused of terrorism.[34]

Taken collectively, the provisions within the NDAA completely circumvent the rule of law and the constitutional rights of American citizens, reorienting our legal landscape in such a way as to ensure that martial law, rather than the rule of law—our U.S. Constitution—becomes the map by which we navigate life in the United States. In short, if legal challenges are unsuccessful,[35] this law will not only ensure that we remain in a perpetual state of war—with this being a war against the American people—but it will also empower the president to unilaterally impose martial law in the United States at any time of his choosing.[36]

A Return to Pre-Revolutionary Days?

Journalist Radley Balko notes, "There's an old Cold War saying commonly attributed to Winston Churchill . . . that goes, 'Democracy means that when there's a knock on the door at 3 a.m., it's probably the milkman.' The idea is that free societies don't send armed government agents dressed in black to raid the private homes of citizens for political crimes."[37] Unfortunately, our once "free" society and the protections that accompany it have been steadily eroded by legislation and court rulings that render the individual completely defenseless against the encroachments of the state. In a very real sense, we truly are back to where we started in those pre-Revolutionary War days, seemingly having learned next to nothing from those early days of tyranny at the hands of the British crown.

We are once again being subjected to broad search warrants, with the police and other government agents trespassing on property without regard for the rights of owners and the blurring of all distinctions—for purposes of searches and seizures—between what is private and public property. Once again, the courts and state legislatures are seen to favor the interests of government officials, especially law enforcement, even at the expense of civil liberties. Indeed, there is no true justice in a court system where the judge, the prosecutor, and the police form a triad against the accused. And once again, Americans are finding themselves underrepresented, overtaxed, and forced at gunpoint, practically to dance to the government's tune.

The similarities to pre-Revolutionary America are startling. For example, since the time of the nation's founding, Americans have taken to heart eighteenth century British Prime Minister William Pitt's sentiment that "every man's home is his castle."[38] However, the right to the sovereignty of one's personal property was sorely challenged by the Quartering Act of 1774, a policy that forced the colonists to provide accommodations for British troops in their homes at night, while these same soldiers terrorized their towns by day. This constant invasion of the colonists' privacy by the British soldiers was condemned in the Declaration of Independence and was ultimately outlawed by the Third Amendment.

People often question whether the Third Amendment, which places our homes off limits to the military, is still germane to our lives today. While Americans no longer have to fear the quartering of troops in their homes, as the cases detailed below illustrate, the safeguards keeping the government out of our homes are fast eroding, especially in an age where military and paramilitary police units such as SWAT teams are treated as superior to the average citizen—all with the approval of the court systems.

For example, in May 2011 the Indiana Supreme Court broadly ruled in *Barnes v. State* that people don't have the right to resist police officers who enter their homes illegally.[39] The court rationalized their 3-2 ruling legitimizing any unlawful police entry into a home as a "public policy" decision. On its face, the case itself is relatively straightforward: an Indiana woman called 911 during an argument with her husband. When the police arrived, the man blocked and then shoved an officer who tried to enter his home without a warrant. Despite the fact that the wife told police her husband hadn't hit her, the man was shocked with a stun gun and arrested. Insisting that it would be safer for all concerned to let police proceed even with an *illegal* action and sort it out later in court with a civil lawsuit, the court held that residents can't resist police who enter their home—whatever the reason. The problem, of course, is that anything short of complete and utter acquiescence and compliance constitutes resistance. Thus, even the supposedly protected act of free speech—a simple "Wait, this is my home. What's this about?"—constitutes resistance.

Added to that, the U.S. Supreme Court effectively decimated the Fourth Amendment in an 8-1 ruling in *Kentucky v. King*[40] by giving police more leeway to smash down doors of homes or apartments *without* a warrant when in search of illegal drugs, which they suspect might be destroyed if the Fourth Amendment requirement of a warrant were followed. In this particular case, police officers pursued a suspect they had seen engage in a parking lot drug deal into an apartment complex. Once there, the police allegedly followed the smell of burning marijuana to an apartment where, after knocking and announcing themselves, they promptly kicked the door in—allegedly on the pretext that evidence of drugs might be destroyed. Despite the fact that it turned out to be the *wrong* person, the *wrong* apartment, and a violation of every tenet that stands between us and a police state, the Supreme Court sanctioned the warrantless raid, saying that police had acted lawfully and that was all that mattered. Yet as Supreme Court Justice Ruth Bader Ginsburg, the lone voice of dissent among the justices, remarked, "How 'secure' do our homes remain if police, armed with no warrant, can pound on doors at will and . . . forcibly enter?"[41]

Courts of Justice?

The varied expressions of the government's growing power, which get more troubling by the day—the excessive use of tasers by police on non-threatening individuals, allowing drones to take to the skies domestically for purposes of surveillance and control of free speech protesters, the government's monitoring of emails and phone calls, just to name a few examples—are merely the outward manifestations of an inner, philosophical shift underway in how the government views not only the Constitution and the Bill of Rights, but "we the people," as well.

What this reflects is a movement away from governmental officials who are bound by the rule of law. If not checked, it will inevitably lead to a government that seeks total control over the populace through the imposition of its own self-serving laws—laws carried out by a police force hired to do the government's bidding and upheld by a judiciary more concerned with legalism, statism, corporatism, and elitism than with preserving the rights of the people.

Many who drove the engines of freedom in pre-Revolutionary America believed that the courts would provide a barrier for the people against governmental encroachments. Unfortunately, that is no longer the case. In fact, what used to be called courts of justice are in reality more like courts of order—that is, maintaining governmental power and authority, even at the expense of the Constitution and citizens' rights. For example, the U.S. Supreme Court's decisions in recent years, characterized most often by its abject deference to government authority, military, and corporate interests, have run the gamut from suppressing free speech activities and justifying suspicionless strip searches and warrantless home invasions to conferring constitutional rights on corporations, while denying them to citizens.

This outright regard for governmental authority at the expense of individual freedoms was most apparent in the Supreme Court's 2012 ruling in *Reichle v. Howards*.[42] In its unanimous decision, the Court actually held that immunity protections for law enforcement officials, specifically Secret Service agents, trump the free speech rights of Americans. In backing the Secret Service, the Supreme Court made it clear that when called on to strike a balance between the reach of government and the rights of Americans, government will win out virtually every time.

Similarly, the Supreme Court let stand a federal appeals court decision in *Brooks v. City of Seattle*, in which police officers who clearly used excessive force when they repeatedly tasered a pregnant woman during a routine traffic stop, were granted immunity from prosecution.[43] The appeals court judges rationalized their ruling by claiming that the officers could not have known beyond a reasonable doubt that their actions—tasering a pregnant woman, who was not a threat in any way, until she was unconscious—violated the Fourth Amendment.

In *Florence v. Burlington*, a divided Supreme Court actually prioritized making life easier for jail officials over the basic right of Americans to be free from dehumanizing strip searches. In its 5-4 ruling, the Court declared that any person who is arrested and processed at a jail house, regardless of the severity of his or her offense (that is, they can be guilty of nothing more than a minor traffic offense), can be subjected to a virtual strip search by police or jail officials, which involves exposing the genitals and the buttocks and could involve touching.[44]

Even the Supreme Court's 9-0 ruling in *U.S. v. Jones* took great pains not to limit the government's ability to monitor our activities.[45] The ruling, which declared that police must get a search warrant before using GPS technology to track criminal suspects, was written so narrowly as to only apply to "physical" intrusions. In an age where law-abiding citizens can easily be tracked using signals from our cell phones, this amounts to little protection at all. In fact, drone technology, cell phones, mobile body scanners and facial recognition software are just a few ways in which the government can conduct surveillance on the American people *without* physically invading their privacy.

Moreover, in its landmark 2010 decision in *Citizens United v. Federal Election Commission*, the Court favored corporate interests over democratic principles, granting unfettered free speech rights to corporations.[46] That case brings us full circle back to the *Reichle* case which, by placing government interests ahead of the free speech rights of the citizenry, reaffirmed the prevailing mindset that reigns supreme at the U.S. Supreme Court today—one that largely defers to government and corporations and, except in the most extreme of circumstances, refrains from limiting or even questioning the reach of government officials, whether it be the president, the police, or the military.

Tip of the Iceberg

These court rulings are merely the tip of the iceberg. However, what these assorted rulings and incidents add up to is a nation that is fast imploding, one that is losing sight of what freedom is really all about and, in the process, is transitioning from a republic governed by the people to a police state governed by the strong arm of the law. In such an environment, the law and the police agencies that enforce them become convenient tools to oppress those whom the government decides to target.

While these decisions on their own may be somewhat disturbing, the courts are not really introducing anything new into our lives—they are merely reflecting and reinforcing the reality of the age in which we live, and that is one in which the citizen is subordinate to the government and what the "state"—be it the police and/or local or federal agents—says goes.

Indeed, this paradigm of abject compliance to the state is also being taught by example in the schools through school lockdowns where police and drug-sniffing dogs enter the classroom, and zero tolerance policies that punish all offenses equally and result in young people being expelled for childish behavior. As a consequence, school districts are increasingly teaming up with law enforcement to create what some are calling the "schoolhouse to jailhouse track" by imposing a "double dose" of punishment: suspension or expulsion from school accompanied by an arrest by the police and a trip to juvenile court. In this way, having failed to learn much in the way of civic education while in school, young people find themselves in a learning environment where they have no true rights and government authorities have near total power over them and can violate their constitutional rights whenever they see fit.

This is true of the average citizen as well, who is helpless in the face of police equipped with an array of sophisticated weapons, both lethal and nonlethal. The increasing militarization of the police, the use of sophisticated weaponry against Americans, and the government's increasing tendency to employ military personnel domestically have taken a toll on more than just our freedoms. They have seeped into our subconscious awareness of life as we know it and colored our very understanding of freedom, justice, and democracy.

CHAPTER 3

On the Road to a Police State

"Totalitarianism differs essentially from other forms of political oppression known to us such as despotism, tyranny and dictatorship. Wherever it rose to power, it developed entirely new political institutions and destroyed all social, legal and political traditions of the country. No matter what the specifically national tradition or the particular spiritual source of its ideology, totalitarian government always transformed classes into masses, supplanted the party system, not by one-party dictatorships, but by a mass movement, shifted the center of power from the army to the police, and established a foreign policy openly directed toward world domination."[47]

—Author HANNAH ARENDT, *The Origins of Totalitarianism*

Movements toward police states are very subtle. As author Naomi Wolf recognizes, police state environments slowly seep into a populace's consciousness:

> It is a mistake to think that early in a fascist shift you see the profile of barbed wire against the sky. In the early days, things look normal on the surface; peasants were celebrating harvest festivals in Calabria in 1922; people were shopping and going to the movies in Berlin in 1931. Early on, as WH Auden put it, the horror is always elsewhere—while someone is being tortured, children are skating, ships are sailing: "dogs go on with their doggy life . . . How everything turns away / Quite leisurely from the disaster."
>
> As Americans turn away quite leisurely, keeping tuned to internet shopping and American Idol, the foundations of democracy are being fatally corroded. Something has changed profoundly that weakens us unprecedentedly: our democratic traditions, independent judiciary and free press do their work today in a context in which we are "at war" in a "long war"—a war without end, on a battlefield described as the globe, in a context that gives the president—without US citizens realising it yet—the power over US citizens of freedom or long solitary incarceration, on his say-so alone.[48]

Welcome to the American Gulag

When most people think of a police state, they think of mass arrests, detention camps, and storm troopers with automatic rifles standing on street corners. But with the rapid advances in technology and the development of a mass media aimed primarily at entertaining the public, such methods of coercion no longer need to be employed on a mass scale. In fact, technology now allows the government to erect an electronic concentration camp over entire populations and countries using much subtler and less jarring means than those employed by past regimes. Nevertheless, the results remain the same: total control.

Total control of whom, though? Despite the government's color-coded alerts and fear-inducing warnings about terrorists lurking among us, the individuals being targeted for government surveillance, control, and detention are, more often than not, Americans merely exercising their constitutional rights. To the government, however, these individuals are known by other labels—extremists, malcontents, activists, rule-breakers, disruptors of the peace, and misfits.

We would do well to remember that the original purpose of concentration camps, which have operated historically as gulags or detainment and/or detention centers, was for the prevention of crime (preventive detention) and re-education (that is, "rehabilitation") of dissidents or "social misfits." Such individuals, depending upon the definition, can mean anyone: peace activists, those involved in the Occupy movement, a Tea Party supporter, an "irritant" at a city council meeting, or grade-school children who engage in a food fight.

As Pulitzer Prize-winning author Anne Applebaum observes in *Gulag: A History*:

> The exile of prisoners to a distant place, where they can "pay their debt to society," make themselves useful, and not contaminate others with their ideas or their criminal acts, is a practice as old as civilization itself. The rulers of ancient Rome and Greece sent their dissidents off to distant colonies. Socrates chose death over the torment of exile from Athens. The poet Ovid was exiled to a fetid port on the Black Sea.[49]

The advent of psychiatry eliminated the need to exile political prisoners, allowing governments instead to declare such dissidents unfit for society. For example, government officials in the Cold War-era Soviet

Union often used psychiatric hospitals as prisons in order to isolate political prisoners from the rest of society, discredit their ideas, and break them physically and mentally[50] through the use of electric shocks, drugs, and various medical procedures. Insisting that "ideas about a struggle for truth and justice are formed by personalities with a paranoid structure," [51] the psychiatric community actually went so far as to provide the government with a diagnosis suitable for locking up such freedom-oriented activists.

In addition to declaring political dissidents mentally unsound, Russian officials also made use of an "administrative" process for dealing with individuals who were considered a bad influence on others or troublemakers. Author George Kennan describes a process in which:

> The obnoxious person may not be guilty of any crime . . . but if, in the opinion of the local authorities, his presence in a particular place is "prejudicial to public order" or "incompatible with public tranquility," he may be arrested without warrant, may be held from two weeks to two years in prison, and may then be removed by force to any other place within the limits of the empire and there be put under police surveillance for a period of from one to ten years. Administrative exile–which required no trial and no sentencing procedure–was an ideal punishment not only for troublemakers as such, but also for political opponents of the regime.[52]

Sound familiar? This age-old practice by which despotic regimes eliminate their critics or potential adversaries by declaring them mentally ill and locking them up in psychiatric wards for extended periods of time is a common practice in present-day China.[53] What is particularly unnerving, however, is that this practice of making individuals disappear is happening with increasing frequency in America.

Disappearing Citizens

Brandon Raub's case exposes the seedy underbelly of a governmental system that is targeting Americans—especially military veterans—for expressing their discontent over America's rapid transition to a police state. On Thursday, August 16, 2012, a swarm of local police, Secret Service, and FBI agents arrived at Raub's home, asking to speak with him about posts he had made on his Facebook page. These posts were made up of song lyrics, political opinions, and dialogue used in a political-thriller virtual card game. Among the posts cited as troublesome were lyrics to a song by the rap group Swollen Members.

After a brief conversation, and without providing any explanation, levying any charges against Raub, or reading him his rights, law enforcement officials then handcuffed Raub and transported him first to police headquarters, then to a medical center, where he was held against his will due to alleged concerns that his Facebook posts were "terrorist in nature." Outraged onlookers filmed the arrest and posted the footage to YouTube, where it quickly went viral, which may have helped prevent Raub from being successfully "disappeared" by the government. A subsequent hearing, reminiscent of the kangaroo courts of earlier days, sentenced the decorated Marine up to thirty days' confinement in a Veterans Administration psych ward.

Under so-called "civil commitment" laws in place in all fifty states, tens of thousands of similar arrests are taking place across the country, with Americans being made to "disappear" into mental institutions. So it was no surprise, then, that within days of Raub being seized and forcibly held in a VA psych ward, news reports started surfacing of other veterans having similar experiences. These incidents were merely the realization of various U.S. government initiatives dating back to 2009. One such initiative, Operation Vigilant Eagle, calls for surveillance of military veterans returning from Iraq and Afghanistan, characterizing them as extremists and potential domestic terrorists because they may be "disgruntled, disillusioned or suffering from the psychological effects of war."[54]

Right- and Left-Wing "Extremists"

Two reports from the Department of Homeland Security, one dubbed "Rightwing Extremism" and the other, "Leftwing Extremism," made a broad swipe at individuals and groups who engage in political activism. For example, the "Rightwing Extremism" report broadly defines as extremists those individuals and groups "that are mainly antigovernment, rejecting federal authority in favor of state or local authority, or rejecting government authority entirely."[55] Obviously, these tactics bode ill for anyone seen as opposing the government.

Although these initiatives caused an initial uproar when announced in 2009, they were quickly subsumed by the ever-shifting cacophony of the news media and its ten-day cycles. Yet while the American public may have forgotten about the government's plans to identify and disable anyone deemed a potential "threat," the government put its plan into action. Thus, what began as a blueprint under the Bush administration was used as an operation manual under the Obama administration to exile those who are challenging the government's authority.

An important point to consider, however, is that the government is not merely targeting individuals who are voicing their discontent—it is also locking up individuals *trained in military warfare* who are voicing feelings of discontent. Under the guise of mental health treatment and with the complicity of government psychiatrists and law enforcement officials, veterans are increasingly being portrayed as ticking time bombs in need of intervention.[56] In 2012, for instance, the Justice Department launched a pilot program aimed at training SWAT teams to deal with confrontations involving highly trained and often heavily armed combat veterans.[57]

As we saw with Brandon Raub, one tactic being used to deal with vocal critics of the government is through the use of civil commitment laws, which have been employed throughout American history to not only silence but cause dissidents to disappear. For example, in 2006, officials with the National Security Agency (NSA) attempted to label former employee Russ Tice, who was willing to testify in Congress about the NSA's warrantless wiretapping program, as "mentally unbalanced" based upon two psychiatric evaluations ordered by his superiors.[58] In 2009, NYPD Officer Adrian Schoolcraft had his home raided, and he was handcuffed to a gurney and taken into emergency custody for an alleged psychiatric episode. It was later discovered by way of an internal investigation that his superiors were retaliating against him for reporting police misconduct. Schoolcraft spent six days in the mental facility, and as a further indignity, was presented with a bill for $7,185 upon his release.[59]

The Electronic Concentration Camp

The farther we advance into the electronic concentration camp, the more the police, as well as the prisons, will be considered responsible for the identification and re-education (that is, "rehabilitation") of "social misfits"—a.k.a. dissidents, rabble-rousers, nonconformists, and extremists. By "police," I am referring to the entire spectrum of law

Line of Riot Police

enforcement and surveillance personnel from local police and state troopers to federal agents (the FBI and intelligence police that work locally through "fusion centers"), as well as the military and agents employed by private corporations who work in tandem with government-funded police.

In order to ferret out individuals who might potentially upset the status quo, police and other government agencies will have to focus more of their resources on preventive detention, which means viewing everyone as potential "suspects" and using surveillance technology to monitor their activities. This has already come to pass.

The end result, as author Hannah Arendt recognized, is that more and more innocent citizens will need to be taken into "protective custody" and "handled as a 'protective police measure,' that is, a measure that deprives people of the ability to act."[60] In today's world, such "protective custody" is technologically induced. Arendt, who survived a Nazi concentration camp and wrote the definitive work on totalitarianism, saw early on that the largest group of inmates in concentration camps were "people who had done nothing whatsoever that, either in their own consciousness or the consciousness of their tormentors, had any rational connection with their arrest."[61] In fact, the "ultimate goal . . . is to have the whole camp population composed of this category of innocent people."[62]

Moreover, the police primarily exist to protect and keep safe the "good" (or compliant) citizens who reside in the electronic concentration camp alongside the less savory elements. The point, however, is that *all* citizens are inhabitants of the electronic concentration camp. In such a society, where the citizens believe the zookeeper to be friendly and looking out for their best interests, there is really no need for overt, generalized tyranny of the masses.

Yet even in such a system, periodic and/or sporadic crackdowns and arbitrary arrests are necessary to ferret out the misfits (even the nonviolent ones), the majority of whom will be innocent. "The arbitrary arrest which chooses among innocent people destroys the validity of free consent," writes Arendt, "just as torture—as distinguished from death—destroys the possibility of opposition."[63] This is now being played out in the streets of some of the larger American cities where stop-and-frisk searches and racial profiling are common occurrences.

Logically, then, if a police state is to operate at optimum level, each and every citizen, even the completely innocent, must be kept track of—geographically, biologically, and economically—from cradle to grave. The police must know or be capable of finding out precisely what every citizen is up to at every moment. The resulting loss of privacy and blurring of any distinction between private and public life and thoughts are common denominators in societies that shift toward state authoritarianism. "The only person who is still a private individual in Germany," boasted Robert Ley, a member of the Nazi hierarchy, after several years of Nazi rule, "is somebody who is asleep."[64]

Indeed, the government is already preparing electronic dossiers on virtually every citizen. Take, for example, the National Security Agency (NSA). A clearinghouse and a depository for vast quantities of data, the NSA makes it possible for the government to keep track of what Americans say and do, from the trivial to the damning, whether it is private or public. Anything and everything you've ever said or done, especially electronically—such as phone calls, Facebook posts, Twitter tweets, Google searches, emails, bookstore and grocery purchases, bank statements, and commuter toll records—can now be tracked, collected, catalogued, analyzed, and placed in an electronic file by the NSA's super computers and teams of government agents. In this way, as former intelligence agent Jim

Bamford writes, the NSA "has transformed itself into the largest, most covert, and potentially most intrusive intelligence agency ever created. In the process—and for the first time since Watergate and the other scandals of the Nixon administration—the NSA has turned its surveillance apparatus on the United States and its citizens."[65]

Human Goldfish

We have to face facts. Mandated by advancing technology, a pervasive surveillance is here to stay. Undoubtedly, we have become human goldfish. Not knowing who is looking in, we have created an electronic concentration camp from which escape is less likely with each passing day, short of living in a cave.

The pressing issues we now face also raise other important philosophical and spiritual questions. What totalitarian ideologies aim at "is not the transformation of the outside world or the revolutionizing transmutation of society," writes Hannah Arendt, "but the transformation of human nature itself."[66] Thus, the questions we wrestle with are profound ones. Will the citizenry be able to limit the government's use of these invasive technologies, or will we be caught in an electronic nightmare from which there is no escape? Can human nature really be altered in such a way that people will forget the longing for freedom, dignity, integrity, and love (longings that often consumed those of past generations)? Can we forget that we are human? Can humanity be obliterated?

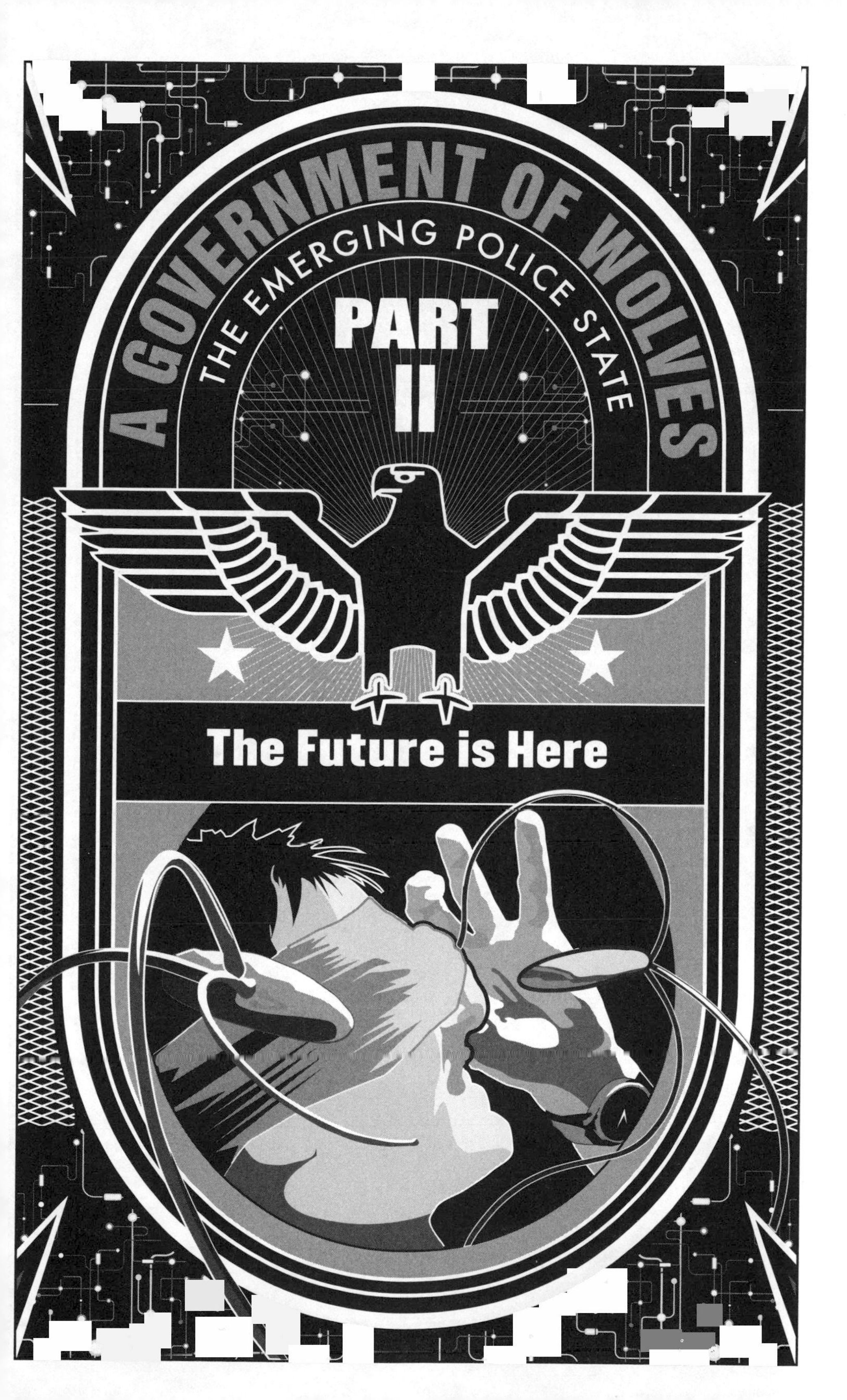
A GOVERNMENT OF WOLVES
THE EMERGING POLICE STATE
PART
II
The Future is Here

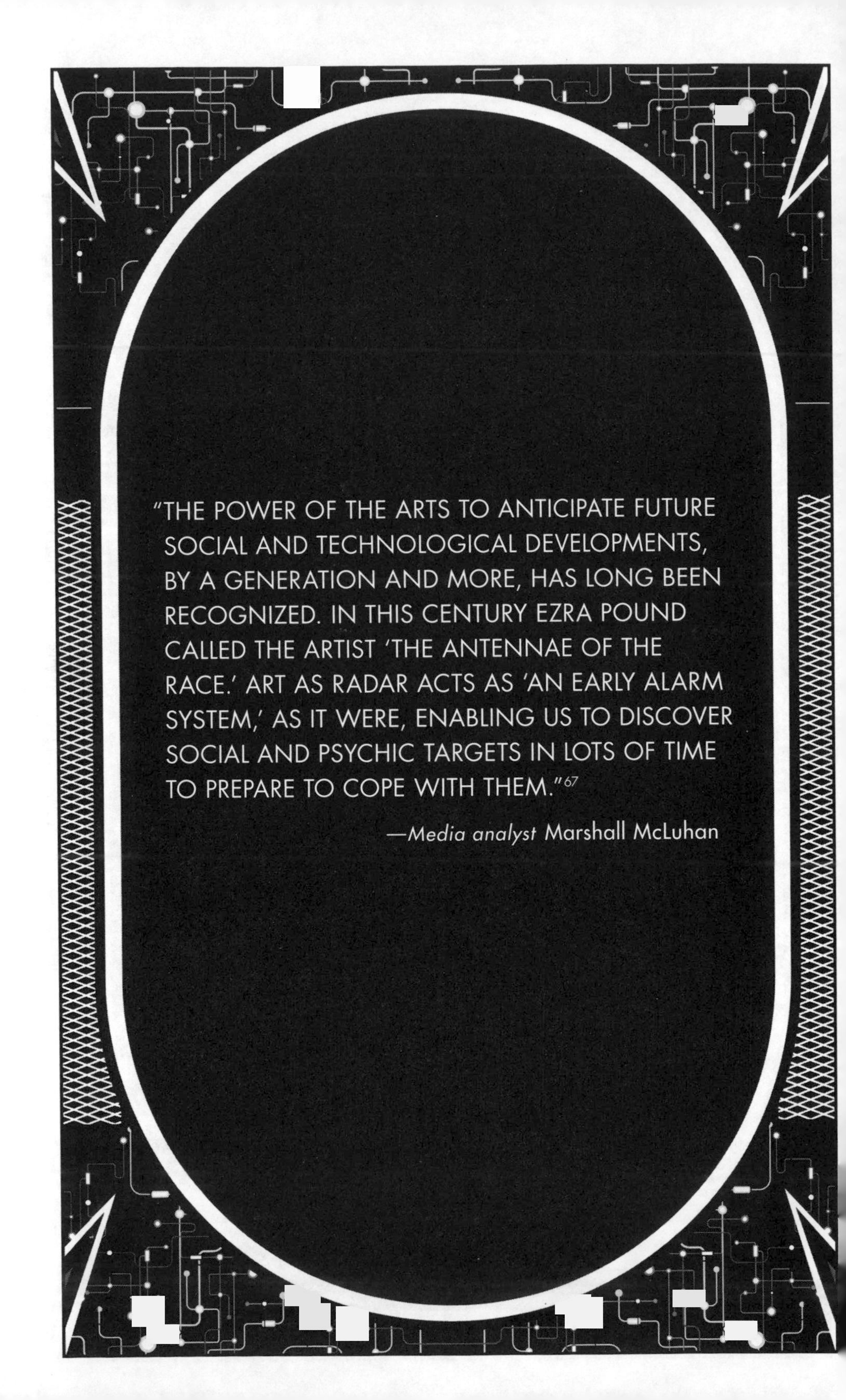

“THE POWER OF THE ARTS TO ANTICIPATE FUTURE SOCIAL AND TECHNOLOGICAL DEVELOPMENTS, BY A GENERATION AND MORE, HAS LONG BEEN RECOGNIZED. IN THIS CENTURY EZRA POUND CALLED THE ARTIST ‘THE ANTENNAE OF THE RACE.’ ART AS RADAR ACTS AS ‘AN EARLY ALARM SYSTEM,’ AS IT WERE, ENABLING US TO DISCOVER SOCIAL AND PSYCHIC TARGETS IN LOTS OF TIME TO PREPARE TO COPE WITH THEM.”[67]

—*Media analyst* Marshall McLuhan

CHAPTER 4

Fiction Has Become Reality

"The Internet is watching us now. If they want to. They can see what sites you visit. In the future, television will be watching us, and customizing itself to what it knows about us. The thrilling thing is, that will make us feel we're part of the medium. The scary thing is, we'll lose our right to privacy. An ad will appear in the air around us, talking directly to us."[68]

—film director STEVEN SPIELBERG

Art—whether in the form of movies, novels, or paintings—has an uncanny way of predicting the future. As the renowned media analyst Marshall McLuhan once recognized, art acts as an early warning system to enable us to cope with inevitable technological change.[69] "Inherent in the artist's creative inspiration is the process of subliminally sniffing out environmental change," observed McLuhan in a 1969 interview. "It's always been the artist who perceives the alterations in man caused by a new medium, who recognizes that the future is the present, and uses his work to prepare the ground for it."[70]

The emerging police/surveillance state that is currently being erected around us has been hinted at and prophesied in novels and movies for years, starting with George Orwell's increasingly relevant novel *1984*. However, it may be that filmmakers, the dominant visual artists of our time, have given and continue to give us the best representation of what we now face as a society. To this end, I shall use some of the best sci-fi films in recent decades as a jumping-off point for a discussion of the emerging police state.

Perhaps the most disturbing fact about these futuristic films is that the future is now. Fiction has become fact. Virtually everything predicted in the following films has come to pass or is about to become reality.

The question, of course, is whether we will accept a totally dehumanized existence or work to retain some semblance of our humanity. Will we actively resist the police state or passively cling to our technological devices and smile as Big Brother and Big Sister dictate the terms of our existence?

Future Films

Fahrenheit 451 (1966), adapted from Ray Bradbury's novel and directed by Francois Truffaut, depicts a futuristic society in which books are banned and firemen are called on to burn contraband books—451 Fahrenheit being the temperature at which books burn. Montag is a fireman who develops a conscience and begins to question the book burning. This film is an adept metaphor for our obsessively politically correct society where virtually everyone now precensors speech and even thoughts. Here, a brainwashed people addicted to television and drugs do little to resist governmental oppressors.

The plot of Stanley Kubrick's masterpiece *2001: A Space Odyssey* (1968), as based on an Arthur C. Clarke short story, revolves around a space voyage to Jupiter. The astronauts soon learn, however, that the fully automated spaceship is orchestrated by a computer system—known as HAL 9000—which has become an autonomous thinking being that will even murder to retain control. The idea is that at some point technology in the form of artificial intelligence will become autonomous, and that human beings will become mere appendages of technology. We are already seeing this come to pass with the massive intelligence systems tasked by the government with amassing information on average citizens and monitoring their communications and activities.

George Lucas' directorial debut, *THX 1138* (1970), presents a somber view of a dehumanized society totally controlled by a police state. The people are force-fed drugs to keep them passive, and they no longer have names, but instead are known only by letter/number combinations such as THX 1138. Any citizen who steps out of line is quickly brought into compliance by robotic police equipped with "pain prods"—electro-shock batons, or in modern terms, tasers.

Director Stanley Kubrick presents a future ruled by sadistic punk gangs and a chaotic government that sporadically cracks down on its citizens in *A Clockwork Orange* (1971). This film may accurately portray the future of Western society that grinds to a halt as oil supplies diminish, environmental crises increase, chaos rules, and the only thing left is brute force exercised by the police and other governmental agencies.

Soylent Green (1973) takes us to the year 2022, when the inhabitants of an overpopulated New York City depend on synthetic foods manufactured by the Soylent Corporation. A policeman investigating a murder discovers the grisly truth about what soylent green is really made of. The theme is chaos in a world ruled by ruthless corporations whose only goal is greed and profit.

Taking a Philip K. Dick novel as his guide, director Ridley Scott introduces us to a twenty-first century Los Angeles in *Blade Runner* (1982), where a world-weary cop tracks down a handful of renegade "replicants" (synthetically produced human slaves). Life is dominated by megacorporations, and people sleepwalk along rain-drenched streets. This is a world where human life is cheap, and where anyone can be exterminated at will by the police (or blade runners). This film questions what it means to be human in an inhuman world.

John Carpenter's bizarre sci-fi social satire action film *They Live* (1988) assumes the future has already arrived. John Nada is a homeless person who stumbles across a resistance movement and finds a pair of sunglasses that enables him to see the real world around him. What he discovers is a monochrome reality in a world controlled by ominous beings who bombard the citizens with subliminal messages such as "obey" and "conform." Carpenter makes an effective political point about the underclass (everyone except those in power, that is): we, the prisoners of our devices, are too busy sucking up the entertainment trivia beamed into our brains and attacking each other to start an effective resistance movement.

The Matrix (1999) centers on computer programmer Thomas A. Anderson, secretly a hacker known by the alias "Neo," who begins a relentless quest to learn the meaning of "The Matrix"—cryptic references that appear on his computer. Neo's search leads him to Morpheus who reveals the truth that the present reality is not what it seems and that Anderson is actually living in the future—2199. Humanity is at war against technology, which has taken the form of intelligent beings, and Neo is actually living in The Matrix, an illusionary world that appears to be set in the present in order to keep the humans docile and under control. Neo soon joins Morpheus and his cohorts in a rebellion against the machines that use SWAT team tactics to keep things under control.

Based on a short story by Philip K. Dick and directed by Steven Spielberg, the setting for *Minority Report* (2002) is 2054 where PreCrime, a specialized police unit, apprehends criminals before they can commit a crime. Captain Anderton (Tom Cruise) is the chief of the Washington, D.C. PreCrime force which uses future visions generated by "pre-cogs" (mutated humans with precognitive abilities) to stop murders. Soon Anderton becomes the focus of an investigation when the precogs predict he will commit a murder. This film poses the danger of technology operating autonomously.

V for Vendetta (2006) depicts a society ruled by a corrupt and totalitarian government where everything is run by an abusive secret police. A vigilante named V dons a mask and leads a rebellion against the state. The subtext here is that authoritarian regimes through repression create their own enemies—that is, terrorists—forcing government agents and terrorists into a recurring cycle of violence. And who is caught in the middle? The citizens, of course. This film has a cult following among various underground political groups such as Anonymous, whose members wear the same Guy Fawkes mask as that worn by V.

Children of Men (2006) transports us to 2027. The world is without hope since humankind has lost its ability to procreate. Civilization has descended into chaos and is held together by a military state and a government that attempts to keep its totalitarian stronghold on the population. Most governments have collapsed, leaving Great Britain as one of the few remaining intact societies. As a result, millions of refugees seek asylum only to be rounded up and detained by the police. Suicide is a viable option as a suicide kit called Quietus is promoted on billboards and on television and newspapers. But hope for a new day comes when a woman becomes inexplicably pregnant.

A dark political satire, *Land of the Blind* (2006) is based on several historical incidents in which tyrannical rulers were overthrown by new leaders who proved just as evil as their predecessors. Maximilian II is a demented fascist ruler of a troubled land named Everycountry who has two main interests: tormenting his underlings and running his country's movie industry. Citizens who are perceived as questioning the state are sent to "re-education camps" where the state's concept of reality is drummed into their heads. Joe, a prison guard, is emotionally moved by the prisoner and renowned author Thorne and eventually joins a coup to remove the sadistic Maximilian, replacing him with Thorne. Soon, however, Joe becomes the target of the new government and comes to realize that the new boss is the same as the old boss.

Much like *Land of the Blind, The Hunger Games* (2012) presents us with a dystopian future. Each year twenty-four young people, representing twelve districts in the nation of Panem (North America), are forced by the government to fight to the death while the nation watches on television. In this way, the Hunger Games, as they are called, provide entertainment for the masses while reminding the people that the state will tolerate no challenge to its power in the form of populist uprisings or mutiny. That all changes with the 74th Hunger Games when 16-year-old Katniss attempts the unthinkable—not only volunteering to take her younger sister's place in the Games but defying those in power at every turn. This film, and the best-selling book on which it was based, stands as a clear indictment of present-day America's fascination with reality TV and mindless entertainment, making no bones about its similarity to the Romans' use of "bread and circuses" (satiating the public's carnal appetites and entertaining them with mindless distraction) to control the masses.

The Future and You

These films and/or their themes portray a bleak, claustrophobic future where there is little or no freedom. However, as you wend your way through the following pages, keep in mind that although fiction is fast becoming reality, it can be altered by an active and alert citizenry. The future, so to speak, is up to you.

CHAPTER 5

Reality Check

"If, as it seems, we are in the process of becoming a totalitarian society ... the ethics most important for survival of the true, human individual would be: cheat, lie, evade, fake it, be elsewhere, forge documents, build improved electronic gadgets in your garage that'll outwit the gadgets used by the authorities."[71]

—PHILIP K. DICK, author of *Minority Report*

Seemingly taking its cue from science fiction, technology has moved so fast in the short time since *Minority Report* premiered in 2002 that what once seemed futuristic is now reality—no longer fiction. The question, of course, is how these technologies will be used by the powers-that-be. Will they be used benevolently or, as Philip K. Dick prophesied, to establish a totalitarian regime?

The following technological marvels from *Minority Report* were envisioned as light years away. As will be made clear, the future is now. For every sci-fi element portrayed in the film, there is now a corresponding gadget in our fast-evolving world that provides a reality check, of sorts.

Set in 2054, Steven Spielberg's futuristic film *Minority Report* (2002), based on a short story by Philip K. Dick, provides a roadmap into how various nascent technologies—iris scanners, massive databases, behavior prediction software, and others—employed today by the U.S. government and corporations alike will in the near future become part of the complex, interwoven cyber network aimed at tracking our movements, predicting our thoughts, and controlling our behavior (complete with dark-clad police SWAT teams for those who dare to step out of line).

The film is set against the backdrop of a city in which there has been no murder committed in six years. This is due in large part to the efforts of John Anderton, Chief of the Department of Pre-Crime in Washington,

D.C., which combines widespread surveillance with behavior prediction technologies to capture would-be criminals before they can do any damage—that is, to prevent crimes before they happen. Unfortunately for Anderton, the technology, which proves to be fallible, identifies him as the next would-be criminal and he flees. In the ensuing chase Anderton finds himself attempting to prove his innocence. He is also forced to take drastic measures in order to avoid capture in a surveillance state that uses biometric data and sophisticated computer networks to track its citizens.

Smart Cars

FICTION: In *Minority Report,* Anderton escapes from the police in a car whose movements are tracked through the use of onboard computers. The autonomous vehicles zip through the city, moving people to their destinations based upon simple voice commands.

REALITY CHECK: In 2009 the Los Angeles Police Department (LAPD) introduced a prototype "smart" police car, which will be made available to law enforcement agencies across the country. This smart cruiser is the most advanced of its kind, equipped with license plate cameras, computers, a GPS projectile launcher, and even a heat detector in the front grill to differentiate between people and animals. The license plate reader can scan and download as many as 8,000 license plates per shift. It saves the information it collects and can access the information instantaneously through the computer system installed in the car. If a stolen or wanted vehicle comes up in the scan, the license plate reader will automatically label the vehicle as a threat and a camera will take a colored picture of the vehicle and send the GPS coordinates of the vehicle to the police station.[72]

In addition to the high-tech license plate readers and cameras, the smart car is equipped with GPS-enabled projectiles, similar to a dart launcher and located near the front bumper of the vehicle. With the aid of a military-grade laser, a law enforcement agent can aim the GPS projectile at the target vehicle with tremendous precision. Once attached, the projectiles can track the target in real time for days.

Aiding the effort to track motorists, Congress is now requiring that all new cars come equipped with event data recorders which can record and transmit data from onboard computers. Similarly, insurance companies are offering discounts to drivers who agree to have tracking bugs installed.[73] As for autonomous vehicles, Google has created self-driving cars which have already surpassed 300,000 miles of road testing.[74] While manufacturers and consumers are still resistant to the technology, self-driving cars should be on American roads within the next twenty years, if not sooner.

Tracking You

FICTION: In *Minority Report,* police use holographic data screens, city-wide surveillance cameras, dimensional maps, and database feeds to monitor the movements of its citizens.

REALITY CHECK: Microsoft, in a partnership with New York City, has developed a crime-fighting system that "will allow police to quickly collate and visualise vast amounts of data from cameras, licence plate readers, 911 calls, police databases, and other sources. It will then display the information in real time, both visually and chronologically, allowing investigators to centralise information about crimes as they happen or are reported."[75]

FICTION: No matter where people go in the world of *Minority Report,* their biometric data precedes them, allowing corporations to tap into their government profiles and target them for advertising based on their highly individual characteristics. So fine-tuned is the process that it goes way beyond gender and lifestyle to mood detection, so that while Anderton flees through a subway station and then later a mall, the stores and billboards call out to him with advertising tuned to his desire to escape and high level of stress. Eventually, in an effort to outwit the identification scanners, Anderton opts for surgery to have his eyeballs replaced.

REALITY CHECK: Google is presently working on context-based advertising that will use environmental sensors in your cell phone, laptop, etc. to deliver "targeted ads tailored to fit with what you're seeing and hearing in the real world."[76] However, long before Google set their sights on context advertising, facial, and iris recognition machines were being employed, ostensibly to detect criminals, streamline security checkpoint processes, and facilitate everyday activities. For example, in preparing to introduce such technology into the United States, the American biometrics firm Global Rainmakers, Inc. (GRI) turned the city of Leon, Mexico into a virtual police state by installing iris scanners, which can scan the irises of thirty to fifty people per minute, throughout the city. As the business and technology magazine *Fast Company* reports:

> When these residents catch a train or bus, or take out money from an ATM, they will scan their irises, rather than swiping a metro or bank card. Police officers will monitor these scans and track the movements of watch-listed individuals. "Fraud, which is a $50 billion problem, will be completely eradicated," says [Jeff] Carter. Not even the "dead eyeballs" seen in *Minority Report* could trick the system, he says. "If you've been convicted of a crime, in essence, this will act as a digital scarlet letter. If you're a known shoplifter, for example, you won't be able to go into a store without being flagged. For others, boarding a plane will be impossible."[77]

The technology is already becoming more commonplace in the U.S. For example, police departments across the country have begun using the Mobile Offender Recognition and Information System, or MORIS, a physical iPhone add-on which allows police officers patrolling the streets to scan the irises and faces of suspected criminals and match them against government databases.[78] By 2014 the FBI plans to launch a nationwide database of iris scans for use by law enforcement agencies in their efforts to track criminals.[79]

Corporations, as well, are beginning to implement eye-tracking technology in their tablets, smartphones, and computers. The technology will allow companies to track which words and phrases users tend to re-read, hover on, or avoid, which can give insight into what they are thinking based upon their eye movements. Some police agencies are already working on developing predictive analysis of "blink rates, pupil dilation, and deception."[80]

Once you add facial recognition software to the mix, it won't be long before we have billboards capable of identifying passersby.[81] IBM has already started developing real-world advertisements that react to people based upon RFID chips embedded in their drivers' licenses and credit cards.[82]

Pre-Cogs

FICTION: In *Minority Report,* John Anderton's Pre-Crime division utilizes psychic mutant humans to predict when a crime will take place.

REALITY CHECK: The Department of Homeland Security is working on its Future Attribute Screening Technology, or FAST, which will utilize a number of personal factors such as "ethnicity, gender, breathing, and heart rate to 'detect cues indicative of mal-intent.'"[83] At least one field test of this program has occurred, somewhere in the northeast United States.

FICTION: In the film, a hacker accesses visions from the "precog" Agatha's mind and plays them back for John Anderton.

REALITY CHECK: While still in its infancy, technology that seeks to translate human thoughts into computer actions is slowly becoming a reality. Jack Gallant, a neuroscientist at UC Berkeley, has created software capable of translating viewers' thoughts into reconstructed visual images.[84] The Emotiv corporation is developing technology which will be capable of reading a person's thoughts and using them as inputs to operate machinery, like voice recognition but with brain signals.[85] Similar devices are being developed to translate thoughts into speech.[86]

Compliance Weapons

FICTION: In *Minority Report,* government agents use less-lethal methods—such as "sick sticks"—to subdue criminal suspects.

REALITY CHECK: A variety of less-lethal weapons have been developed and deployed in the years since *Minority Report* hit theaters. In 2007 the Department of Homeland Security granted a contract to Intelligent Optical Systems for an "LED Incapacitator," a flashlight-like device that emits a dazzling array of pulsating lights, incapacitating its target by causing nausea and vomiting.[87] A heat ray device from the Raytheon corporation, the "Assault Intervention Device" causes an unbearable burning sensation on its target's skin.[88] The Long Range Acoustic Device, which emits painful noises in order to disperse crowds, has been seen at the London Olympics[89] and G20 protests in Pittsburgh.

FICTION: In *Minority Report*, tiny robots shaped like spiders and equipped with lasers and scanners attempt to locate John Anderton using his stored biometric data.

REALITY CHECK: The Defense Advanced Research Projects Agency (DARPA), a division of the U.S. Department of Defense, is also working on turning insects into "cybugs" by utilizing and expanding upon the insects' natural abilities (e.g., using bees' olfactory abilities for bomb detection). Researchers hope to outfit June beetles with tiny backpacks complete with various detection devices, microphones, and cameras. These devices could be powered by the very energy produced by the bugs beating their wings, or the heat they give off while in flight.[90]

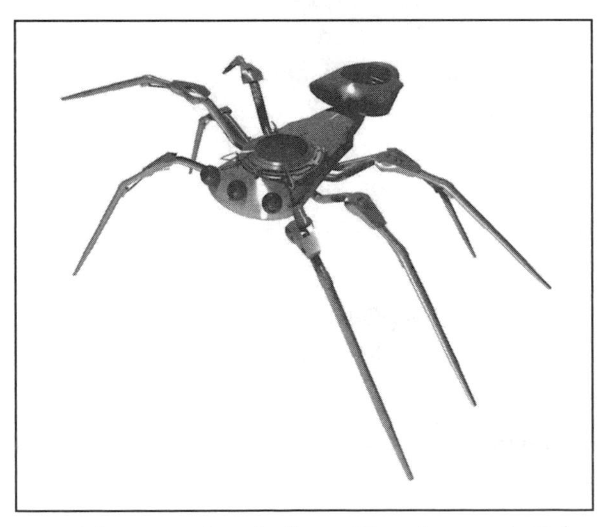

A Representation of a Future Micro Autonomous Robot
(BAE Systems)

Many models of small robotic fliers have been developed by the military since World War II. As far back as the 1970s the CIA was working on an "insectothopter," a gasoline-powered dragonfly-style aerial surveillance drone. A 2007 article in the *Washington Post* used reported sightings of dragonfly drones at protests in Washington, D.C. and New York as the springboard for an in-depth look at the government's ability to utilize robobug technology.[91] That same year, Japanese scientists at the International Symposium on Flying Insects and Robots unveiled radio-controlled drones resembling hawk moths, complete with four-inch wingspans.[92]

Gadgets

These are but a few of the technological devices now in the hands of those who control the corporate police state. Will we be able to evade these "gadgets" and those that will follow? Hide from them? Refuse them? If not, then the future we face is a rather frightening one, especially now that fiction, in essence, has become fact.

Remember, we all look like suspects to police state surveillance cameras and computers. Before long, we all may be mere extensions or appendages of the police state—all suspects in a world commandeered by "gadgets."

CHAPTER 6

Smiling at Big Brother

> "What Orwell feared were those who would ban books. What Huxley feared was that there would be no reason to ban a book, for there would be no one who wanted to read one. Orwell feared those who would deprive us of information. Huxley feared those who would give us so much that we would be reduced to passivity and egoism. Orwell feared we would become a captive audience. Huxley feared the truth would be drowned in a sea of irrelevance. Orwell feared that we would become a captive culture. Huxley feared we would become a trivial culture, preoccupied with some equivalent of the feelies, the orgy porgy, and the centrifugal bumblepuppy. As Huxley remarked in Brave New World Revisited, the civil libertarians and rationalists who are ever on the alert to oppose tyranny "failed to take into account man's almost infinite appetite for distractions." In *Brave New World*, they are controlled by inflicting pleasure. In short, Orwell feared that what we hate would ruin us. Huxley feared that what we love will ruin us."[93]
>
> —PROFESSOR NEIL POSTMAN

Long before there was Steven Spielberg's *Minority Report* or any of the other futuristic films and books prophesying a totalitarian future, there were George Orwell's *1984* and Aldous Huxley's *Brave New World*. Published decades ago as political satires, both novels have become nothing short of political prophecies—prophecies that are being fulfilled in our own times.

Both novels present differing blueprints for how police states come into power. In the Orwellian scenario, the culture conforms to a prison complete with terror, storm trooper raids, and detention camps. The Huxleyan scenario presents a culture so consumed with and distracted by entertainment (and/or technological gadgets) that the citizenry does not realize they occupy a prison until it is too late. Both scenarios rely on the education system to instill compliance in young minds.

Orwell or Huxley?

Visualizing the total loss of freedom in a world dominated by technology and its misuse, and the crushing inhumanity of an omniscient state, Orwell's *1984* portrays a global society of total control in which people are not allowed to have thoughts that in any way disagree with the corporate state. There is no personal freedom, and advanced technology has become the driving force behind a surveillance-driven society. Snitches and cameras are everywhere, and people are subject to the Thought Police, who arrest and "re-educate" anyone guilty of thought crimes. The government, or "Party," is headed by Big Brother, who appears on posters everywhere with the words: "Big Brother is watching you." Orwell's story revolves around Winston Smith, a doubter who turns to self-expression through his diary and then begins questioning the ways and methods of Big Brother before being "re-educated."

Huxley's *Brave New World* provides a different vision about how a totalitarian society arrives. It is one dominated by a consumer society driven by entertainment—thus, lessening the need for the coercion evident in Orwell's *1984*. As professor Neil Postman writes:

> What Huxley teaches is that in the age of advanced technology, spiritual devastation is more likely to come from an enemy with a smiling face than from one whose countenance exudes suspicion and hate. In the Huxleyan prophecy, Big Brother does not watch us, by his choice. We watch him, by ours. There is no need for wardens or gates or Ministries of Truth. When a population becomes distracted by trivia, when cultural life is redefined as a perpetual round of entertainments, when serious public conversation becomes a form of baby talk, when, in short, a people become an audience and their public business a vaudeville act, then a nation finds itself at risk; culture-death is a clear possibility.[94]

Television and the Internet (as it extends itself through cell phones, laptops, and tablets) are the new mediums that equip those who control society with an efficient program for change. Huxley believed, as

Postman writes, that we are in "a race between education and disaster, and he wrote continuously about the necessity of our understanding the politics and epistemology of media. For in the end, he was trying to tell us that what afflicted the people in *Brave New World* was not that they were laughing instead of thinking, but that they did not know what they were laughing about and why they had stopped thinking."[95] Nevertheless, they kept smiling.

Here and Now

Coupled with the Huxleyan vision, much of what Orwell envisioned in his futuristic society has now come to pass. Surveillance cameras are everywhere. Government agents listen in on our telephone calls and read our emails. Political correctness (a precursor to "thought crimes")—a philosophy that discourages diversity and challenges the right of certain people to speak—has become a guiding principle of modern society. The courts have eviscerated the Fourth Amendment protections against unreasonable searches and seizures of our bodies, homes, and personal possessions. In fact, SWAT teams battering down doors without search warrants and FBI agents acting as a secret police that investigate and "detain" dissenting citizens have become all-too-common occurrences in contemporary America. We are increasingly ruled by multi-corporations wedded to the police state. And much of the population is either hooked on illegal drugs or legal ones marketed heavily by the pharmaceutical industry.

When all is said and done, however, "An Orwellian world is much easier to recognize, and to oppose, than a Huxleyan. Everything in our background has prepared us to know and resist a prison when the gates begin to close around us." As professor Neil Postman writes in *Amusing Ourselves to Death*:

> We take arms against such a sea of troubles, buttressed by the spirit of Milton, Bacon, Voltaire, Goethe, and Jefferson. But what if there are no cries of anguish to be heard? Who is prepared to take arms against a sea of amusements? To whom do we complain, and when, and in what tone of voice, when serious discourse dissolves into giggles? What is the antidote to a culture's being drained by laughter?[96]

A GOVERNMENT OF WOLVES
THE EMERGING POLICE STATE
PART
III
Welcome to the Police State
INGSOC

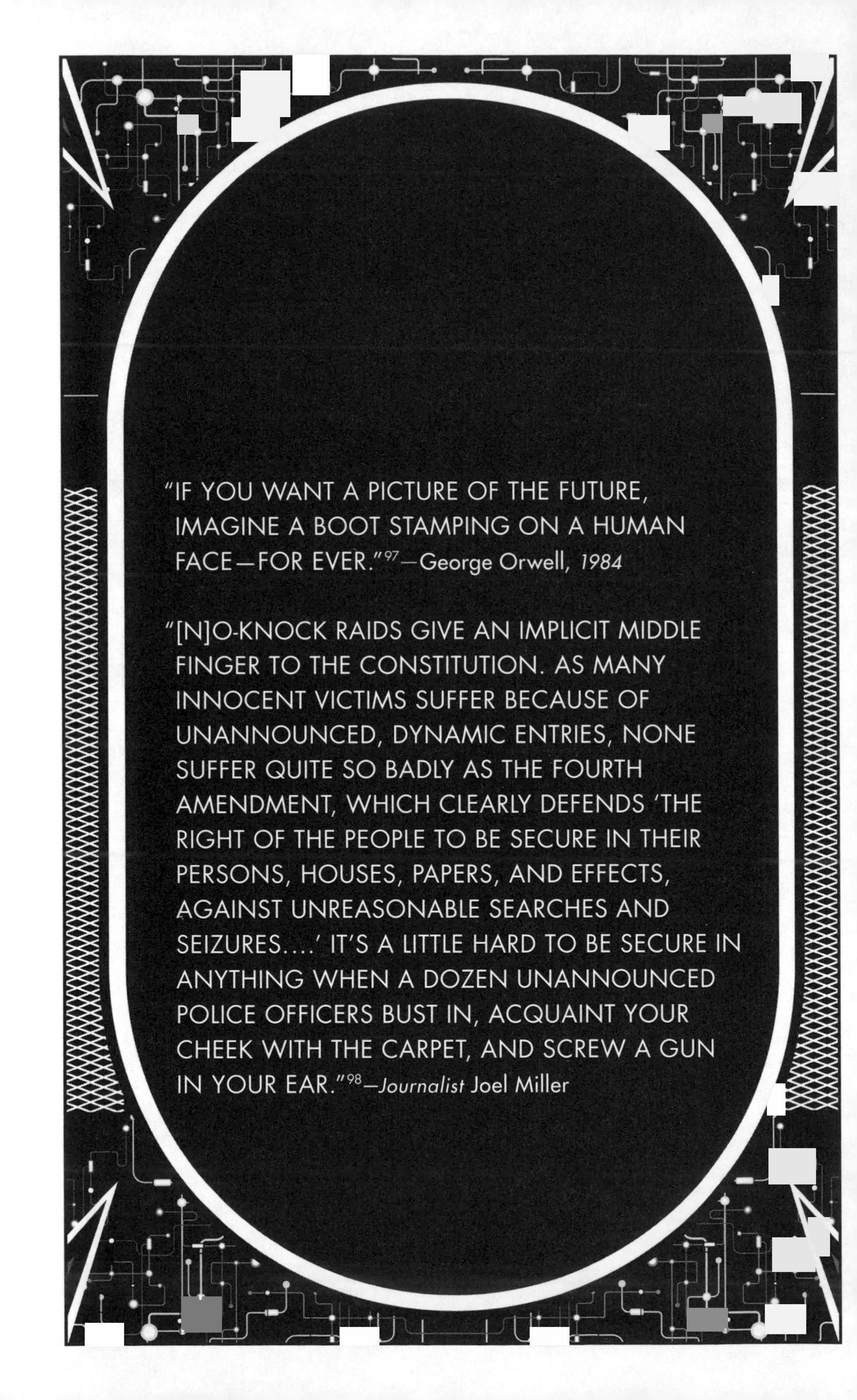
"IF YOU WANT A PICTURE OF THE FUTURE, IMAGINE A BOOT STAMPING ON A HUMAN FACE—FOR EVER."[97]—George Orwell, *1984*
"[N]O-KNOCK RAIDS GIVE AN IMPLICIT MIDDLE FINGER TO THE CONSTITUTION. AS MANY INNOCENT VICTIMS SUFFER BECAUSE OF UNANNOUNCED, DYNAMIC ENTRIES, NONE SUFFER QUITE SO BADLY AS THE FOURTH AMENDMENT, WHICH CLEARLY DEFENDS 'THE RIGHT OF THE PEOPLE TO BE SECURE IN THEIR PERSONS, HOUSES, PAPERS, AND EFFECTS, AGAINST UNREASONABLE SEARCHES AND SEIZURES....' IT'S A LITTLE HARD TO BE SECURE IN ANYTHING WHEN A DOZEN UNANNOUNCED POLICE OFFICERS BUST IN, ACQUAINT YOUR CHEEK WITH THE CARPET, AND SCREW A GUN IN YOUR EAR."[98]—*Journalist* Joel Miller

CHAPTER 7

1984

"The very first essential for success is a perpetually constant and regular employment of violence."[99]

—ADOLPH HITLER, *Mein Kampf*

The stomping boot is something most people never really thought they would see in America, but like all authoritarian trends in government, it has crept up on us while we were unaware.

"What happened here," observed historian Milton Mayer, "was the gradual habituation of the people, little by little, to being governed by surprise; to receiving decisions deliberated in secret; to believing that the situation was so complicated that the government had to act on information which the people could not understand, or so dangerous that, even if the people could understand it, it could not be released because of national security."[100] Although Mayer was writing about how authoritarianism rose to power in Nazi Germany, his description of the emergence of a police state echoes what we are seeing in modern America.

Big Brother—a euphemism for Big Government—is here. In fact, it looks as if the government is taking George Orwell's novel *1984* and implementing it as government policy.

George Orwell saw what might come to pass and it frightened him—a society where thinking the wrong thing (a "thought crime"), disagreeing with the prevailing view of society, or being the wrong skin color and/or from the wrong social class would bring the stomping boot down upon you. In a police state, you're either part of the state's ruling elite or you're its subject. As police chief Bryant says to Ric Deckard when trying to recruit him to return to police work in the 1982 film *Blade Runner*: "You're either a cop or little people." Likewise, when Winston Smith decides to subtly resist Big Brother in *1984*, he finds out rather quickly what it means to be "little people"—isolation, torture, and "re-education."

Yet it is not Big Brother that defeats us in the end. It is what we fear that subdues us. We have been conditioned to fear the criminal, the terrorist, the protester, the police, and now even our next-door neighbor. "An atmosphere of fear is itself a powerful force," writes former presidential advisor Bertram Gross in his book *Friendly Fascism*. "Present fears, to recall Macbeth's words, are even 'less than horrible happenings.' With but slight expectations of force, an all-pervasive sense of fright may be produced in the invisible spheres of life. An ounce of actual violence can yield a pound of terror."[101]

SWAT team raids occurring across America? Protesters tasered, pepper sprayed, beaten, and shot? The military on American streets? Yes, it is here. And it is definitely time to realize that what we call "the government" is not what it seems. Unfortunately, most Americans have come to believe that the zookeeper is friendly. All the while, freedom continues to diminish. We had better wake up or we will become the Winston Smiths of our time.

CHAPTER 8

America's New Way of Life

"Uncontrolled search and seizure is one of the first and most effective weapons in the arsenal of every arbitrary government . . . Among deprivations of rights, none is so effective in cowing a population, crushing the spirit of the individual and putting terror in every heart."[102]

—JUSTICE ROBERT JACKSON
Chief U.S. prosecutor at the Nuremberg Trials

The role of law enforcement, especially local police officers, has drastically changed from when I was a child in the 1950s. The friendly local sheriff in *The Andy Griffith Show* has been replaced by grim-faced, armed warriors quick to do the government's bidding, with little to no thought for the Constitution.

The changing face of law enforcement (Thinkstock)

One clear distinction between local police and military forces used to be the kinds of weapons at their disposal. With the advent of modern police weaponry and the introduction of SWAT teams into almost every police force in the nation, that is no longer the case. Standard SWAT team weaponry includes battering rams, ballistic shields, "flashbang" grenades, smoke grenades, pepper spray, and tear gas. Moreover, while "non-lethal" weapons such as tasers, stun guns, rubber bullets, and other weapons of compliance might pale in comparison to the arsenal of deadly weapons available to local law enforcement, their effect on our freedoms is no less severe.

Permanent Armies

Undoubtedly, as the militarization of law enforcement continues to grow, armed police officers (and federal agents armed to the hilt) have become a force to be reckoned with. Consequently, at all levels—federal, local, and state—the government and the police have merged. In the process, they have become a "standing" or permanent army, one composed of full-time professional soldiers who do not disband.

These permanent armies are exactly what those who drafted the U.S. Constitution and Bill of Rights feared. They knew that despotic governments have used standing armies to control the people and impose tyranny. For example, James Madison, in a speech before the Constitutional Convention in the summer of 1789, warned: "A standing military force, with an overgrown Executive will not long be safe companions to liberty. The means of defence against foreign danger, have been always the instruments of tyranny at home."[103] As Madison foresaw, "instruments of tyranny" can be used by a government to wage war against its citizens.

Tanks on Main Street

In communities large and small across America, local law enforcement are arming themselves to the teeth with weapons previously only seen on the battlefield.[104] Local police—clad in jackboots, helmets, and shields and wielding batons, pepper spray, stun guns, and assault rifles—have increasingly come to resemble occupying forces in our communities. As investigative journalists Andrew Becker and G.W. Schulz point out, "Many police, including beat cops, now routinely carry assault rifles. Combined with body armor and other apparel, many officers look more and more like combat troops serving in Iraq and Afghanistan."[105]

The fifty-person police department in Oxford, Alabama, for example, has acquired $3 million worth of equipment, including M-16s, infrared goggles, and an armored vehicle.[106] All of these new toys lead to specious SWAT team raids that eviscerate the Fourth Amendment, conditioning us to the vision of police in jackboots with assault rifles patrolling our streets.

Military Tanks Used Domestically (AP Photo/Eric Gay)

"Today," notes Paul Craig Roberts, former Assistant Secretary of the Treasury and associate editor of *The Wall Street Journal,* "17,000 local police forces are equipped with such military equipment as Blackhawk helicopters, machine guns, grenade launchers, battering rams, explosives, chemical sprays, body armor, night vision, rappelling gear, and armored vehicles. Some have tanks."[107]

Thus, what began with the militarization of the police in the 1980s during the government's war on drugs has snowballed into a full-fledged integration of military weaponry, technology, and tactics into police protocol. For example, in 1981 Congress passed the Military Cooperation with Law Enforcement Act, which granted the military the power to help local police forces wage the "war on drugs" by sharing equipment, training, and intelligence. In 1997 Congress approved the 1033 Program, which allows the Secretary of Defense to transfer surplus military supplies and weapons to local law enforcement agencies without charge—the only thing that local police departments have to pay for is shipping and future maintenance. And police departments aren't just getting boots and medkits—they're receiving assault rifles, mini-tanks, grenade launchers, and remote controlled robots.

Since 1997 more than 17,000 agencies have taken advantage of the federal government's 1033 Program, acquiring $2.6 billion dollars' worth of weapons and equipment,[108] and demand is only getting higher. In fact, a record-setting half a billion dollars' worth of military equipment flowed from the U.S. Department of Defense to local police in 2011, with another $400 million worth of equipment reaching local police by May 2012.[109]

As Becker and Schulz report, more than $34 billion in federal government grants made available to local police agencies in the wake of 9/11 "ha[ve] fueled a rapid, broad transformation of police operations . . . across the country. More than ever before, police rely on quasi-military tactics and equipment."[110] For example:

> If terrorists ever target Fargo, N.D., the local police will be ready. In recent years, they have bought bomb-detection robots, digital communications equipment and Kevlar helmets, like those used by soldiers in foreign wars. For local siege situations requiring real firepower, police there can use a new $256,643 armored truck, complete with a rotating turret.[111]

Moreover:

> No one can say exactly what has been purchased in total across the country or how it's being used, because the federal government doesn't keep close track. State and local governments don't maintain uniform records. But a review of records from forty-one states obtained through open-government requests, and interviews with more than two-dozen current and former police officials and terrorism experts, shows police departments around the United States have transformed into small army-like forces.[112]

For example:

> In Montgomery County, Tex., the sheriff's department owns a $300,000 pilotless surveillance drone. In Garland County, Ark., known for its pleasant hot springs, a local law enforcement agency acquired four handheld bulletproof protective shields costing $600 each. In East Baton Rouge, La., it was $400 ballistic helmets. In Augusta, Maine, with fewer than 20,000 people and where an officer hasn't died from gunfire in the line of duty in more than 125 years, police bought eight $1,500 tactical vests. And for police in Des Moines, Iowa, it was two $180,000 bomb robots.[113]

High-Flying Drone (AP Photo)

The purchases get even more extravagant the deeper you go. For instance, police in Cobb County, Georgia, have an amphibious tank,[114] while Richland County, South Carolina, police have a machine-gun-equipped armored personnel carrier called "The Peacemaker," the likes of which had previously only been seen in war zones.[115] One popular piece of equipment, the BearCat, a "16,000-pound bulletproof truck equipped with battering rams, gun ports, tear-gas dispensers and radiation detectors," which costs $237,000, has been sold to over 500 local agencies.[116] Police in Hanceville, Alabama, (population 3,000) have acquired $250,000 worth of equipment.[117]

While these so-called "free" surplus military weapons may seem like a windfall for cash-strapped communities, the maintenance costs for such extraneous equipment can quickly skyrocket. For example, police in Tupelo, Mississippi, spent about $274,000 over five years servicing a helicopter that flew an average of ten missions per year.[118]

In addition to the military equipment acquired by police departments via the 1033 Program, police agencies are also beginning to use drones—pilotless, remote-controlled aircraft that have been used extensively in Iraq, Afghanistan, and Pakistan—domestically. In fact, the Federal Aviation Administration has already issued testing permits to local police agencies across the country seeking to employ drone technology.[119] AeroVironment, Inc., a manufacturer of drones, intends to sell 18,000 five-pound drones controlled via tablet computer to police departments throughout the country.[120] They are also touting the "Switchblade," a small, one-use drone that has the ability to track a person from the air and then fly down to their level and explode.[121] Moreover, some police officials are already discussing outfitting these spy drones with "nonlethal" weapons.[122]

Civilian Branches of the Military

In appearance, weapons, and attitude, law enforcement agencies are increasingly being transformed into civilian branches of the military. This militarization of American police—no doubt a blowback effect of the military empire—has become an unfortunate part of American life. In fact, it says something about our reliance on the military that federal agencies having nothing whatsoever to do with national defense now see the need for their own paramilitary units.

Consider that federal agencies now employ more than 100,000 full-time personnel authorized to make arrests and carry firearms.[123]Among those federal agencies laying claim to their own law enforcement divisions are the Department of Homeland Security, State Department, Department of Education,[124] Department of Energy, U.S. Fish and Wildlife Service, and the National Park Service, to name just a few.[125] These agencies have secured the services of fully-armed agents—often in SWAT team attire—through a typical bureaucratic sleight-of-hand provision allowing for the creation of Offices of Inspectors General (OIG). Each OIG office is supposedly charged with not only auditing their particular agency's actions but also uncovering possible misconduct, waste, fraud, theft, or certain types of criminal activity by individuals or groups related to the agency's operation.[126] At present, there are 73 such OIG offices[127] in the federal government that, at times, perpetuate a police state aura about them.

For example, it was heavily armed agents from one such OIG office, working under the auspices of the U.S. Department of Education, who forced their way into the home of a California man, handcuffed him and placed his three children (ages three, seven, and eleven) in a squad car while they conducted a search of his home.[128]

This federal SWAT team raid on the home of Kenneth Wright on Tuesday, June 7, 2011,[129] was allegedly intended to ferret out information on Wright's estranged wife, Michelle, who no longer lived with him

Kenneth Wright (News 10 Central Stockton)

and who was suspected of financial aid fraud[130] (early news reports characterized the purpose of the raid as being over Michelle's delinquent student loans[131]). Wright was awakened at 6 a.m. by the sound of agents battering down his door and, upon descending the stairs, was immediately subdued by police. One neighbor actually witnessed the team of armed agents surround the house and, after forcing entry, they "dragged [Wright] out in his boxer shorts, threw him to the ground and handcuffed him."[132]

A Dangerous Paranoia

The total militarization of government, which has taken place since the 1980s and rapidly advanced since 9/11, is most clearly illustrated by the Department of Homeland Security's (DHS) transformation from a security agency into a domestic army, with its teams of paramilitary forces roaming the country. This disconcerting transformation has been made all the more troubling by a dangerous paranoia that seems to have overtaken the governmental bureaucracy, especially in regard to an increasingly discontent citizenry.

Speculation has been understandably rife as to the government's motivation in ordering vast quantities of hollow-point bullets, which are designed to explode upon entry into the body, causing massive organ damage, thus resulting in death. For example, in March 2012, defense contractor ATK agreed to produce 450 million hollow-point rounds to be used by the DHS and its Immigration and Customs Enforcement (ICE) office.[133] DHS placed another order for 750 million rounds of various ammunition in August 2012.[134] In August 2012 the Social Security Administration (SSA) placed an order for 174,000 rounds of hollow point ammunition.[135] Supposedly, the SSA sent the ammunition to forty-one locations throughout the United States, including major cities such as Los Angeles, Detroit, and Philadelphia, among others.[136]

It's unclear why the SSA would need hollow-point bullets. However, it's worth noting that DHS and SSA have already collaborated in police exercises. In January 2012 Federal Protective Service officers with DHS conducted a training exercise at the SSA office in Leesburg, Florida. One officer carrying a semi-automatic assault rifle randomly checked IDs as people filed into the building, while other officers combed the building with K-9 units. The exercise was part of the larger Operation Shield, which, according to DHS officials, involves federal officers randomly showing up to government buildings throughout the country in order to test the effectiveness of their security procedures.[137]

DHS and SSA aren't the only agencies beefing up their ammunition stockpiles. In August 2012 the National Oceanic and Atmospheric Administration (NOAA), which houses the National Weather Service, requested 46,000 hollow-point bullets to be sent to locations in Maine, Massachusetts, New Jersey, and Florida,[138] as well as 500 paper targets.[139] The NOAA later released a statement claiming that the ammunition is intended for the Fisheries Office of Law Enforcement which is entrusted to "enforce laws that conserve and protect our nation's living marine resources and their natural habitat."[140]

A New Way

Hollow-point bullets, local police armed to the teeth, and SWAT team raids on unarmed citizens. A spurious trend? Or America's new way of life?

CHAPTER 9

SWAT Team Mania

"On July 29, 2008, my family and I were terrorized by an errant Prince George's County SWAT team. This unit forced entry into my home without a proper warrant, executed our beloved black Labradors, Payton and Chase, and bound and interrogated my mother-in-law and me for hours as they ransacked our belongings ... As I was forced to kneel, bound at gun point on my living room floor, I recall thinking that there had been a terrible mistake. However, as I have learned more, I have to understand that what my family and I experienced is part of a growing and troubling trend where law enforcement is relying on SWAT teams to perform duties once handled by ordinary police officers."[141]

—Maryland MAYOR CHEYE CALVO in testimony before the Maryland Senate

What we are witnessing is an inversion of the police-civilian relationship. Rather than compelling police officers to remain within constitutional bounds as servants of the people, ordinary Americans are being placed at the mercy of law enforcement and the stomping boot, especially with the increasing reliance on SWAT teams for matters that once could have been satisfactorily performed by traditional civilian officers.

Frequently justified as vital tools necessary to combat terrorism and deal with rare but extremely dangerous criminal situations, such as those involving hostages, SWAT teams—which first appeared on the scene in California in the 1960s[142]—have now become intrinsic parts of local law enforcement operations.[143] This is thanks in large part to substantial "donations" of military equipment from the federal government[144] and a law enforcement bureaucracy pressured to put such resources to use.

Consequently, 75-80 percent of SWAT callouts are now for mere warrant service.[145] In some jurisdictions, SWAT teams are responsible for servicing 100 percent of all drug warrants issued.[146] A Maryland

SWAT Team Raid (AP Photo/The Daily World, MacLeod Pappidas)

study[147] indicated that SWAT teams are deployed 4.5 times per day in Maryland with 94 percent of those deployments being for something as minor as serving search or arrest warrants.[148] In one county, more than 50 percent of SWAT operations carried out were for misdemeanors or non-serious felonies.[149]

Mimicking the Military

The pervasive culture of militarism in domestic law enforcement is largely the result of the militarization of *local* police forces, which are increasingly militaristic in their uniforms, weaponry, language, training, and tactics.[150] Police mimicry of the military is enhanced by the war-heavy imagery and metaphors associated with law enforcement activity: the *war* on drugs, the *war* on crime, and so on.[151] Moreover, it is estimated that at least 46 percent of paramilitary units (SWAT teams) are trained by "active-duty military experts in special operations."[152] In turn, the military mindset adopted by many SWAT members encourages a tendency to employ lethal force.[153] After all, soldiers are authorized to terminate enemy combatants and not act, as local police should, as "peace" officers. As Lawrence Korb, a former official in the Reagan Administration, put it, soldiers are "trained to vaporize, not Mirandize."[154]

Ironically, despite the fact that SWAT team members are subject to greater legal restraints than their counterparts in the military, they are often less well-trained in the use of force than are the special ops soldiers on which they model themselves. In fact, SWAT teams frequently fail to conform to the basic precautions required in military raids.[155]

Nonviolent "Suspects"

Remember, SWAT teams originated as specialized units dedicated to defusing extremely sensitive, dangerous situations. As the role of paramilitary forces has expanded, however, to include involvement in nondescript police work targeting nonviolent suspects, the mere presence of SWAT units has actually injected a level of danger and violence into police-citizen interactions that was not present when these interactions were handled by traditional civilian officers.[156] In one drug raid, for instance, an unarmed pregnant woman was shot as she attempted to flee the police by climbing out a window.[157] In another case, the girlfriend of a drug suspect and her young child crouched on the floor in obedience to police instructions during the execution of a search warrant. One officer proceeded to shoot the family dogs. His fellow officer, in another room, mistook the shots for hostile gunfire and fired blindly into the room where the defendant crouched, killing her and wounding her child.[158]

General incompetence, collateral damage (fatalities, property damage, etc.) and botched raids tend to go hand in hand with an overuse of paramilitary forces.[159] In some cases, officers misread the address on the warrant.[160] In others, they simply barge into the wrong house[161] or even the wrong building.[162]

In another subset of cases (such as the Department of Education's raid on Kenneth Wright's home), police conduct a search of a building where the suspect no longer resides.[163] SWAT teams have even on occasion conducted multiple, sequential raids on wrong addresses[164] or executed search warrants despite the fact that the suspect is already in police custody.[165] Police have also raided homes on the basis of mistaking the presence or scent of legal substances for illegal drugs.

No-Knock Raids

At least 50,000—but more like 70,000—no-knock raids are carried out each year, usually conducted by teams of heavily armed paramilitary units dressed not as police officers but as soldiers prepared for war. However, as one retired police officer warns: "One tends to throw caution to the wind when wearing 'commando-chic' regalia, a bulletproof vest with the word 'POLICE' emblazoned on both sides, and when one is armed with high tech weaponry."[166]

At first, no-knock raids were generally employed only in situations where innocent lives were determined to be at imminent risk. That changed in the early 1980s, when a dramatic and unsettling rise in the use of paramilitary units in routine police work resulted in a militarization of American civilian law enforcement. The government's militaristically labeled "war on drugs" also spurred a significant rise in the use of SWAT teams for raids. In some jurisdictions, drug warrants are only served by SWAT teams or similar paramilitary units and oftentimes are executed with forced, unannounced entry into the home.

Unfortunately, while few of these raids ever make the news, they are happening more and more frequently. As David Borden, the Executive Director of the Drug Reform Coordination Network, pointed out, "In 1980 there were fewer than 3,000 reported SWAT raids. Now, the number is believed to be over 50,000 per year . . . About 3/4 of these are drug raids, perhaps more by now, the vast majority of them low-level."[167]

Various news stories over the years document the fact that police have on numerous occasions battered down doors, entered the wrong houses, and killed innocent people. Journalist Radley Balko's research reinforces this phenomenon. There have been at least "40 cases in which a completely innocent person was killed. There are dozens more in which nonviolent offenders (recreational pot smokers, for example...) or police officers were needlessly killed. There are nearly 150 cases in which innocent families, sometimes with children, were roused from their beds at gunpoint, and subjected to the fright of being apprehended and thoroughly searched at gunpoint. There are other cases in which a SWAT team seems wholly inappropriate, such as the apprehension of medical marijuana patients, many of whom are bedridden."[168]

There was a time when communities would have been up in arms over a botched SWAT team raid resulting in the loss of innocent lives. Unfortunately, today, we are increasingly being conditioned by both the media and the government to accept the use of SWAT teams by law enforcement agencies for routine drug policing and the high incidence of error-related casualties that accompanies these raids.

All too often, botched SWAT team raids have resulted in one tragedy after another for civilians with little consequences for law enforcement.

In fact, judges tend to afford extreme levels of deference to police officers who have mistakenly killed innocent civilians but do not afford similar leniency to civilians who have injured police officers in acts of self-defense.[169] Even homeowners who mistake officers for robbers can be sentenced for assault or murder if they take defensive actions resulting in harm to police.[170]

Tragic Mistakes

Once upon a time, the motto emblazoned on police cars was "To Protect and Serve." However, as police forces have been transformed into paramilitary units, complete with riot gear and a take-no-prisoners attitude, the fear that police are increasingly overstepping their limits in carrying out these no-knock raids is on the rise. Unfortunately, the "tragic mistake" of police bursting into a house, apprehending the residents, and only afterwards corroborating their facts is also on the rise.

For example, an 88-year-old African-American woman was shot and killed in 2006 when policemen barged unannounced into her home, reportedly in search of cocaine. Police officers broke down Kathryn Johnston's door while serving a "no-knock" warrant to search her home on a run-down Atlanta street known for drugs and crime, prompting the woman to fire at what she believed to be the "intruders" in self-defense. The officers returned fire, killing the octogenarian. No cocaine was found.[171]

Police tasered and gunned to death Derek Hale, a decorated 25-year-old U.S. Marine who was talking to a woman and two children in front of a house in a Delaware neighborhood that police suspected was the home of an outlaw motorcycle gang member. Ordering Hale to place his hands in view, the police reportedly tasered him three times and fired three 40-caliber rounds into his chest, ultimately leading to his death. Hale had no criminal or arrest record in Delaware, and witnesses insist that he was no threat to the police. In fact, after police tasered Hale the second time, one of the independent witnesses yelled at the police that what they were doing was "overkill," to which one of the officers responded, "Shut . . . up or we'll show you overkill."[172]

Fifty-seven-year-old Alberta Spruill was getting ready for work on May 16, 2003, when a police raiding party in search of a drug dealer broke down the door of her Harlem apartment, tossed in a "flashbang" stun grenade and handcuffed her to a chair. After realizing their mistake—the man they wanted lived in the same building but had been arrested by a different police unit four days earlier—the police uncuffed Ms. Spruill, checked her vital signs, and sent her to the Emergency Room. Spruill, however, who suffered from a heart condition, died on the way to the hospital.[173]

Similarly, in Boston, thirteen heavily-armed policemen in black fatigues smashed into the apartment of Acelynne Williams, a 75-year-old retired African-American preacher. Supposedly, they had been working off an anonymous tip that four Jamaican drug dealers lived somewhere in the apartment building. Williams died of a heart attack from the "shock and awe" of being visited by commando-like cops.[174]

Sometimes, even when confronted with obvious errors, law enforcement officials proceed anyway. For example, after having his house raided, Glen Williamson of Louisiana pointed out to the arresting officer that the search warrant actually said "Glen Williams," not "Williamson." In response, the officer added "on" to the name on the warrant and arrested Williamson.[175]

The Killing of Aiyana Jones

No-knock raids illustrate just how little protection Americans have against gun-wielding government agents forcing their way into our homes, especially when those agents shoot first and ask questions later.

Aiyana Jones

Consider what happened to 7-year-old Aiyana Jones. At 12:40 a.m. on Sunday, May 16, 2010, a flash grenade was thrown through the Jones family's living room window, followed by the sounds of police bursting into the apartment and a gun going off. Rushing into the room, Charles Jones found himself tackled by police and forced to lie on the floor, his face in a pool of blood. His daughter Aiyana's blood.

It would be hours before Charles would be informed that his daughter, who had been sleeping on the living room sofa, was dead. According to news reports, the little girl was shot in the neck by the lead officer's gun after he allegedly collided with Aiyana's grandmother during a police raid gone awry. The 34-year-old suspect the police had been looking for would later be found during a search of the building. Ironically, a camera crew shadowing the police SWAT team for the reality television show "The First 48" (cop shows are among the most popular of the television reality shows) caught the unfolding tragedy on film.[176]

Killing a Marine

As we saw with the case of Aiyana Jones, the shock-and-awe tactics utilized by many SWAT teams during no-knock raids only increase the likelihood that someone will get maimed or killed. Drug warrants, for instance, are typically served by paramilitary units late at night or shortly before dawn.[177] Unfortunately, to the unsuspecting homeowner—especially in cases involving mistaken identities or wrong addresses—a raid can appear to be nothing less than a violent home invasion by armed criminals crashing through their door. The natural reaction would be to engage in self-defense.[178] Yet such a defensive reaction on the part of a homeowner, particularly a gun owner, will spur the police to employ lethal force.[179]

Jose Guerena

Take, for example, the case of Jose Guerena. On May 5, 2011, at around 9:30 a.m., several teams of Tucson, Ariz., police officers from various police agencies armed with SWAT gear and an armored personnel carrier raided at least four homes as part of what was described at the time as an investigation into alleged marijuana trafficking.[180] One of those homes belonged to 26-year-old Guerena, a former Marine who had served two tours of duty in Iraq, and his wife, Vanessa.

Asleep after returning from a twelve-hour overnight shift at a local mine, Guerena was awakened by his wife who heard noises outside their house, later identified as flashbang grenades deployed by police in the backyard as a diversion.[181] Seeing a man pointing a gun at her, Vanessa Guerena yelled, "Don't shoot! I have a baby!"[182] Vanessa thought the gunman might be part of a home invasion by criminals, especially because two members of her sister-in-law's family were killed in 2010, with their two children in their Tucson home.[183] She shouted for her husband in the next room. Jose woke up and told his wife to hide in the closet with their 4-year-old.[184]

As the SWAT team forced its way into his home, Guerena armed himself with a rifle and confronted them from the far end of a long, dark hallway. The police opened fire, releasing more than seventy rounds in about seven seconds, at least sixty of which struck Guerena.[185] He was pronounced dead a little over an hour later.

The police initially claimed Guerena fired his weapon at the SWAT team.[186] However, the police later acknowledged that not only did Guerena not fire but the safety on his gun was still activated when he was killed.

Incredibly, after ushering Jose's wife and son out of the house, the police refused to allow paramedics to attend to Guerena for more than an hour, leaving the young father to bleed to death, alone, in his own home.[187] Guerena had no prior criminal record, and the police found nothing illegal in his home. The raids on the other homes carried out that same morning, all part of the same operation, resulted in no arrests and turned up little if any actual marijuana.[188]

Rendering Us Helpless

The problems inherent in these home raids are further compounded by the fact that SWAT teams are granted "no-knock" warrants at such high rates that the warrants themselves are rendered practically meaningless.[189] This sorry state of affairs is made even worse by U.S. Supreme Court rulings that have essentially done away with the need for a "no-knock" warrant altogether, giving the police authority to disregard the protections afforded American citizens by the Fourth Amendment.

In the process, Americans are rendered altogether helpless and terror-stricken as a result of these confrontations with the police. Indeed, "terrorizing" is a mild term to describe the effect on those who survive such vigilante tactics. "It was terrible. It was the most frightening experience of my life. I thought it was a terrorist attack," said 84-year-old Leona Goldberg, a victim of such a raid.[190]

Of course, SWAT team raids and other extreme shows of force by the police are only possible because of the acquiescence of the American people to all government programs relating to "security" since 9/11. Despite the fact that violent crime rates are low,[191] and terrorist attacks are statistically rare (in fact, one is more likely to die in a car wreck or be struck by lightning than be killed by a terrorist),[192] we are being subjected to government agencies "protecting" us in the name of security.

This is the inertia of government bureaucracy. Created during moments of fear, such agencies and the corporate entities that benefit from them always resist change once a citizenry gathers their senses and demands are made for the restoration of free government.

The War on Drugs

Fear, coupled with violence, have been the tools utilized by past historical regimes to control an unruly populace—that is, those citizens brave enough to exercise their rights and vocally disagree with the powers-that-be.

A perfect example of this masterful use of the politics of fear to cow the populace is the government's War on Drugs. Reputedly a response to crime and poverty in inner cities and suburbia, it has been the driving force behind the militarization of the police, at all levels, over the past 40 years.[193] While it has failed to decrease drug use, it has exacerbated social problems by expanding America's rapidly growing prison system and allowing police *carte blanche* access to our homes and personal property.[194]

The foot soldiers in the government's increasingly fanatical war on drugs, particularly marijuana, are state and local police officers dressed in SWAT gear and armed to the hilt. As author and journalist Radley Balko reports, "The vast majority of these raids are to serve routine drug warrants, many times for crimes no more serious than possession of marijuana . . . Police have broken down doors, screamed obscenities, and held innocent people at gunpoint only to discover that what they thought were marijuana plants were really sunflowers, hibiscus, ragweed, tomatoes, or elderberry bushes. (It's happened with all five.)"[195]

Every nineteen seconds, someone in the U.S. is arrested for violating a drug law.[196] Every thirty seconds, someone in the U.S. is arrested for violating a marijuana law,[197] making it the fourth most common cause of arrest in the United States.[198]

For those Americans who find themselves on the wrong end of a SWAT team raid in search of marijuana, the end result is a tragic loss of countless lives, including children and the elderly. Usually, however, as Radley Balko details in "The Drug War Goes to the Dogs," the first to be shot are the family dogs.

> When police in Fremont, California, raided the home of medical marijuana patient Robert Filgo, they shot his pet Akita nine times. Filgo himself was never charged. Last October [2005] police in Alabama raided a home on suspicion of marijuana possession, shot and killed both family dogs, then joked about the kill in front of the family. They seized eight grams of marijuana, equal in weight to a ketchup packet. In January [2006] a cop en route to a drug raid in Tampa, Florida, took a short cut across a neighboring lawn and shot the neighbor's two pooches on his way. And last May [2005], an officer in Syracuse, New York, squeezed off several shots at a family dog during a drug raid, one of which ricocheted and struck a 13-year-old boy in the leg. The boy was handcuffed at gunpoint at the time.[199]

Incentives for Drug Busts

Adding fuel to the fire, the government is providing financial incentives to the SWAT teams carrying out these raids through federal grants such as the Edward Byrne memorial grants and the Community Oriented Policing Services (COPS) grants. These grants seem to focus on the number of arrests made, particularly drug arrests, in addition to funding the purchase of equipment for SWAT teams.[200]

As always, the special interests have a lot to say in these matters, and it is particularly telling that those lobbying hard to keep the prohibition on marijuana include law enforcement officials, the pharmaceutical corporations, and alcoholic beverage producers.[201] However, when the war on drugs becomes little more than a thinly veiled attempt to keep SWAT teams employed and special interests appeased, it's time to revisit our drug policies and laws. As Professors Eric Blumenson and Eva Nilson recognize:

> During the 25 years of its existence, the "War on Drugs" has transformed the criminal justice system, to the point where the imperatives of drug law enforcement now drive many of the broader legislative, law enforcement, and

corrections policies in counterproductive ways. One significant impetus for this transformation has been the enactment of forfeiture laws which allow law enforcement agencies to keep the lion's share of the drug-related assets they seize. Another has been the federal law enforcement aid program, revised a decade ago to focus on assisting state anti-drug efforts. Collectively these financial incentives have left many law enforcement agencies dependent on drug law enforcement to meet their budgetary requirements, at the expense of alternative goals such as the investigation and prosecution of non-drug crimes, crime prevention strategies, and drug education and treatment.[202]

CHAPTER 10

"Dominate. Intimidate. Control."

"They're trying to scare the pants off the American people that we need these things ... Fear is a commodity and they're selling it. The more they can sell it, the more we buy into it. When American people are afraid, they will accept anything."[203]

—KATE HANNI, passengers' rights advocate

Perhaps you, reader, have yet to experience the particular thrill, and I use that word loosely, of being patted down by government agents, having your personal possessions rummaged through, and your activities and associations scrutinized. If so, not to worry. It may only be a matter of time before such a military task force comes knocking at your door. Only, chances are that it won't be a knock, and you might not even be at home when government agents decide to "investigate" you. Indeed, you may be at a shopping mall or a grocery store when you're subjected to a pat down. As increasing numbers of Americans are discovering, these so-called "soft target" security inspections are taking place whenever and wherever the government deems appropriate, at random times and places, and without needing the justification of a particular threat.

What I'm describing—something that was once limited to authoritarian regimes—is only possible thanks to an unofficial rewriting of the Fourth Amendment by the courts that essentially does away with any distinctions over what is "reasonable" when it comes to searches and seizures by government agents. The rationale, of course, is that anything is "reasonable" in the war on terrorism.

Airport Security Patdown (Thinkstock)

Ritualized Humiliation

The Transportation Security Administration (TSA) continues to draw ire from various travelers because of security procedures which have subjected airline travelers of all ages, most of whom clearly do not in any way fit the profile of a terrorist, to invasive virtual strip searches, excessive enhanced pat downs, and unreasonable demands by government agents—what one journalist refers to as "ritualized humiliation of travelers."[204] In 2011, for example, TSA agents at a Florida airport forced a 95-year-old wheelchair-bound cancer patient to remove her adult diaper during the course of a security check.[205] Ninety-year-old Marian Peterson, also confined to a wheelchair, was pulled out of line for a random security check and according to her son, Joe, TSA agents "groped her. All of her body: her crotch, her breasts, and everything else." She was also made to get out of her wheelchair and stand with her arms outstretched for over ten minutes.[206] Then there was the incident with 4-year-old Isabella, who was forced to undergo a pat down after she ran to hug her grandmother goodbye during a security screening at a Kansas airport. The little girl, who became hysterical during the course of the pat down, was declared "an uncooperative suspect."[207]

VIPR Strikes

Unfortunately, in light of TSA's Chief John Pistole's determination to "take the TSA to the next level," there will soon be no place safe from the TSA's groping searches.[208] Only this next time around, the "ritualized humiliation" won't be restricted to airports but will be spreading to train stations, bus terminals, shopping malls, and concert venues, meted out by Visible Intermodal Prevention and Response (VIPR) task forces comprised of federal air marshals, surface transportation security inspectors, transportation security officers, behavior detection officers and explosive detection canine teams.[209] As a sign of where things are headed, Pistole, a former FBI agent, wants to turn the TSA into a "national-security, counterterrorism organization, fully integrated into U.S. government efforts."[210]

VIPR is the first major step in the government's efforts to secure so-called "soft" targets such as malls, stadiums, bridges, etc.[211] In fact, some security experts predict that checkpoints and screening stations will eventually be established at *all* soft targets,[212] such as department stores, restaurants, and schools. Given the virtually limitless number of potential soft targets vulnerable to terrorist attack, subjection to intrusive pat downs and full-body imaging (scanners, that is) will become an integral component of everyday life in the United States. As Jim Harper of the Cato Institute observed, "The natural illogic of VIPR stings is that terrorism can strike anywhere, so VIPR teams should search anywhere."[213]

The goal of VIPR is to have an omnipresent anti-terrorist force deployed at every moderate or high-density site: malls, stadiums, restaurants, grocery stores, and so on. Expanding VIPR to its logical conclusion necessitates a police state. Additionally, VIPR, by expanding intrusive searches beyond the spatially circumscribed confines of airports, regularizes abusive behavior by government officials and inculcates submissiveness and subservience on the part of the average citizen.

In effect, VIPR paves the way psychologically for the implementation of Orwellian apparatuses of control. Furthermore, by entrenching frequent, intrusive searches in the American mindset as an unquestioned component of everyday life, programs like VIPR actually serve to reduce the level of protection afforded citizens by the Constitution. And once VIPR has accrued a sufficient bureaucracy, it will be virtually impossible to eradicate.

Getting After the "Bad" Guys

For now, under the pretext of protecting the nation's infrastructure (roads, mass transit systems, water and power supplies, telecommunications systems, and so on) against criminal or terrorist attacks, these VIPR teams are being deployed to do random security sweeps of nexuses of transportation, including ports, railway and bus stations,[214] airports,[215] ferries, and subways.[216] VIPR teams are also being deployed to elevate the security presence at certain special events such as political conventions, baseball games, and music concerts.[217] Sweep tactics include the use of x-ray technology,[218] pat downs and drug-sniffing dogs, among other things.[219] Unfortunately, these sweeps are not confined to detecting terrorist activity. Federal officials have admitted that transit screening is also intended, at least in some instances, to detect illegal immigration or even cash smuggling.[220]

Incredibly, in the absence of any viable threat, VIPR teams—roving SWAT teams, with no need for a warrant—conducted over 8,000 such searches in public places in 2011 alone.[221] For example, in February 2011, a VIPR team conducted a raid at an Amtrak station in Georgia, not only patting down all passengers—both adults and small children alike—entering the station but also those departing.[222] In a characteristic display of incompetence, TSA agents co-opted the station and posted a sign on the door informing patrons that anyone who entered would be subject to mandatory screening[223] (this, despite the fact that boarding passengers can easily bypass the station entirely and access the boarding area directly).[224] One officer rummaged through a passenger's hand luggage and even smelled her perfume.[225] A vacationing firefighter roped into the search commented, "It was just not professional. It was just weird . . . we are being harassed by the TSA."[226] In fact, when Amtrak Police Chief John O'Connor was informed of VIPR's activities, he "hit the ceiling" and banned VIPR personnel from entering Amtrak property.[227]

These raids, conducted at taxpayer expense on average Americans going about their normal, day-to-day business, run the gamut from the ridiculous to the abusive. In Santa Fe, TSA agents were assigned to conduct searches at a high school prom.[228] At the port of Brownsville, Texas, VIPR units searched all private and commercial vehicles entering and exiting the port. Although the TSA admitted the search was not conducted in response to any specific threat, VIPR agents nonetheless engaged in "thorough" inspections of each and every vehicle.[229] In a training exercise in Atlanta, VIPR teams allegedly arrested a man after discovering a small amount of marijuana in his semi-trailer.[230] In San Diego, a VIPR investigation at a trolley station resulted in the deportation of three teenagers apprehended on their way to school.[231]

In April 2011 Homeland Security official Gary Milano stated that VIPR teams involved in a raid at a Tampa bus station, again conducted in the absence of any threat, were there "to sort of invent the wheel in advance in case we have to, if there ever is specific intelligence requiring us to be here. This way us and our partners are ready to move in at a moment's notice."[232] He added, "We'll be back. We won't say when we'll be back. This way the bad guys are on notice we'll be back."[233]

Likewise, in an intimidating display of force in June 2011, VIPR conducted a vast training exercise—that is, a military raid—covering more than 5,000 square miles' worth of crucial infrastructure sites such as bridges, gas lines, and power plants between Ohio, West Virginia, and Kentucky.[234] The raid included members of seventy different agencies, over 400 state and federal agents, Black Hawk helicopters, fixed-wing aircraft,[235] and Coast Guard vessels.[236] Although the surveillance activities constituted an exercise rather than a response to an actual terrorist threat, the sweep was clearly calculated to produce a deterrent effect. According to TSA official Michael Cleveland, the purpose of the exercise was to "have a visible presence and let people know we're out here . . . It can be a deterrent."[237]

On September 11, 2012, the Cincinnati Police Department SWAT team conducted a training raid on the University of Cincinnati campus without first warning the student population. Concerned students videotaped the incident and uploaded it to YouTube,[238] documenting a dozen or so armed men with masks and shields exiting a black SWAT team vehicle. When a concerned student asked one of the lead officers what they were doing on campus, the officer was evasive, refusing to confirm or deny that any federal agencies were involved. The SWAT vehicle did, however, have the words "Department of Homeland Security" emblazoned on the side.[239]

Public Enemy Number One?

The question that must be asked, of course, is whom exactly is the TSA trying to target and intimidate? Not would-be terrorists, given that scattershot pat-down stings are unlikely to apprehend or deter terrorists.[240]

In light of the fact that average citizens are the ones receiving the brunt of the TSA's efforts, it stands to reason that we've become public enemy number one. We are all suspects. And how does the TSA deal with perceived threats? Its motto, posted at the TSA's air marshal training center headquarters in the wake of 9/11, is particularly telling: "Dominate. Intimidate. Control."[241]

Those three words effectively sum up the manner in which the government now relates to its citizens, making a travesty of every democratic ideal our representatives spout so glibly and reinforcing the specter of the police state. After all, no government that truly respects or values its citizens would subject them to such intrusive, dehumanizing, demoralizing, suspicionless searches. Yet by taking the TSA's airport screenings nationwide with VIPR and inserting the type of abusive authoritarianism already present in airports into countless other sectors of American life, the government is expanding the physical and psychological scope of the police state apparatus.

Security Theater

VIPR activities epitomize exactly the kind of farcical security theater the government has come to favor through its use of coded color alerts and other largely superficial and meaningless maneuvers. These stings do, however, inculcate and condition citizens to a culture of submissiveness towards authority and regularize intrusive, suspicionless searches as a facet of everyday life. In April 2010, for instance, at a Tampa bus station, VIPR patted down passengers and used dogs to search the luggage.[242] That type of small-scale, random operation provides little actual value but does impart to some citizens a false sense of security. A passenger in Tampa, for instance, commented, "I feel safe, knowing that I get on a bus and I'm not going to blow up."[243]

It's an ingenious plan: the incremental ratcheting-up of intrusive searches combined with the gradual rollout of VIPR teams permits the normalization of the TSA's police state tactics while inciting minimal resistance, thereby muting dissent and enabling the ultimate implementation of totalitarian-style authoritarianism.

VIPR Teams (AP Photo/Yuri Gripas)

Sadly, this repeated degradation by government officials of Americans engaged in common activities inevitably normalizes what is essentially an abusive relationship to such an extent that government agents are permitted to trample Americans' constitutional rights with impunity. And those abused are prevented even from protesting. Reinforcing this latter point is the TSA's admission that those who merely exercise their First Amendment rights by *complaining* about intrusive airport security exhibit a behavioral indicator of a "high risk" passenger that, in combination with other behavioral indicators, warrants additional screening.[244]

There is also a chilling effect to TSA activity. For instance, when a group of peace protesters composed of high school students and Catholic priests and nuns were detained at an airport after showing up on a federal watch list, a sheriff's deputy, according to one member of the group, explained, "You're probably being stopped because you are a peace group and you're protesting against your country."[245]

TSA and VIPR searches also indoctrinate children to accept pat downs, full-body scans, and other invasive procedures as a regular component of the relationship between government and its citizens. In this way, Orwellian police state tactics will gradually grow in acceptance as simply "the way things are." A child who has been molested by government officials since before he could read is unlikely to question such activities as an unjustified exercise of authority when an adult.

Furthermore, the normalization of intrusive searches arguably reworks the content of the protections provided by the Constitution, particularly the Fourth Amendment. Increasing use of pat downs and other controversial screening procedures changes the definition of what is a "reasonable" search and seizure from a cultural perspective and therefore actually re-engineers the constitutional fabric by altering the definition of what is "reasonable" under the Fourth Amendment.

Black Hawks over America

Obviously, the bedrock of the American republic is fracturing. The Constitution is being eviscerated by government leaders and their corporate allies. The system of checks and balances embodied in that document, the mechanism which prevents the United States from sliding into tyranny, is eroding. The walls separating the three branches of government, as well as those separating the government from corporations and the military, have collapsed. With the rise of the national security state, this process has accelerated. Now, thanks to the collusion between domestic police forces and the military, we are being subjected to an onslaught of VIPR and military drills carried out in major American cities, SWAT team raids on unsuspecting homeowners, and Black Hawk helicopters patrolling American skies.

Black Hawk Helicopters Take to the Skies
(U.S. Department of Defense)

Throughout 2011 and into 2012, for example, cities such as Boston,[246] Miami,[247] Little Rock,[248] and Los Angeles[249] have all served as staging grounds for military training exercises involving Black Hawk helicopters and uniformed soldiers. These military training exercises occur in the middle of the night, with the full cooperation of the local police forces and generally without forewarning the public. They involve helicopters buzzing buildings and performing landing and takeoff maneuvers.

Justified on the grounds that they prepare troops for urban warfare situations and future deployments, these training exercises also condition Americans to an environment in which the buzz of Black Hawk helicopters and the sight of armed forces rappelling onto buildings is commonplace.

CHAPTER 11

The New York Prototype

"I have my own army in the NYPD, which is the seventh biggest army in the world. I have my own State Department, much to Foggy Bottom's annoyance. We have the United Nations in New York, and so we have an entree into the diplomatic world that Washington does not have."[250]—MAYOR MICHAEL BLOOMBERG

NYPD Police Officers (Burger International Photography)

New York City has long been celebrated as the cultural capital of the world, renowned for its art, music, and film. The "city that never sleeps," however, is serving as the staging ground for a fast-evolving police state through the use of cutting-edge technology, sophisticated surveillance, random crackdowns, and old-fashioned scare tactics, all of which keep New Yorkers in a state of compliance. A *60 Minutes* report describes the police state atmosphere: "At random, 100 police cars will swarm parts of the town just to make a scene. It happens with complete unpredictability. Cops signal subway trains to stop to be searched. And sometimes they hold the trains until they've eyeballed every passenger."[251]

A Dangerous Leviathan

Some New Yorkers can see the dangerous leviathan that is wrapping its tentacles around the Bill of Rights. Representative Yvette Clarke of Brooklyn notes, "We're quickly moving to an apartheid situation here in the city of New York where we don't recognize the civil liberties and the civil rights of all New Yorkers."[252] Indeed, boasting a $4.5 billion budget,[253] a counterterrorism unit that includes 35,000 uniformed police officers and 15,000 civilians,[254] and a $3 billion joint operations center with representatives from the FBI, FEMA, and the military,[255] the New York Police Department (NYPD) operates much like an autonomous Department of Homeland Security—only without the constraints of the Constitution. The capabilities of the department are astounding. The leviathan can even take down an aircraft should the need arise.[256]

The NYPD has radiation detectors on their boats, helicopters, and officers' belts that are so sensitive they even alert officers to citizens who have had radiation treatment for medical reasons. Moreover, the NYPD has a $150 million surveillance system comprised of a network of more than 2000 cameras, monitored by an advanced computer system that can detect suspicious packages.[257] The NYPD also possesses portable scanners created in cooperation with the U.S. Department of Defense that can peer under people's clothing as they walk the streets.[258]

Minority Report?

In yet another partnership, this time with Microsoft, the NYPD is working to develop a Minority Report–type program that would allow law enforcement to collate various surveillance feeds in an effort to better target potential criminals. Dubbed the Domain Awareness System, the spy program "will allow police to quickly collate and visualise vast amounts of data from cameras, licence plate readers, 911 calls, police databases, and other sources."[259]

The system, which cost $30-40 million to develop, relies on 3,000 Closed-Circuit Television (CCTV) cameras positioned throughout the city, as well as a network of 2,600 radiation detectors.[260] Watchful government eyes can track a suspicious package or person over a number of days throughout the city by cross-referencing video feeds, license plate identifications, and criminal records. The system can, for example, pull up all recorded images of someone wearing a red shirt, thus streamlining

An NYPD Stop and Frisk (AP Photo/Gregory Bull)

the process of tracking New Yorkers.[261] And if a suspect's car is located via a license plate reader, the system will bring up not only its current location, but its past locations. The system will also consider "all other plates that have ever been scanned in the vicinity of the target vehicle within a 60-second window, allowing officers to determine if a culprit might be part of a larger, theretofore unknown caravan."[262]

With such an expansive amount of information being gathered under such dubious circumstances, this sophisticated surveillance program makes spying on civilians a routine part of the job for all law enforcement officials, not just the NYPD. (New York City and Microsoft intend to shop the jointly produced software to other cities, with New York City getting a 30% cut of the profits.[263]) But it will be par for the course in the near future.

Profiling, NYPD Style

In addition to its overt surveillance programs, the NYPD has also gained notoriety in recent years for its overt racial profiling, a spying program which targets Muslim communities and political activists, and a stop-and-frisk program that has targeted more than 4 million New Yorkers—the majority of whom were black or Latino and had done nothing wrong—over the course of the past decade or so.[264]

Cracking Down on Protesters (Angel Chevrestt / New York Daily News)

In 2011 alone, 684,330 people were stopped and frisked by the police: 88% were totally innocent. Of those stopped, the majority were either black or Latino.[265]

Building on the NYPD's blatant practice of racial profiling, police officers in New York have also initiated a spying program which includes amassing data on New York Muslims, such as where they buy groceries and which cafes they visit.[266] Among the tactics employed by the NYPD include the use of so-called "mosque crawlers," who document activities taking place at mosques; "rakers," who spy on Muslims in cafes and bookstores within the Muslim community[267] (both involve clear violations of state laws against religious profiling); and the forcible detention and recruiting of informants, who are threatened with arrest unless they comply with police demands.[268]

Cracking Down on Protesters

The NYPD is also infamous for its historic crackdowns on protesters, dating back to the 2004 Republican National Convention when 1,806 protesters were arrested (most of the arrests were later thrown out at a cost of $8 million to the city).[269] More recently, the NYPD flexed its substantial muscles to not only minimize the efforts of Occupy Wall Street protesters but also keep the media at a distance. One photographer who tried to take a picture of a bloodied protester being dragged away by police found himself slammed into a barricade and informed that he wasn't allowed to take photos.[270]

Loving Big Brother

What's happening in New York illustrates how easily people are led into the Orwellian illusion that security should trump freedom. However, as past regimes illustrate, such security measures eventually become tools of terror against the citizens themselves. "There are no safeguards to ensure that the NYPD doesn't break the law," warned author Leonard Levitt. "So far as I know, there are no mechanisms in place to ensure that the NYPD does not become a rogue organization."[271]

One thing is clear: if we as Americans continue to play into the desires of the government elite, if we continue to give credence to the political rat race, the foreign wars, the outrageous government spending, and the rigid conditioning of school children, we are simply digging our own graves. And on our tombstones it would be appropriate to have inscribed: "Here lie those who refused to listen to the warnings and speak up when freedom hung in the balance." And beneath that will be inscribed the last sentence in Orwell's *1984*, which describes Winston Smith following his re-education by the government. It reads simply: "He loved Big Brother."

A GOVERNMENT OF WOLVES

THE EMERGING POLICE STATE

PART IV

The Electronic Concentration Camp

OBEY OBEY

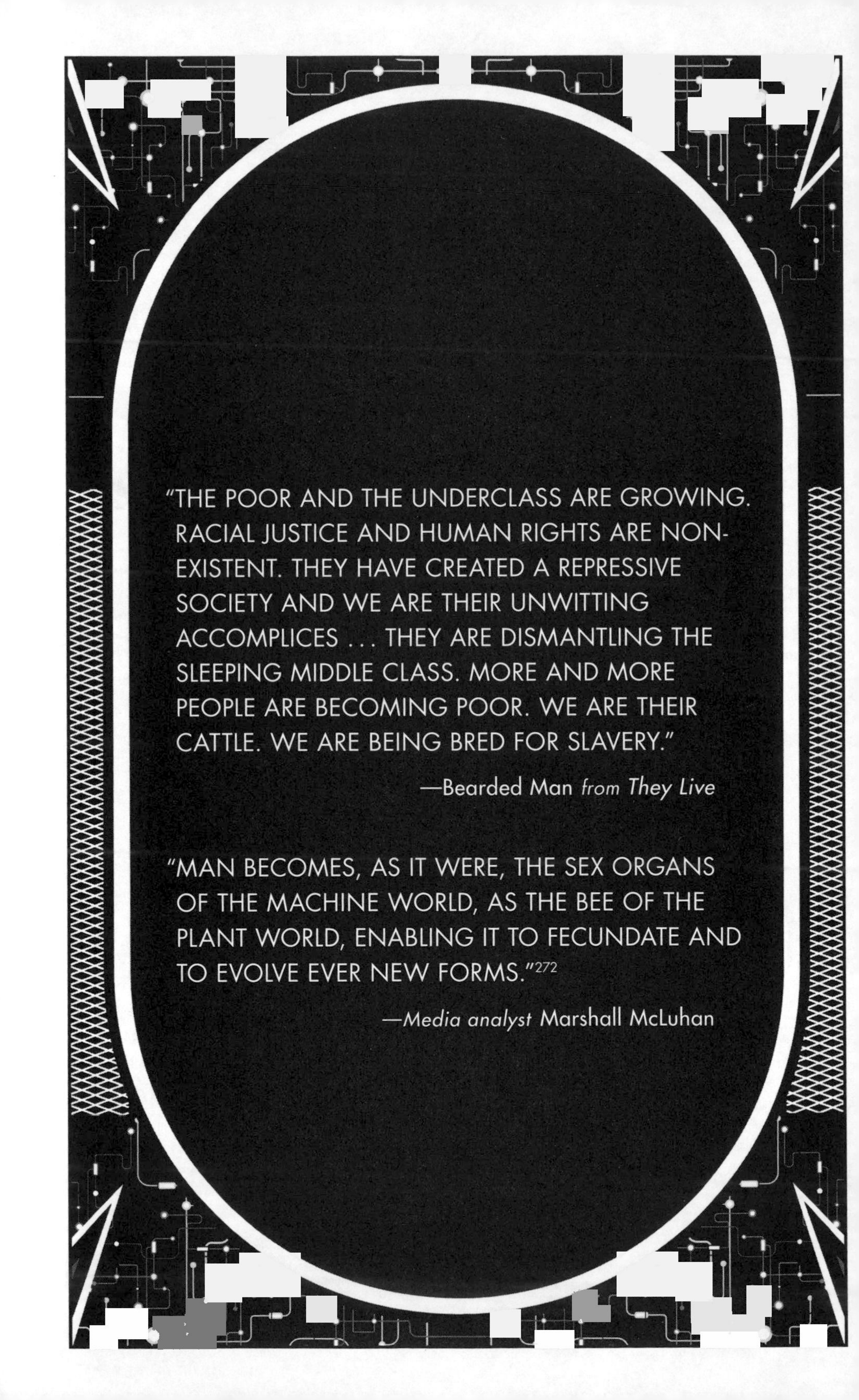
"THE POOR AND THE UNDERCLASS ARE GROWING. RACIAL JUSTICE AND HUMAN RIGHTS ARE NON-EXISTENT. THEY HAVE CREATED A REPRESSIVE SOCIETY AND WE ARE THEIR UNWITTING ACCOMPLICES . . . THEY ARE DISMANTLING THE SLEEPING MIDDLE CLASS. MORE AND MORE PEOPLE ARE BECOMING POOR. WE ARE THEIR CATTLE. WE ARE BEING BRED FOR SLAVERY."
—Bearded Man *from They Live*
"MAN BECOMES, AS IT WERE, THE SEX ORGANS OF THE MACHINE WORLD, AS THE BEE OF THE PLANT WORLD, ENABLING IT TO FECUNDATE AND TO EVOLVE EVER NEW FORMS."[272]
—*Media analyst* Marshall McLuhan

CHAPTER 12

The Matrix: Where They Live

"The Matrix is a system, Neo. That system is our enemy. But when you're inside, you look around, what do you see? Businessmen, teachers, lawyers, carpenters. The very minds of the people we are trying to save. But until we do, these people are still a part of that system and that makes them our enemy. You have to understand, most of these people are not ready to be unplugged. And many of them are so inured, so hopelessly dependent on the system, that they will fight to protect it."

—Morpheus, *The Matrix*

Technology is developing at such a rapid pace that it is inconceivable that mere human beings can control it. What has prompted such rapidity? The pressure, fear, and uncertainty resulting from the 9/11 attacks and their aftermath. War, fear of war and/or terrorist attacks "have always been considered the main incentives," writes media analyst Marshall McLuhan, "to the technological extension of our bodies." Furthermore:

> More even than the preparation for war, the aftermath of invasion is a rich technological period; because the subject culture has to adjust all its sense ratios to accommodate the impact of the invading culture. It is from such intensive hybrid exchange and strife of ideas and forms that the greatest social energies are released, and from which arise the greatest technologies.[273]

Combine America's expanding overseas military empire (where technology is tested for domestic use) with a fear of potential terrorist attacks (or "invasions"), and the resulting proliferation of invasive technologies that are littering the national landscape is explainable. The problem such technologies—what McLuhan calls "extensions of man"—pose is that they are so advanced as to operate autonomously. As a result, we are increasingly caught in an electronic concentration camp.

Cue *The Matrix*. In the 1999 film, computer programmer Thomas A. Anderson is secretly a hacker known as "Neo," who is intrigued by the cryptic references to the "Matrix" that appear on his computer. Eventually, Neo learns that intelligent computer systems which were created in the twenty-first century are acting autonomously and have taken control of all life on earth and now watch and control everyone. These computer systems harvest the bio-electrical energy of humans who are kept docile and distracted by the illusions that the entertainment media provides. And when Neo joins a resistance group led by Morpheus, he finds out that the police are more than willing to crack heads to keep dissidents in line with the status quo.

As this section will reveal, the U.S. government has an arsenal of technology that not only eviscerates the last vestiges of our privacy but controls us as well. No matter what you say, write, or do, there is a good chance that Big Brother—or perhaps more appropriately "Peeping Sam"—knows it. But why no outcry from the major media outlets? Why no alerts from those talking heads on television? Could it be that those who control the corporate media in conjunction with the government want to keep us distracted from the nefarious reality that surrounds us?

This was the essential plot of director John Carpenter's 1988 film *They Live*, where a group of down and out homeless men discover that people have been, in effect, so hypnotized by media distractions that they do not see that alien creatures control them. Caught up in the subliminal messages such as "obey" and "conform" being beamed out on television, billboards, and the like, people are unaware of the elite controlling their lives. And, of course, resistance is met with police aggression.

Carpenter, who also wrote the film's screenplay, was reacting to the commercialization of popular culture and politics. "I began watching TV again," said Carpenter. "I quickly realized that everything we see is designed to sell us something... The only thing they want to do is take our money."[274] Thus, the film echoes the mindless consumption of modern American culture that is engineered through the corporate media.

Again, as we have seen with other novels and films, the realms of fiction have now become our reality. Numb to the onslaught of technology, many continue to consume and smile as those who administer the electronic concentration camp invade every aspect of our lives. Although we live in a matrix administered by our own controllers, there is yet time to educate ourselves and take action. The reason "they live" is because we sleep. Time to wake up.

CHAPTER 13

The Federal "Gestapo"?

"The minute the FBI begins making recommendations on what should be done with its information, it becomes a Gestapo."[275]—J. EDGAR HOOVER (July 14, 1955)

If America is an electronic concentration camp, the FBI and its many agents are our wardens.

Sadly, the history of the Federal Bureau of Investigation (FBI) is the history of how America—once a nation that abided by the rule of law and held the government accountable for its actions—has steadily devolved into a police state where laws are unidirectional and intended as a tool for government to control the people.

J. Edgar Hoover (FBI Gallery)

Established in 1908 by President Theodore Roosevelt, the FBI started out as a small task force assigned to deal with specific domestic crimes, its first being to survey houses of prostitution in anticipation of enforcing the White Slave Traffic Act. Initially quite limited in its abilities to investigate so-called domestic crimes, the FBI has dramatically expanded in size, scope, and authority over the course of the past century.

Today, the FBI employs more than 35,000 individuals and operates more than 56 field offices in major cities across the U.S., as well as 400 resident agencies in smaller towns, and more than 50 international offices. In addition to their "data campus," which houses more than 96 million sets of fingerprints from across the United States and elsewhere, the FBI is also, according to *The Washington Post*, "building a vast repository controlled by people who work in a top-secret vault on the fourth floor of the J. Edgar Hoover FBI Building in Washington. This one stores the profiles of tens of thousands of Americans and legal residents who are not accused of any crime. What they have done is appear to be acting suspiciously to a town sheriff, a traffic cop or even a neighbor."[276]

The agency's reach is more invasive than ever. This is thanks, no doubt, to its nearly unlimited resources (its budget for fiscal year 2012 was $7.9 billion[277]), the government's vast arsenal of technology, the interconnectedness of government intelligence agencies, and information sharing through fusion centers. The latter are data collecting intelligence agencies spread throughout the country which constantly monitor communications (including those of American citizens), meaning everything from Internet activity and web searches to text messages, phone calls, and emails.

Neutralizing Dissidents

It was during the social and political upheaval of the 1960s, however, that the FBI's transformation into a federal policing and surveillance agency really began, one aimed not so much at the criminal element but at anyone who challenged the status quo—namely, those expressing anti-government sentiments. According to J. Edgar Hoover, the FBI's first and most infamous director, the United States was confronted with "a new style in conspiracy—conspiracy that is extremely subtle and devious and hence difficult to understand . . . a conspiracy reflected by questionable moods and attitudes, by unrestrained individualism, by nonconformism in dress and speech, even by obscene language, rather than by formal membership in specific organizations."[278]

Martin Luther King Jr.
(Dick DeMarsico/World Telegram & Sun)

Among those most closely watched by the FBI during that time period was Martin Luther King Jr., a man labeled by the FBI as the "most dangerous and effective Negro leader in the country."[279] With wiretaps and electronic bugs planted in his home and office, King was kept under constant surveillance by the FBI from 1958 until his death in 1968, all with the aim of "neutralizing King as an effective Negro leader."[280] King even received letters written by FBI agents suggesting that either he commit suicide or the details of his private life would be revealed to the public.[281] The FBI file on King is estimated to contain 17,000 pages of materials documenting his day-to-day activities. Incredibly, nearly fifty years later, the FBI maintains a stranglehold on information relating to this "covert" operation. Per a court order, information relating to the FBI wiretaps on King will not be released until 2027.

John Lennon, the ex-Beatle, was another such activist targeted for surveillance by the FBI. Fearing Lennon might incite antiwar protests, the Nixon administration directed the FBI to keep close tabs on the ex-Beatle, resulting in close to 400 pages of files on his activities during the early 1970s. But the government's actions didn't stop with mere surveillance. The agency went so far as to attempt to have Lennon deported on drug charges. As professor Jon Wiener, a historian who sued the federal government to have the files on Lennon made public, observed, "This is really the story of F.B.I. misconduct, of the President using the F.B.I. to get his enemies, to use federal agencies to suppress dissent and to silence critics."[282]

Violating the Law

Unfortunately, not even the creation of the Intelligence Oversight Board (IOB) by President Ford in 1976 could keep the FBI's surveillance activities within the bounds of the law. Whether or not those boundaries were respected in the ensuing years, they all but disappeared in the wake of the 9/11 attacks. This was true, especially with the passage of the USA Patriot Act, which gave the FBI and other intelligence agencies carte blanche authority to investigate Americans suspected of being anti-government. While the FBI's powers were being strengthened, President George W. Bush dismantled the oversight capabilities of the IOB, which was supposedly entrusted with keeping the FBI in check.

Even Barack Obama, a vocal critic of the Bush policies, failed to restore these checks and balances on the FBI. In fact, the Obama administration went so far as to insist that the FBI may obtain telephone records of international calls made from the United States without any formal legal process or court oversight. This rationale obviously applies to emails and text messages, as well.

Little wonder, then, that FBI abuses keep mounting. A 2011 report by the Electronic Frontier Foundation revealed that since 9/11 the FBI has been responsible for at least 40,000 violations of the law. Most of the violations dealt with "internal oversight guidelines," while close to one-third were "abuse of National Security Letters," and almost one-fifth were "violations of the Constitution, FISA, and other legal authorities."[283]

Created in the 1970s for espionage and terrorism investigations, National Security Letters (NSL) allow the FBI to bypass the Fourth Amendment's requirement of a court-sanctioned search warrant by allowing an agent to demand information merely on his say-so. The NSLs were originally intended as narrow exceptions in consumer privacy law, enabling the FBI to review in secret the customer records of suspected foreign agents. However, they have since been used for clandestine scrutiny of American citizens, U.S. residents, and visitors who are not alleged to be terrorists or spies.

As journalist Barton Gellman noted in *The Washington Post,* "The FBI now issues more than 30,000 national security letters a year, a hundredfold increase over historic norms. The letters—one of which can be used to sweep up the records of many people—are extending the bureau's reach as never before into the telephone calls, correspondence and financial lives of ordinary Americans."[284] It has since been revealed that the FBI issued more than 140,000 national security letters between 2003 and 2005, many involving people with no obvious connections to terrorism. Some of the FBI's clandestine surveillance on U.S. residents lasted for as long as eighteen months at a time without a search warrant, proper paperwork, or oversight.[285]

Pursuing Peace Activists

In many cases, those targeted by the FBI are ordinary American citizens doing nothing more than exercising their First Amendment right to free speech by criticizing the government or engaging in nonviolent, peaceful protest activities. As Michael German, a former FBI agent, observed, "You have a bunch of guys and women all over the country sent out to find terrorism. Fortunately, there isn't a lot of terrorism in many communities. So they end up pursuing people who are critical of the government."[286]

For example, on September 24, 2010, FBI agents raided the homes of five peace activists in the Minneapolis area. The agents filtered through all of the possessions in the activists' homes, seizing computers and cell phones, as well as other documents. An attorney for those targeted describes his clients—who include an activist-minded couple that sells silkscreened baby outfits and other clothes with phrases like "Help Wanted: Revolutionaries"—as "public non-violent activists with long, distinguished careers in public service, including teachers, union organizers and antiwar and community leaders."[287]

The activists targeted in the Minneapolis raid had been members in the antiwar and labor communities for many years.[288] Other targets of bureau surveillance, according to the *New York Times*, have included antiwar activists in Pittsburgh, animal rights advocates in Virginia, and liberal Roman Catholics in Nebraska. "When such investigations produce no criminal charges," notes the *Times*, "their methods rarely come to light publicly."[289]

Scott Crow (Todd Sanchioni)

One investigation that produced no charges but *did* come to light, thanks to a Freedom of Information Act request, focused on Scott Crow, a relatively obscure political activist who has been the object of intense surveillance by FBI counterterrorism agents.

At a massive 440 pages, Crow's FBI file speaks volumes about the way in which the government views the American people as a whole—as potential threats to national security—not to mention what it says about the FBI's complete disregard for the Fourth Amendment. Over the course of at least three years, Crow had agents staking out his house; tracking the comings and goings of visitors; monitoring his phone calls, mail, and email; sifting through his trash; infiltrating his circle of friends; and even monitoring him round the clock with a video camera attached to a phone pole across the street from his house.[290]

Given that no criminal charges were ever levied against Crow, it might appear that the agency went overboard in its efforts to monitor his activities. However, as we are discovering, such surveillance—even in the absence of credible evidence suggesting wrongdoing—is par for the course. For the federal government to go to such expense (*taxpayer* expense, that is) and trouble over a political activist, in particular, might seem rather paranoid. However, that is exactly what we are dealing with—a government that is increasingly paranoid about having its authority challenged and determined to discourage such challenges by inciting fear in the American people.

Make-Work Projects

The FBI has made a practice of singling out outspoken critics of the government for scrutiny (especially peace activists), attempting to assign them terrorist ties, and continuing the investigations long past the point at which they were found not guilty of having committed any crimes.

The question that must be asked is why. Why is the government expending so much energy on a relatively small group of peace and antiwar activists whose First Amendment activities comprise the totality of their "suspicious" behavior? Having acquired all of these new tools and powers post-9/11, of course the government wants to hold onto them and what better way to do so than by using them to ferret out "potential" threats.

This is what is described in government circles as a "make-work" project. A prime example of this occurred in 2002 when the FBI dispatched a special agent, armed with a camera, to a peace rally to search for terrorism suspects who might happen to be there, just to "see what they are doing."[291] The protest was sponsored by the Thomas Merton Center, an organization dedicated to advocating peaceful solutions to international conflicts,[292] and was composed primarily of individuals distributing leaflets.[293] The Office of Inspector General, in its report on FBI surveillance of domestic organizations, characterized the task provided to the special agent assigned to the Merton protest as a "make-work" project.[294]

Reversing the Burden of Proof

It gets worse. In late 2009 it was revealed that the FBI was granting its 14,000 agents expansive *additional* powers that include relaxing restrictions on a low-level category of investigations termed "assessments." This allows FBI agents, much like secret police, to investigate individuals using highly intrusive monitoring techniques, including infiltrating suspect organizations with confidential informants and photographing and tailing individuals,[295] without having any factual basis for suspecting them of wrongdoing.[296] (Incredibly, during the four-month period running from December 2008 to March 2009, the FBI initiated close to 12,000 assessments of individuals and organizations, and that was *before* the rules were further relaxed.)[297]

These newest powers, detailed in the FBI's operations manual, extend the agency's reach into the lives of average Americans and effectively transform the citizenry into a nation of suspects, reversing the burden of proof so that we are now all guilty until proven innocent. Thus, no longer do agents need evidence of possible criminal or terrorist activity in order to launch an investigation. Now, they can "proactively" look into people and organizations, as well as searching law enforcement and private electronic databases without making a record about it, conducting lie detector tests, searching people's trash, and deploying surveillance teams.

The point, of course, is that if agents aren't required to maintain a paper trail documenting their activities, there can be no way to hold the government accountable for subsequent abuses. Moreover, as an FBI general counsel revealed, agents want to be able to use the information found in a subject's trash or elsewhere to pressure that person to assist in a government investigation.[298] Under the new guidelines, surveillance squads can also be deployed repeatedly to follow "targets," agents can infiltrate organizations for longer periods of time before certain undisclosed "rules" kick in, and public officials, members of the news media or academic scholars can be investigated without the need for extra supervision.

All of this was sanctioned by the Obama administration, which, as the *New York Times* aptly notes, "has long been bumbling along in the footsteps of its predecessor when it comes to sacrificing Americans' basic rights and liberties under the false flag of fighting terrorism" and now "seems ready to lurch even farther down that dismal road than George W.

Bush did."[299] In fact, this steady erosion of our rights started long before Bush came into office. Indeed, it has little to do with political affiliation and everything to do with an entrenched bureaucratic mindset—call it the "Establishment," if you like—that, in its quest to amass and retain power, seeks to function autonomously and independent of the Constitution.

The Law of the Instrument

What we are experiencing with the FBI is a phenomenon that philosopher Abraham Kaplan referred to as the law of the instrument.[300] Or to put it another way: to a hammer, everything looks like a nail. Unfortunately, in the scenario that has been playing out in recent years, we have all become the nails to the government's hammer. After all, having equipped government agents with an arsenal of tools, weapons, and powers with which to vanquish the so-called forces of terror, it was inevitable that that same arsenal would eventually be turned on the citizenry.

CHAPTER 14

Living in Oceania

"We are taking a giant leap into the unknown, and the consequences for ourselves and our children may be dire and irreversible. Some day, soon, we may wake up and find we're living in Oceania."[301]—CHIEF JUDGE ALEX KOZINSKI, Ninth Circuit Court of Appeals, (voicing his discontent with the Ninth Circuit Court of Appeals' ruling in *United States v. Pineda-Moreno*, which declared the warrantless use of a GPS device by police to be constitutional)

Having outstripped our ability as humans to control it, technology, while useful and beneficial at times, seems to be turning into our Frankenstein's monster. Delighted with technology's conveniences, its ability to make our lives easier by doing an endless array of tasks faster and more efficiently, we have given it free rein in our lives with little thought to the legal or moral ramifications of doing so. Thus, we have no one but ourselves to blame for the fact that technology now operates virtually autonomously according to its own invasive code. It respects no one's intimate moments or privacy and is impervious to the foibles of human beings and human relationships. And with the proliferation of the police as conjoined with the FBI and other intelligence agencies, everyone—whether innocent or not—is now a suspect, much like living in Orwell's Oceania where Big Brother watched everyone.

Technology, thus, while providing benefits, has negatives which most are willing to overlook. For example, consider how enthusiastically we welcomed Global Positioning System (GPS) devices into our lives. We've installed this satellite-based technology, which is funded and operated by none other than the U.S. Department of Defense,[302] in everything from our phones to our cars to our pets. Yet by ensuring that we never get lost, never lose our loved ones, and never lose our wireless signals, we also made it possible for the government to never lose sight of us, as well.

Indeed, while many Americans are literally lost without their cell phones and GPS devices, they have also become ubiquitous conveniences for law enforcement agencies, which use them to track our every move.

GPS Devices

In January 2012 the U.S. Supreme Court issued a unanimous 9-0 ruling[303] in *United States v. Jones*, declaring that police must get a search warrant before using GPS technology to track criminal suspects. The ruling arose out of a September 2005 incident in which police, lacking a valid search warrant, placed a GPS device on the undercarriage of Antoine Jones' Jeep while it was parked in a public lot in Maryland. Jones, the co-owner of a nightclub in Washington, D.C., was suspected of being part of a cocaine-selling operation.

Every day—24 hours a day, seven days a week—for four weeks, the police used the GPS device to track Jones' movements and actions. Based upon the detailed information they were able to obtain about Jones' movements (including a trip to a Maryland stash house in which police reportedly found cocaine, crack, and $850,000 in cash), on October 24, 2005, police arrested and charged Jones with conspiring to distribute drugs. Jones was later convicted and sentenced to life in prison.

As the case made its way through the courts, the Obama Administration defended the actions of the Maryland police, insisting that GPS devices have become a common tool in crime fighting and that a person traveling on public roads has "no reasonable expectation of privacy" in his movements. In his ruling against such an unwarranted use of a tracking device by government officials, Judge Douglas H. Ginsburg of the District of Columbia Court of Appeals declared:

> It is one thing for a passerby to observe or even to follow someone during a single journey as he goes to the market or returns home from work. It is another thing entirely for that stranger to pick up the scent again the next day and the day after that, week in and week out, dogging his prey until he has identified all the places, people, amusements, and chores that make up that person's hitherto private routine . . . A reasonable person does not expect anyone to monitor and retain a record of every time he drives his car, including his origin, route, destination, and each place he stops and how long he stays there; rather, he expects each of those movements to remain disconnected and anonymous.[304]

Ginsburg rightly recognized the dangers of such a vast, uninhibited use of GPS technology: "A person who knows all of another's travel can deduce whether he is a weekly churchgoer, a heavy drinker, a regular at the gym, an unfaithful husband, an outpatient receiving medical treatment, an associate of particular individuals or political groups—and not just one such fact about a person, but all such facts."[305]

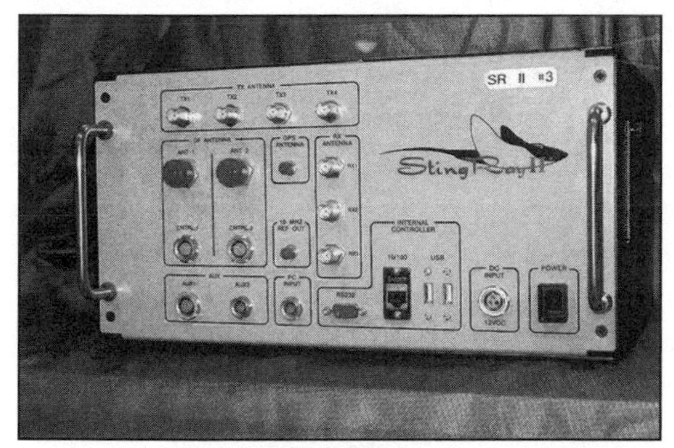

Stingray Surveillance Device Used to Track Mobile Phone Calls (US Patent and Trademark Office)

By the time *U.S. v. Jones* reached the U.S. Supreme Court, it had generated heated debate regarding where to draw the line when it comes to the collision of privacy, technology, constitutional rights and government surveillance. The arguments on both sides were far-ranging, with law enforcement agencies on one side defending warrantless searches and civil liberties advocates on the other insisting that if police can stick a GPS on a car, why not on a piece of clothing, or everyone's license plate?

Yet while a unanimous Supreme Court sided with Jones, declaring that the government's *physical* attachment of a GPS device to Antoine Jones' vehicle for the purpose of tracking Jones' movements[306] constitutes an unlawful search under the Fourth Amendment, the ruling failed to delineate the boundaries of permissible government surveillance within the context of rapidly evolving technologies.[307] Nor did it curb the government's ceaseless, suspicionless technological surveillance of innocent Americans. As Supreme Court Justice Samuel Alito recognized in his concurring judgment,[308] physical intrusion is now unnecessary to many forms of invasive surveillance. As we have seen, the government's current arsenal of surveillance technologies includes a multitude of devices which enable its agents to comprehensively monitor an individual's private life without necessarily introducing the type of *physical* intrusion into his person or property covered by the Court's ruling.

Your Cell Phone Tracks Your Every Move

Cell phones are a perfect example of how the government can track your every move without physically attaching a tracking device to your person or property. Unfortunately, the courts have provided little in the way of protection against such intrusions.[309] For example, an August 2012 ruling by the Sixth Circuit Court of Appeals declared that police can track the location of a cell phone *without* a warrant.[310]

In fact, using "stingray" devices, often housed in mobile surveillance vans, federal agents can not only target *all* cell phone signals, they can also track your *every* move by tapping into the data transferred from, received by, and stored in your cell phone. (Incredibly, one agent can track 200 or 300 people at a time.[311]) Your texts, web browsing, and geographic location are also up for grabs.[312]

Tens of thousands of cell tracking orders are issued every year, allowing police agencies to accurately pinpoint people's locations within a few yards. Unless they're charged with a crime, most people remain unaware that their cell data has been tracked.[313] In July 2012 it was revealed that cell phone carriers had responded to an astonishing 1.3 million requests from police agencies for personal information taken from people's cell phones. Sprint receives an average of 1,500 such requests per day.[314] A relatively small carrier, C Spire Wireless, received 12,500 requests in 2011 alone.[315] Keep in mind that a single request often involves targeting multiple people.[316] Even small police departments—at least, those willing to shell out upwards of $244,000 to get the technology necessary to track cell phones—are engaging in cell phone tracking with little to no oversight.[317]

In this way, Americans have been sold to the highest corporate bidder. This is nothing less than the corporate police state at work, with cell phone companies as willing accomplices in the government's efforts to track individuals using their cell phones. Cell phone companies actually make a handsome profit from selling the details of your private life to the government (AT&T collected $8.3 million in 2011 for their surveillance activities).[318]

Helping the government spy on Americans using their cell phones has become so profitable for cell phone carriers that they've come up with price lists for easy reference for police agencies. "Surveillance fees"—that is, your tax dollars at work—for sharing information on a person's location and activities can range from a few hundred to a few thousand dollars per request.[319] For example, Sprint, which has more than 100 employees dedicated to handling information requests from the government, "charged $120 per target number for 'Pictures and Video,' $60 for 'E-Mail,' $60 for 'Voicemail,' and $30 for 'SMS Content.'"[320]

On the rare occasion that a telecom corporation resists efforts by the police to spy on a particular cell phone customer, there are methods by which companies are coerced to comply with the data requests. Telecoms are frequently harassed by the FBI with National Security Letters, which are demands for user information without warrant or judicial oversight. These include a gag order, which prevents the recipient from discussing the demand with others, including the media. Roughly 300,000 of these NSLs have been sent out since 2000.[321]

"It's Not Even Past"

Unfortunately, with telecommunications companies storing user data, including text messages and Internet browsing history, for months to years at a time,[322] it will not be long before William Faulkner's observation that "The past is never dead. It's not even past"[323] becomes the truism of our age. Already, British researchers have created an algorithm that accurately predicts someone's future whereabouts at a certain time based upon where she and her friends have been in the past.[324]

Soon there really will be no place to escape from the government's electronic concentration camp. As journalist Pratap Chatterjee has noted, "[T]hese tools have the potential to make computer cables as dangerous as police batons."[325] With intelligence gathering and surveillance becoming booming business ventures, and with corporations rolling out technologies capable of filtering through vast reams of user data, tapping into underseas communication cables, and blocking websites for entire countries, privacy as we have known it will be extinct.

It must be noted that there is both an intrinsic and instrumental value to privacy. Intrinsically, privacy is precious to the extent that it is a component of liberty. Part of citizenship in a free society is the expectation that one's personal affairs and physical person are inviolable so long as one remains within the law. A robust conception of freedom includes the freedom from constant and intrusive government surveillance of one's life. From this perspective, Fourth Amendment violations are objectionable for the simple fact that the government is doing something it has no license to do—that is, invading the privacy of a law-abiding citizen by monitoring her daily activities and laying hands on her person without any evidence of wrongdoing.

Privacy is also instrumental in nature. This aspect of the right highlights the pernicious effects, rather than the inherent illegitimacy, of intrusive, suspicionless surveillance. For example, encroachments on individual privacy undermine democratic institutions by chilling free speech.[326] When citizens—especially those espousing unpopular viewpoints—are aware that the intimate details of their personal lives are pervasively monitored by government, or even that they could be singled out for discriminatory treatment by government officials as a result of their First Amendment expressive activities, they are less likely to freely express their dissident views.

No Place to Hide

So where does this leave us?

One of the hallmarks of citizenship in a free society is the expectation that one's personal affairs and physical person are inviolable so long as one conforms his or her conduct to the law. In other words, we should not have to worry about constant and covert government surveillance—whether or not that intrusion is physical or tangible and whether it occurs in public or private.

Unfortunately, in modern society, there really is no place to hide. Caught within the matrix of the American Oceania, we have arrived at a new paradigm where the concept of private property is eroding and along with it, the right against unreasonable searches and seizures once protected by the Fourth Amendment. In such a climate, everyone is a suspect. And you're guilty until you can prove yourself innocent.

Worse yet, those in control are using life's little conveniences, such as GPS devices and cell phones, to do much of the spying. And worst of all, the corporations who produce these little conveniences are happy to hand your personal information over to the police so long as their profit margins increase. To put it simply, the corporate-surveillance state is in full effect.

As Judge Kozinski concludes:

You can preserve your anonymity from prying eyes, even in public, by traveling at night, through heavy traffic, in crowds, by using a circuitous route, disguising your appearance, passing in and out of buildings and being careful not to be followed. But there's no hiding from the all-seeing network of GPS satellites that hover overhead, which never sleep, never blink, never get confused and never lose attention. Nor is there respite from the dense network of cell towers that honeycomb the inhabited United States. Acting together these two technologies alone can provide law enforcement with a swift, efficient, silent, invisible and *cheap* way of tracking the movements of virtually anyone and everyone they choose. Most targets won't know they need to disguise their movements or turn off their cell phones because they'll have no reason to suspect that Big Brother is watching them.[327]

CHAPTER 15

The Watchers and the Watched

"There was of course no way of knowing whether you were being watched at any given moment. How often, or on what system, the Thought Police plugged in on any individual wire was guesswork. It was even conceivable that they watched everybody all the time. But at any rate they could plug in your wire whenever they wanted to. You had to live—did live, from habit that became instinct—in the assumption that every sound you made was overheard, and, except in darkness, every movement scrutinized."[328]—GEORGE ORWELL, *1984*

As George Orwell warned, you have to live with the assumption that everything you do, say and see is being tracked by those who run the corporate surveillance state. That has also become the assumption under which we, too, must live given that advanced technology provided by the corporate state now enables government agents and police officers with the ability to track our every move. The surveillance state is our new society. It is here, and it is spying on you, your family, and your friends every day.

The government has inexhaustible resources when it comes to tracking our movements, from electronic wiretapping devices, traffic cameras, and biometrics to radio-frequency identification cards and satellites. Speech recognition technology now makes it possible for the government to carry out massive eavesdropping by way of sophisticated computer systems. Phone calls can be monitored, the audio converted to text files and stored in computer databases indefinitely. And if any "threatening" words are detected—no matter how inane or silly—the record can be flagged and assigned to a government agent for further investigation. In recent years, federal and state governments, as well as private corporations, have been amassing tools aimed at allowing them to monitor content. Users are profiled and tracked in order to identify, target, and even prosecute them.

The resulting loss of privacy highlights very dramatically the growing problem of the large governmental bureaucracy working in tandem with the megacorporations to keep tabs on the American citizenry. As such, what we are witnessing, in the so-called name of security and efficiency, is the creation of a new class system comprised of the *watched* (average Americans such as you and me) and the *watchers* (government bureaucrats, law enforcement agents, technicians, and private corporations). The growing need for technicians necessitates the bureaucracy. Thus, the massive bureaucracies—now technologically advanced—that administer governmental policy are a *permanent* form of government. Presidents come and go, but the nonelected bureaucrats remain.

Security-Industrial Matrix

The increasingly complex security demands of the massive federal governmental bureaucracy, especially in the areas of defense, surveillance, and data management, have been met within the corporate sector, which has shown itself to be a powerful ally that both depends on and feeds the growth of governmental bureaucracy. For example, *USA Today* reports that five years after the 9/11 terrorist attacks, the homeland security "business" was booming to such an extent that it eclipsed mature enterprises like moviemaking and the music industry in annual revenue.[329] This security spending by the government to private corporations is forecast to exceed $1 trillion in the near future.

Surveillance State Watchers (FBI Gallery)

Money, power, control. There is no shortage of motives fueling the convergence of megacorporations and government. But who is paying the price? The American people, of course, and it's taking a toll on more than our pocketbooks. "You have government on a holy mission to ramp up information gathering and you have an information technology industry desperate for new markets," says Peter Swire, the nation's first privacy counselor, who served during the Clinton Administration. "Once this is done, you will have unprecedented snooping abilities. What will happen to our private lives if we're under constant surveillance?"[330]

We're at that point now. Americans are subtly being conditioned to accept routine incursions on their privacy rights. However, at one time, the idea of a total surveillance state tracking one's every move would have been abhorrent to most Americans. That all changed with the 9/11 attacks. As professor Jeffrey Rosen observes, "Before Sept. 11, the idea that Americans would voluntarily agree to live their lives under the gaze of a network of biometric surveillance cameras, peering at them in government buildings, shopping malls, subways and stadiums, would have seemed unthinkable, a dystopian fantasy of a society that had surrendered privacy and anonymity."[331]

We have been sold a bill of goods. A good example of this is the ubiquitous surveillance cameras that are popping up everywhere across the country, despite the fact that they have been shown not to reduce crime. Indeed, a 2005 study by the British government, which boasts the most extensive surveillance camera coverage in the world at approximately 4 million cameras (one for every 14 people), found that of all the areas studied, surveillance cameras generally failed to achieve a reduction in crime. Indeed, while these snooping devices were supposed to reduce premeditated or planned crimes such as burglary, vehicle crime, criminal damage, and theft, they failed to have an impact on more spontaneous crimes, such as violence against the person and public order offenses such as public drunkenness.

Surveillance cameras have also been found to have a "displacement" effect on crime. Thus, rather than getting rid of crime, surveillance cameras force criminal activity to move from the area being watched to other surrounding areas.[332] And while a surveillance camera might help law enforcement identify a suicide bomber after the fact, as Marc Rotenberg of the Electronic Privacy Information Center notes, "Cameras are not an effective way to stop a person that is prepared to commit that kind of act." Rotenberg points to the 2005 terrorist subway bombings in London as an example. He explained that surveillance cameras "did help determine the identity of the suicide bombers and aided the police in subsequent investigations, but obviously they had no deterrent effect in preventing the act, because suicide bombers are not particularly concerned about being caught in the act."[333]

Electronic Footprints

Wherever you go and whatever you do, you are now being watched—especially if you leave behind an electronic footprint. And, of course, we leave plenty of electronic footprints for the watchers to follow.

When you buy food at the supermarket, purchase a shirt online or through a toll-free number, these transactions are recorded by data collection and information companies. In this way, you are specifically targeted as a particular type of consumer by private corporations. As if that were not worrisome enough, government intelligence agencies routinely collect these records—billions of them—about what you have done and where you have lived your entire life: every house or apartment, all your telephone numbers, the cars you've owned, ad infinitum.

When you use your cell phone you leave a record of when the call was placed, who you called, how long it lasted, and even where you were at the time. When you use your ATM card you leave a record of where and when you used the card. There is even a video camera at most locations. When you drive a car enabled with GPS you are tracked by satellite. And all of this once-private information about your consumer habits, your whereabouts, and your activities is now being fed to the U.S. government intelligence agencies.

Under the USA Patriot Act your bank is required to analyze your transactions for any patterns that raise suspicion and to see if you are connected to any "objectionable" people—ostensibly in the hunt for terrorists. If there are questions, your bank alerts the government, which shares such information with intelligence and law enforcement agencies across the country (local, county, state, and federal).

Fusion Centers

As if it weren't bad enough that the government is tracking individuals electronically, we're also being subjected to the peering, watchful eyes of Terrorism Liaison Officers (TLOs). TLOs are firefighters, police officers, and even corporate employees that are sprinkled across the country and have received training to spy on their fellow citizens and report back to

Control Center

government entities on their day-to-day activities. They are entrusted to report "suspicious activity," which includes taking pictures with no apparent aesthetic value, making measurements and drawings, taking notes, conversing in code, espousing radical beliefs, and buying items in bulk.[334]

TLOs report back to "fusion centers" where information is aggregated into government computers and pieced together to create profiles of citizens. Then information analysts determine if there are any individuals worth tracking down. "Fusion centers," which integrate local police and federal intelligence agencies, are a driving force behind the government's quest to collect, analyze, and disseminate information on American citizens. Fusion centers grew dramatically between the fiscal years of 2004 and 2008 with the help of more than $327 million in taxpayer-provided funding.[335]

Virtually every state has a fusion center in operation or formation.[336] More than seventy such data collecting agencies are already spread throughout the country,[337] constantly monitoring our communications, everything from our Internet activity and web searches to text messages, phone calls, and emails. This data is then fed to government agencies, which are now interconnected: the CIA to the FBI, the FBI to local police.

Too often, the partnership between law enforcement officials and fusion centers gives rise to procedures lacking in transparency and which skate alarmingly close to the edge of constitutional prohibitions against unreasonable searches, when they're not flouting them altogether.[338] Equally problematic is the fact that there is no nationally recognized structure for a fusion center, so each fusion center essentially establishes its own protocol, a shortcoming acknowledged by the Department of Homeland Security (DHS).[339]

The information gathered at these fusion centers travels not only up the chain of command, but down as well, and flows throughout the country.[340] All of this information-sharing from a vast number of sources means that a local police officer in Washington State can tap into the traveling or shopping habits of someone, innocent or not, in Florida.

On top of the extreme level of information-sharing among government entities, there has been a strong push to get private corporations to work with the government on information gathering. Boeing, the country's largest aircraft manufacturer and second-largest defense contractor, has pushed to take part in intelligence gathering, going so far as to try placing one of their representatives at the Washington Joint Analytical Center (WAJAC), a massive fusion center in Washington State.[341] Starbucks, Alaska Airlines, and Amazon have also expressed interest in working with the WAJAC.

Pools of Ineptitude

Incredibly, despite the roughly $1.4 billion[342] in taxpayer dollars poured into these fusion centers, they have, in the words of investigative journalist Robert O'Harrow, proven to be little more than "pools of ineptitude, waste and civil liberties intrusions."[343] This sorry impression is bolstered by a bipartisan report released in 2012 by the Senate Permanent Subcommittee on Investigations alleging that DHS has done very little to aid counterterrorism efforts with its seventy-seven (and growing) fusion centers, which suffer from a lack of oversight[344] and wasteful spending of "hundreds of millions of dollars."[345] Among the high-dollar purchases attributed to the fusion centers' wasteful spending are flat-screen TVs, a $6,000 laptop, and a $45,000 SUV used for commuting.[346]

Some DHS officials at the various fusion centers throughout the country received no more than five days of training in intelligence gathering. Despite this, they were being paid upwards of $80,000 a year. This lack of adequate training may help explain why innocent, constitutionally protected activities have been flagged as potentially terrorist in nature. For example, one intelligence report warned against a "Russian cyberattack," which turned out to be nothing more than an American employee accessing a work computer remotely.[347]

Unfortunately, the liberal application of the phrase "suspicious activity" has allowed fusion centers and intelligence agents to label pretty much any activity as a potential terror threat. The idea is to track "suspicious" individuals who are performing innocent activities which may add up to something more sinister. More often than not, however, the result is just a lot of dead ends. For example, of the 386 unclassified fusion center homeland intelligence reports reviewed by the Senate Permanent Subcommittee, "close to 300 of them had no discernible connection to terrorists, terrorist plots, or threats."[348]

Then again, you're bound to end up with few legitimate leads on "terrorist" activity if you classify unemployment as a cause for suspicion, which is actually one of the criteria used by TLOs.[349] The problem with tracking innocent behavior is that more often than not innocent people will be investigated for heinous crimes. For example, in 2007 a police officer filed a report on a man who had been seen purchasing "large quantities of liquid chlorine bleach and ammonia" on consecutive days. When that information traveled to the fusion center, it was picked out as a "suspicious activity" and the individual was investigated. It turned out that the man was a golf course owner attempting to circumvent a ban on gopher traps by killing the rodents with chlorine gas.[350]

Among the many groups of innocent people labeled suspicious and targeted for surveillance are pro-choice advocates, pro-life advocates, environmental activists, Tea Party members, Second Amendment rally attendees, third-party voters, Ron Paul supporters, anti-death penalty advocates, and antiwar activists.[351] According to a fusion center in Virginia, universities and religious institutions are potential hubs of extremism and terrorist activity. Another fusion center specifically cited historically black and Christian evangelical colleges as cause for concern.[352]

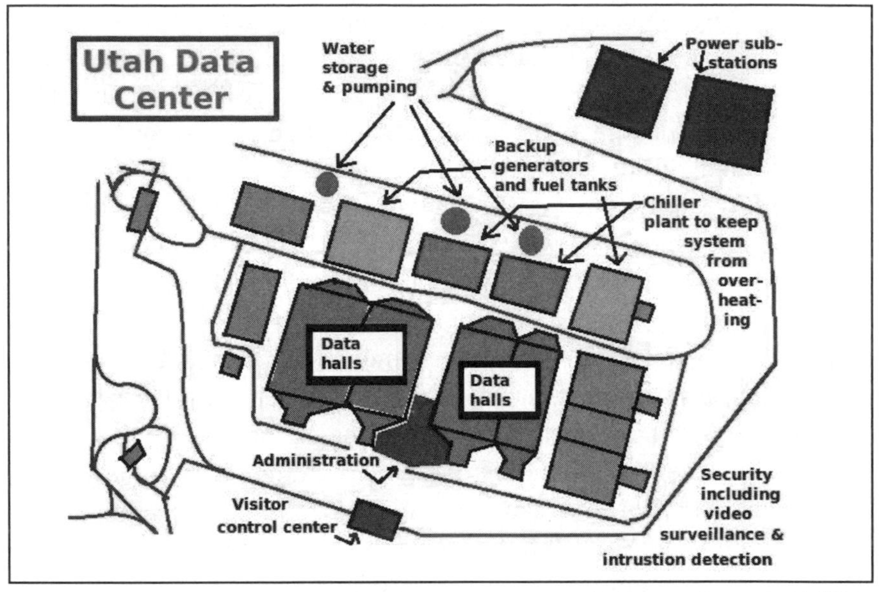

NSA Data Center in Bluffdale

America's Crown Jewel

Even with the preponderance of fusion centers and their poor track records, the government continues to push for more access, more control, and more surveillance of American citizens. The Utah Data Center (UDC), a $2 billion behemoth that houses a network of computers, satellites, and phone lines that stretches across the world,[353] serves as the crown jewel of the federal government's surveillance empire.

Situated in the small desert town of Bluffdale, Utah, not far from bustling Salt Lake City, the UDC is the central hub of the National Security Agency's (NSA) vast spying infrastructure. At five times the size of the U.S. Capitol,[354] the UDC is a clearinghouse and a depository for every imaginable kind of information[355] to be tracked, collected, catalogued, and analyzed by the UDC's supercomputers and its teams of government agents. In this way, by sifting through the detritus of your once-private life, the government will come to its own conclusions about who you are, where you fit in, and how best to deal with you should the need arise.[356]

What little we know about this highly classified spy center and its parent agency, the NSA, comes from James Bamford, a former intelligence analyst and an expert on the highly secretive government agency.

Bamford provides a chilling glimpse into the government's plans for total control, a.k.a., total information awareness. As Bamford notes, the NSA "has transformed itself into the largest, most covert, and potentially most intrusive intelligence agency ever created. In the process—and for the first time since Watergate and the other scandals of the Nixon administration—the NSA has turned its surveillance apparatus on the United States and its citizens."[357]

Supposedly created by the NSA in order to track foreign threats to America, as well as to shore up cybersecurity and battle hackers,[358] the UDC's technological capabilities are astounding. As the central depository for all of the information gathered by the NSA's vast spy centers, the UDC's supercomputers can download data amounting to the entire contents of the Library of Congress *every six hours*. However, the data targeted goes far beyond the scope of terrorist threats. In fact, as Bamford points out, the NSA is interested in nothing less than the "so-called invisible web, also known as the deep web or deepnet—data beyond the reach of the public. This includes password-protected data, U.S. and foreign government communications, and noncommercial file-sharing between trusted peers."[359]

Everybody's a Target

That the NSA, which has shown itself to care little for constitutional limits or privacy, is the driving force behind this spy center is no surprise. The agency—which is three times the size of the CIA, consumes one third of the intelligence budget and has a global spy network[360]—has a long history of spying on Americans, whether or not it has always had the authorization to do so. Take, for instance, the warrantless wiretapping program conducted during the George W. Bush years,[361] which resulted in the NSA monitoring the private communications of millions of Americans—a program that continues unabated today—with help from private telecommunications companies such as AT&T. The program recorded 320 million phone calls *a day* when it first started.[362] It is estimated that the NSA has intercepted at least 20 trillion communications by American citizens since 9/11.[363]

Clearly, the age of privacy in America is coming to a close. We have moved into a new paradigm in which surveillance technology that renders everyone a suspect is driving the bureaucratic ship that once was our democratic republic. We are all becoming data collected in government files. As a senior intelligence official previously involved with the National Security Agency's Utah Data Center remarked, "Everybody's a target; everybody with communication is a target."[364]

The author and dissident Aleksandr Solzhenitsyn, who suffered under the secret police in the Soviet Union, wrote about this process some years ago:

> As every man goes through life he fills in a number of forms for the record, each containing a number of questions . . . There are thus hundreds of little threads radiating from every man, millions of threads in all. If these threads were suddenly to become visible, the whole sky would look like a spider's web, and if they materialized like rubber bands, buses and trams and even people would lose the ability to move and the wind would be unable to carry torn-up newspapers or autumn leaves along the streets of the city.[365]

CHAPTER 16

A Total Control Society

"The privacy and dignity of our citizens [are] being whittled away by sometimes imperceptible steps. Taken individually, each step may be of little consequence. But when viewed as a whole, there begins to emerge a society quite unlike any we have seen—a society in which government may intrude into the secret regions of a [person's] life."[366]

—Former U.S. Supreme Court Justice WILLIAM O. DOUGLAS

The obvious goal of the corporate state, of course, is to create a total control society—one in which the government is able to track the movements of people in real time and control who does what, when, and where. This is accomplished through mass surveillance, sold to the American people by way of the two highly manipulative, siren-song catchwords of our modern age—security and convenience.

Surveillance once relied primarily on government or corporate agents peering through binoculars, listening to conversations through a bugged telephone, or actively monitoring a camera. However, the government's mass surveillance tools are many and growing. This includes, at a bare minimum, surveillance cameras, electronic eavesdropping devices, traffic cameras, biometrics, radio-frequency identification cards, and satellites, all of which persistently monitor the behaviors and actions of the public while intruding on one's privacy.

Technology is on the march and there are virtually no limitations to its uses against American citizens. The U.S. government and its corporate allies are looking out for you—literally—with surveillance tools intended to identify you, track your whereabouts, monitor your activities and allow or restrict your access to people, places, or things deemed suitable by the government.

Surveillance Cameras

As of 2007 there were approximately 30 million surveillance cameras located throughout the United States. At that time, the average American was captured on film by a surveillance camera more than 200 times a day.[367] Thus, surrounded at every turn by surveillance cameras in one form or another on street corners, at the ATM, at convenience stores, and even in public restrooms, Americans have proven to be relatively adaptable to life in a goldfish bowl.

Indeed, surveillance cameras, which operate in real time, and can be seen perched on traffic lights, alongside highways and roads, on bridges, expressways, and even on school buses, are perhaps the perfect example of how easy it was for the government to lead us down that slippery slope into a surveillance state. Sold to the public as safety devices to monitor traffic jams, catch drivers who break the law by speeding or perhaps running a red light, these cameras—often operated by private corporations—are little more than surveillance and revenue-raising devices for corporations, states, and municipalities, which use them to levy fines against alleged lawbreakers.[368] Yet when coupled with license-plate readers, mobile scanners, and iris scanners to full-body scanners in airports, biometric ID cards, etc., they become yet another layer in our surveillance society.

Mobile Scanners

There is no limit to what these technological gadgets can do in the so-called name of efficiency, expediency, economy, and security. For example, law enforcement agencies now have license-plate recognition scanners that can sweep a parking lot full of cars in under a minute and check them against police databases. "Police like the devices for their speed and efficiency but mostly for their ability to record thousands of plates and their locations each day," writes journalist Christine Vendel. "The information is loaded wirelessly into a police database and archived for possible searches later."[369]

With such a tool at its disposal, the government can retroactively pinpoint exactly where you were on any given day. And if you have the bad luck of being in the wrong place at the wrong time, the burden of proving your innocence will rest with you.

For some years now, Americans have been conditioned to full-body scans and invasive pat downs at airports. Now a mobile version of an airport full-body scanner is already roaming some of America's streets and neighborhoods. Mounted in nondescript delivery vehicles that enable police or other government agents to blend into urban and other landscapes, these roving x-ray scanners "bounce a narrow stream of x-rays off and through nearby objects, and read which ones come back," thereby producing instantaneous photo-like images of whatever the van passes—whether cars, trucks, containers, homes, or people.[370]

In other words, the government can now do drive-by strip searches of your person and your home, including monitoring what you are doing in the privacy of your home. Even though you may be innocent of any wrongdoing whatsoever, *every* aspect of your life, as well as *every* room of your house and *everything* you do in your house, will be under scrutiny by government agents—and can and will be recorded and used against you at a later date.

Biometrics

Biometrics, a method of identifying someone based upon their individual biological traits, has enabled the government to go far beyond fingerprinting to pinpoint a person based on his most unique characteristics, whether it is the shape of his face, iris patterns, gait, or veins.[371] Thanks to the corporate world's eagerness to jump on the biometric bandwagon by requesting people's fingerprints rather than a password, for example, or an iris scan in lieu of a key, the government (its partner in crime, so to speak) now has an infinite number of ways in which to track each individual citizen.

With biometrics promising to be an $11 billion industry by 2017, the demand by government and corporate entities for these disguised data collection systems will only accelerate, as will the accuracy of the programs.[372] For example, facial recognition, once thwarted by basic methods of evasion, can now identify "people obscured by sunglasses, hats, and windshields." Soon, it is expected that basic consumer items like cell phones will have the ability to carry out iris scans and fingerprint recognition.[373] "In 10 years," predicts Joseph Atick, co-founder of the International Biometrics and Identification Association, "[facial recognition] technology is going to be so good you can identify people in public places very easily."[374]

Facial and iris recognition machines have come into greater use in recent years, ostensibly to detect criminals, streamline security checkpoints processes, and facilitate everyday activities. However, their uses are becoming more routine every day. For example, ticket holders at Walt Disney World must use their fingerprints to access the park. Some fitness centers, like 24 Hour Fitness, rely on fingerprint scans to give customers access to their facilities.[375] In the summer of 2011, Facebook implemented a new facial recognition feature which automatically tagged individuals in photos uploaded by their friends.[376]

Iris Scanners

Iris scanning works by reading the unique pattern found on the iris, the colored part of the eyeball. This pattern is unique even among individuals with the exact same DNA.

The perceived benefits of iris scan technology, we are told, include a high level of accuracy, protection against identity theft, and the ability to quickly search through a database of the digitized iris information. It also provides corporations and the government—that is, the corporate state—with a streamlined, uniform way to track and access *all* of the information amassed about us, from our financial and merchant records, to our medical history, activities, interests, travels, and so on.

In this way, iris scans become de facto national ID cards, which can be implemented without our knowledge or consent. In fact, the latest generation of iris scanners can even capture scans on individuals in motion who are six feet away. And as these devices become more sophisticated, they will only become more powerfully invasive. As Jeff Carter, CDO of Global Rainmakers, stated, "In the future, whether it's entering your home, opening your car, entering your workspace, getting a pharmacy prescription refilled, or having your medical records pulled up, everything will come off that unique key that is your iris. Every person, place, and thing on this planet will be connected [to the iris system] within the next 10 years."[377]

As *Fast Company* reports:

> For such a Big Brother-esque system, why would any law-abiding resident ever volunteer to scan their irises into a public database, and sacrifice their privacy? GRI hopes that the immediate value the system creates will alleviate any concern. "There's a lot of convenience to this—you'll have nothing to carry except your eyes," says Carter, claiming that consumers will no longer

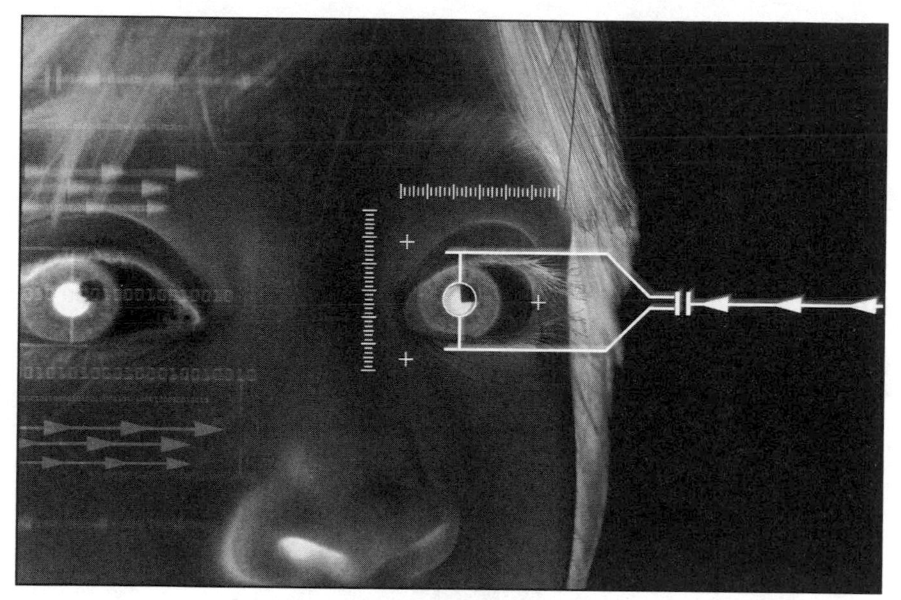

Iris Scanners at Work

be carded at bars and liquor stores. And he has a warning for those thinking of opting out: "When you get masses of people opting-in, opting out does not help. Opting out actually puts more of a flag on you than just being part of the system. We believe everyone will opt-in."[378]

Iris scanning technology has already been implemented in the United States. For example, the U.S. Department of Homeland Security ran a two-week test of iris scanners at a Border Patrol station in McAllen, Texas, in October 2010. That same month, in Boone County, Missouri, the sheriff's office unveiled an Iris Biometric station purchased with funds provided by the U.S. Department of Justice.[379] Unknown by most, the technology is reportedly already being used by law enforcement in forty states throughout the country.[380]

There's even an iPhone app in the works that will allow police officers to use their iPhones for on-the-spot, on-the-go iris scanning of American citizens. The manufacturer, B12 Technologies, has already equipped police with iPhones armed with facial recognition software linked to a statewide database which, of course, federal agents also have access to. (And for those who have been protesting the whole-body imaging scanners at airports as overly invasive, just wait until they include the iris scans in their security protocol. The technology has already been tested in about twenty U.S. airports as part of a program to identify passengers who could skip to the front of security lines.)

AOptix Technologies, a force behind cutting-edge biometrics, proudly boasts that its scanners are not only fully automated but can capture high quality images at eighteen meters and perform stand-off iris recognition at two meters. Moreover, the company credits itself with the successful iris enrollment of children as young as five months of age.[381] Of course, iris enrollment of five-month-old babies serves little purpose other than to ensure that future generations will be registered and catalogued in a database long before they're old enough to realize its sinister implications. Then again, it's a safe bet that those same young people will be so immersed in the surveillance culture as to never recognize the electronic concentration camp closing in on them.

Facial Recognition Software

The FBI's $1 billion Next Generation Identification (NGI) system, which expands the government's current ID database from a fingerprint system to a facial recognition system using a variety of biometric data, cross-referenced against the nation's growing network of surveillance cameras, not only tracks your every move but creates a permanent "recognition" file on you within the government's massive databases.[382]

By the time it's fully operational in 2014,[383] NGI will serve as a vast data storehouse of "iris scans, photos searchable with face recognition technology, palm prints, and measures of gait and voice recordings alongside records of fingerprints, scars, and tattoos." One component of NGI, the Universal Face Workstation, already contains some 13 million facial images, gleaned from "criminal mug shot photos" taken during the booking process. However, with major search engines having "accumulated face image databases that in their size dwarf the earth's population,"[384] it's only a matter of time before the government taps into the trove of images stored on social media and photo sharing websites such as Facebook.

Real-Time Surveillance

Also aiding and abetting police in the government's efforts to track our every movement in real time is Trapwire, which allows for the quick analysis of live feeds of people's facial characteristics from CCTV

SkyWatch Mobile Surveillance Tower

surveillance cameras. Some of Trapwire's users range from casinos in Las Vegas to police in Washington, D.C., New York, Los Angeles, Canada, and London.[385] Utilizing Trapwire in conjunction with NGI, police and other government agents will be able to pinpoint anyone by checking the personal characteristics stored in the database against images on social media websites, feeds from the thousands of CCTV surveillance cameras installed throughout American cities (there are 3,700 CCTV cameras tracking the public in the New York subway system alone[386]), as well as data being beamed down from the more than 30,000 surveillance drones taking to the skies within the next eight years.

Given that the drones' powerful facial recognition cameras will be capable of capturing minute details, including every mundane action performed by every person in an entire city simultaneously,[387] soon there really will be nowhere to run and nowhere to hide.

A Noxious Mix

The government's massive identification databases include criminals and non-criminals alike—in other words, innocent American citizens. The information is being amassed through a variety of routine procedures, with the police leading the way as prime collectors of biometrics for something as non-threatening as a simple moving violation.[388] This effort is helped along by the Mobile Offender Recognition and Information System, or MORIS, a physical iPhone add-on that allows officers patrolling the streets to scan the irises and faces of individuals and match them against government databases.[389]

The nation's courts are also doing their part to "build" the database, requiring biometric information as a precursor to more lenient sentences. In March 2012 New York Governor Andrew Cuomo signed a law allowing DNA evidence to be collected from anyone convicted of a crime, even if it's a non-violent misdemeanor.[390] New York judges have also begun demanding mandatory iris scans before putting defendants on trial.

Then there are the nation's public schools, where young people are being conditioned to mindlessly march in lockstep to the pervasive authoritarian dictates of the surveillance state. It was here that surveillance cameras and metal detectors became the norm. It was here, too, that schools began reviewing social media websites in order to police student activity. With the advent of biometrics, school officials have gone to ever more creative lengths to monitor and track students' activities and whereabouts, even for the most mundane things. For example, students in Pinellas County, Florida, are actually subjected to vein recognition scans when purchasing lunch at school.[391]

Of course, the government is not the only looming threat to our privacy and bodily integrity. As with most invasive technologies, the groundwork to accustom the American people to the so-called benefits or conveniences of facial recognition is being laid quite effectively by corporations. For example, a new Facebook application, Facedeals, is being tested in Nashville, Tennessee, which enables businesses to target potential customers with specialized offers. Yet another page borrowed from Stephen Spielberg's film *Minority Report,* the app works like this: businesses install cameras at their front doors which, using facial recognition technology, identify the faces of Facebook users and then send coupons to their smartphones based upon things they've "liked" in the past.[392]

Even store mannequins have gotten in on the gig. According to the *Washington Post,* mannequins in some high-end boutiques are now being outfitted with cameras that utilize facial recognition technology. A small camera embedded in the eye of an otherwise normal looking mannequin allows storekeepers to keep track of the age, gender, and race of all their customers. This information is then used to personally tailor the shopping experience to those coming in and out of their stores. As the *Washington Post* report notes, "a clothier introduced a children's line after the dummy showed that kids made up more than half its mid-afternoon traffic . . . Another store found that a third of visitors using one of its doors after 4 p.m. were Asian, prompting it to place Chinese-speaking staff members by that entrance."[393]

At $5,072 a pop, these EyeSee mannequins come with a steep price tag, but for storeowners who want to know more—*a lot more*—about their customers, they're the perfect tool, able to sit innocently at store entrances and windows, leaving shoppers oblivious to their hidden cameras.[394] Italian mannequin maker Almax SpA, manufacturer of the EyeSee mannequins, is currently working on adding ears to the mannequins, allowing them to record people's comments in order to further tailor the shopping experience.[395]

Making this noxious mix even more troubling is the significant margin for error and abuse that goes hand in hand with just about every government-instigated program, only more so when it comes to biometrics and identification databases. Take, for example, the Secure Communities initiative. Touted by the Department of Homeland Security as a way to crack down on illegal immigration, the program attempted to match the inmates in local jails against the federal immigration database. Unfortunately, it resulted in Americans being arrested for such things as reporting domestic abuse and occasionally flagged U.S. citizens for deportation.[396] More recently, in July 2012, security researcher Javier Galbally demonstrated that iris scans can be spoofed, allowing a hacker to use synthetic images of an iris to trick an iris-scanning device into thinking it had received a positive match for a real iris over 50 percent of the time.[397]

The Writing Is on the Wall

With technology moving so fast and assaults on our freedoms and privacy occurring with increasing frequency, there is little hope of turning back this technological, corporate, and governmental juggernaut. Even trying to avoid inclusion in the government's massive identification database will be nearly impossible. The hacktivist group Anonymous suggests wearing a transparent plastic mask, tilting one's head at a 15 degree angle, wearing obscuring makeup, and wearing a hat outfitted with infrared LED lights as methods for confounding the cameras' facial recognition technology.[398]

Yet for those who can read the writing on the wall, the message is clear: we're living in *The Matrix* of the corporate police state from which there is little hope of escape. The government has taken on the identity of the corporation, which exists to make money and amass power—not protect freedoms. Together, these surveillance tools form a toxic cocktail for which there is no cure. By subjecting Americans to biometric scans in public and other insidious forms of surveillance without their knowledge or compliance and then storing the data for later use, the government—in conjunction with the corporate state—has erected the ultimate suspect society. In such an environment, there is no such thing as "innocent until proven guilty." We are all potentially guilty of some wrongdoing or other.

They Live

Ultimately, the erection of the electronic concentration camp comes back to power, money, and control—how it is acquired and maintained, and how those who seek it or seek to keep it tend to sacrifice anything and everything in its name. In the meantime, like those caught within the confines of *They Live*, we are to conform and obey.

This is the same scenario that George Orwell warned about in *1984*. It is a warning we have failed to heed. As veteran journalist Walter Cronkite observed in his preface to a commemorative edition of *1984*:

> *1984* is an anguished lament and a warning that vibrates powerfully when we may not be strong enough nor wise enough nor moral enough to cope with the kind of power we have learned to amass. That warning vibrates powerfully when we allow ourselves to sit still and think carefully about orbiting satellites that can read the license plates in a parking lot and computers that can read into thousands of telephone calls and telex transmissions at once and other computers that can do our banking and purchasing, can watch the house and tell a monitoring station what television program we are watching and how many people there are in a room. We think of Orwell when we read of scientists who believe they have *located* in the human brain the seats of behavioral emotions like aggression, or learn more about the vast potential of genetic engineering. And we hear echoes of that warning chord in the constant demand for greater security and comfort, for less risk in our societies. We recognize, however dimly, that greater efficiency, ease, and security may come at a substantial price in freedom, that "law and order" can be a *doublethink* version of oppression, that individual liberties surrendered for whatever good reason are freedoms lost.[399]

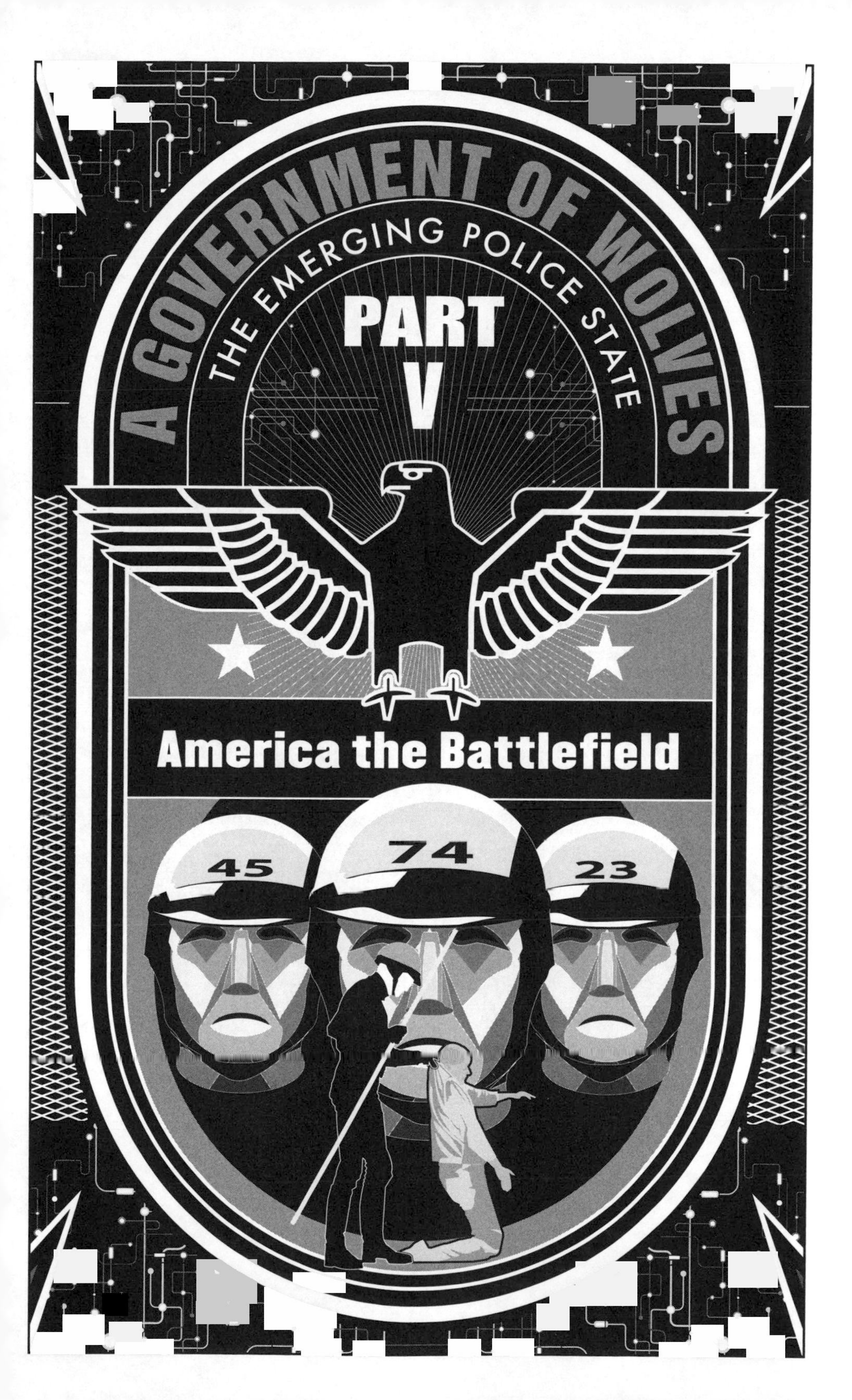
A GOVERNMENT OF WOLVES
THE EMERGING POLICE STATE
PART
V
America the Battlefield
45
74
23

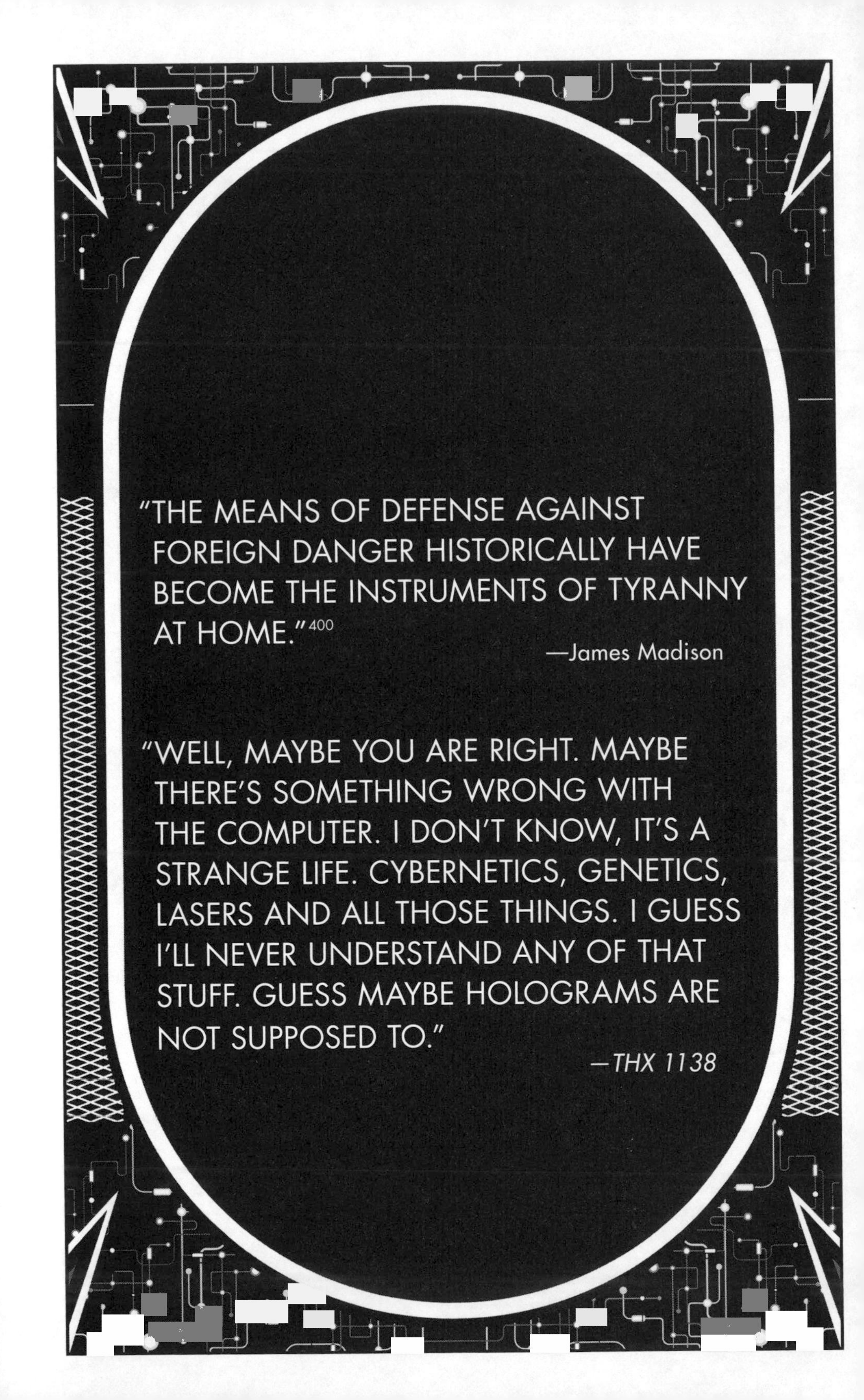
"THE MEANS OF DEFENSE AGAINST FOREIGN DANGER HISTORICALLY HAVE BECOME THE INSTRUMENTS OF TYRANNY AT HOME."[400]
—James Madison
"WELL, MAYBE YOU ARE RIGHT. MAYBE THERE'S SOMETHING WRONG WITH THE COMPUTER. I DON'T KNOW, IT'S A STRANGE LIFE. CYBERNETICS, GENETICS, LASERS AND ALL THOSE THINGS. I GUESS I'LL NEVER UNDERSTAND ANY OF THAT STUFF. GUESS MAYBE HOLOGRAMS ARE NOT SUPPOSED TO."
—*THX 1138*

CHAPTER 17

Subduing a Populace: THX 1138

"Government by clubs and firing squads ... is not merely inhumane (nobody cares much about that nowadays); it is demonstrably inefficient and, in an age of advanced technology, inefficiency is the sin against the Holy Ghost."[401]

—ALDOUS HUXLEY

Killing people is a messy thing—especially if it happens to be a government killing its own citizens. Shooting protesters who get rowdy, for example, invariably attracts more media attention and bad press for the police. The solution? Weapons of compliance, such as tasers, which inflict pain and subdue dissidents but which don't incite quite as much public outrage.

A far more effective way to subdue a population, more so than through the use of compliance weapons, is to numb them with drugs, which come in all shapes and sizes. Of the many drugs available, legal and illicit alike, the drug of materialism—the endless pursuit of consumerism—is the most effective at distracting the populace from what is happening around them. Coupled with the wall-to-wall corporate entertainment complex and the distractions of everyday life, it's a wonder that there is any resistance at all to the emerging police state.

Then there are the actual prescription drugs that permeate American society. For example, the National Center for Health Statistics released a report in 2010 indicating that there has been a steady increase in the number of Americans taking at least one prescription drug. According to the study, 48% of Americans are on at least one prescription drug, 31% are on two or more, and 11% are on five or more. One in five children are on a prescription drug and 90% of older Americans use prescription drugs. Adolescents most commonly use "central nervous system stimulants," such as those used to treat conditions such as ADD/ADHD. Middle aged individuals most often use antidepressants.

In 2008, $234.1 billion were spent on prescription drugs, twice the amount spent in 1999.[402] At the same time, we have seen an increase in the pharmaceutical corporations advertising directly to "consumers." For example, Oxycontin advertising spending increased to $30 million annually between the years 1996 and 2001.[403] The manufacturers of these dangerous drugs are basically legally protected drug dealers, except that their impact is much more widespread and deadly than the guy selling marijuana on the corner.

Such is the scenario in director George Lucas' *THX 1138*, where the use of mind-altering drugs is mandatory. In this future world, narcotics—prescription drugs, that is—are critical in both maintaining compliance and for ensuring that the citizenry can endure the mindless but demanding jobs required of them. In this futuristic world, people no longer have names but letters and numbers such as THX 1138, who works in a factory producing android policemen. Eventually, THX 1138, with the help of a girl who weans him off the drugs, begins to wake up to the monochrome reality surrounding him. From there, THX 1138 tries to escape, chased by robots and android cops.

Unlike THX 1138, the great majority of Americans, while being fed a diet of bread, circuses, and prescription drugs, don't seem to want to escape. All the while, the corporate state is erecting an electronic concentration camp around us. And to those who dare complain and take active steps in exercising their rights, the police are armed with a whole host of stinging devices to corral them.

Welcome to the battlefield that is America.

CHAPTER 18

Tactics of Intimidation

"I was astonished, bewildered. This was America, a country where, whatever its faults, people could speak, write, assemble, demonstrate without fear. It was in the Constitution, the Bill of Rights. We were a democracy ... But I knew it wasn't a dream; there was a painful lump on the side of my head ... The state and its police were not neutral referees in a society of contending interests. They were on the side of the rich and powerful. Free speech? Try it and the police will be there with their horses, their clubs, their guns, to stop you. From that moment on, I was no longer a liberal, a believer in the self-correcting character of American democracy. I was a radical, believing that something fundamental was wrong in this country—not just the existence of poverty amidst great wealth, not just the horrible treatment of black people, but something rotten at the root. The situation required not just a new president or new laws, but an uprooting of the old order, the introduction of a new kind of society—cooperative, peaceful, egalitarian."[404]—HOWARD ZINN

We're entering the final phase of America's transition to authoritarianism, a phase notable for its co-opting of civilian police as military forces. Not only do the police now look like the military—with their foreboding uniforms and phalanx of lethal weapons—but they function like them, as well. As we have seen, in many instances, no longer do they act as peace officers guarding against violent criminals. And no more do we have a civilian police force entrusted with serving and protecting the American people. Instead, today's militarized law enforcement officials, have, it seems, shifted their allegiance from the citizenry to the state, acting preemptively to ward off any possible challenges to the government's power.

NYPD Disorder Control Unit (CS Muncy)

We're the Enemy

In such an environment, free speech is little more than a nuisance to be stamped out. Nowhere is this more evident than in the way police deal with those who dare to exercise their First Amendment right to "peaceably assemble, and to petition the Government for a redress of grievances." For example, Chicago police in riot gear and gas masks, as well as SWAT teams,[405] clashed with thousands of antiwar protesters who gathered to air their discontent during the NATO summit that took place in May 2012.[406]

Anticipating a fracas, police during the weeks leading up to the NATO summit had equipped themselves with $1 million worth of militarized riot gear.[407] Then, a few days before the summit commenced, fighter jets—including Air Force KC-135 tankers, Air Force F-16s, and Coast Guard HH-65 Dolphin helicopters—took to the skies over Chicago as part of a "security" drill. Surveillance drones were also sighted.[408] Police also arrested six activists and held them in solitary confinement for 18 hours, then released them without charge. News reports indicated that some of those "arrested" may have been undercover officers.[409]

All of these tactics of intimidation—the show of force by heavily armed police, the security drills by fighter planes and surveillance drones, even the arrests of protesters—were done with one goal in mind: to deter and subdue any would-be protesters. Yet what many Americans fail to realize, caught up as they are in the partisan-charged rhetoric being pumped out by politicians and the media, is that the government does not discriminate when it comes to clamping down on dissent. We are all the enemy. Thus it doesn't matter what the content of the speech might be, whether it's coming from protesters speaking out against corrupt government practices or peace activists attempting to advance an antiwar message. In the face of the government's growing power, we are all lumped into the same category: potential nuisances and rabble-rousers who must be surveilled, silenced, and, if necessary, shut down.

Case in point: in anticipation of the 2012 Democratic and Republican National Conventions that took place in Charlotte and Tampa, government agencies in conjunction with the militarized police prepared to head off any protests by refusing to issue permits, cordoning off city blocks, creating "free speech" zones and passing a litany of laws banning everything from protesters wearing masks to carrying string. The few protesters who managed to take to the streets were faced with an array of non-lethal weapons meant to incapacitate them.

"Subduing" Protesters in Seattle (Steve Kaiser)

"Non-Lethal" Weapons

Americans would do well to remember that modern police weaponry was introduced with a government guarantee of safety for the public. "Non-lethal" weapons such as tasers, stun guns, rubber pellets, and the like, were adopted by police departments across the country purportedly because they would help restrain *violent* individuals. Unfortunately, the "non-lethal" label has resulted in police using these dangerous weapons more often and with less restraint—even against women and children—and in some instances, even causing death. For instance, a 9-year-old Arizona runaway was tasered as she sat in the back seat of a police car with her hands cuffed behind her back.[410] In Texas, a 72-year-old great-grandmother was tasered after refusing to sign a speeding ticket.[411] Equally troubling is law enforcement's use of these weapons to intimidate and silence protesters.

Unfortunately, advances in crowd control technology are providing police with ever-greater weapons of compliance. For example, Intelligent Optics Systems, Inc. has developed a handheld, flashlight-like device that uses light emitting diodes "to emit super-bright pulses of light at rapidly changing wavelengths, causing disorientation, nausea and even vomiting in whomever it's pointed at."[412] Raytheon has developed a "pain ray"[413] which shoots an electromagnetic beam composed of high frequency radio waves, causing a burning sensation on the target's skin. In December 2011, the *Telegraph* reported that police in the UK were equipped with a shoulder-mounted laser that temporarily blinds protesters and rioters.[414]

Sound cannons are used by both military and police to emit high-pitched tones of 153 decibels,[415] well beyond the threshold for causing hearing damage and auditory pain,[416] with the potential to damage eardrums and cause fatal aneurysms.[417] The Pittsburgh police used a sound cannon to subdue protesters during the G20 Summit in 2009, their first use on American citizens.[418]

Drones, outfitted with the latest in high-definition cameras[419] and crowd control technology such as impact rounds, chemical munitions rounds, and tasers[420] will eventually be star players in the government's efforts to clamp down on protest activities and keep track of protesters. The Shadowhawk drone, which is already being sold to law enforcement agencies throughout the country, is outfitted with lethal weapons, including a grenade launcher or a shotgun, and weapons of compliance, such as tear gas[421] and rubber buckshot.[422]

Languishing

Does the way protesters are treated in major cities across America really have any bearing on how law-abiding citizens are treated in small-town America? Of course it does. The militarization of the police, the use of sophisticated weaponry against Americans, and the government's increasing tendency to clamp down on dissent have colored our very understanding of freedom, justice, and democracy. The end result is a people cowed into submission by an atmosphere of intimidation. And as this militarization spreads to small-town America, just the whispered threat of police action can be a powerfully intimidating force.

This may explain why some people who are tyrannized by violent regimes languish under oppression with little resistance. As early as 1776, Thomas Jefferson noted in the Declaration of Independence that "all experience has shown that mankind are more disposed to suffer, while evils are sufferable, than to right themselves by abolishing the forms to which they are accustomed." Proving Jefferson's point, the Soviet dissident Aleksandr Solzhenitsyn noted how the Russian people would kneel inside the door of their apartments, pressing their ears to listen when the KGB (the secret police) came at midnight to arrest a neighbor. He commented that if *all* the people had come out and driven off the officers, sheer public opinion would have demoralized the effort to subdue what should have been a free people. But the people hid and trembled.

CHAPTER 19

Tasering Us into Compliance

"When the government . . . begins to stamp out the freedom of dissent that is the hallmark of a democratic society, can there be any turning back?"[423]—DANIEL KURTZMAN

Dorli Rainey (Hearst Newspapers, LLC/Seattle P-I/Joshua Trujillo)

As we have seen, in appearance, weapons, and attitude, local police agencies are increasingly being transformed into civilian branches of the military. However, one clear distinction between local police and military forces used to be the kinds of weapons at their disposal. With the advent of modern police weaponry, such as tasers, that is no longer the case.

Indeed, compliance weapons such as tasers, pepper spray, and sound cannons have become increasingly popular with police agencies around the world. On paper, these weapons seem like a welcome alternative to bloodshed, especially if it means protecting law enforcement officials from dangerous criminals and minimizing civilian casualties. Yet the dangers posed by these so-called "non-lethal" weapons, especially to defenseless non-criminals, cannot be lightly dismissed. And as technology makes possible the widespread availability and acceptance of these weapons, their impact on police tactics and the exercise of civil liberties is far-reaching.

"Chilling" Free Speech

Examples abound. For instance, in a September 2011 incident, the New York police responded to Occupy Wall Street protesters by throwing people to the ground and using pepper spray on nonviolent protesters trapped behind a barricade.[424] Then the police became savvier. Rather than using brute force to discourage the protests, they resorted to freezing out the protesters by confiscating their electric generators and the fuel that runs them.[425]

Police in Oakland used tear gas canisters, rubber bullets, sound cannons, and flashbang grenades to disperse the Occupy Oakland protest. An Iraq War veteran, 24-year-old Scott Olsen, who was taking part in the protest, was struck in the head with a police projectile. His skull was fractured and he was listed in critical condition due to his brain swelling. When protesters came to his aid, they were driven back by a flashbang grenade.[426]

Police in Atlanta rounded up more than fifty protesters who had been camped out in a city park as part of Occupy Atlanta, while police in Philadelphia arrested fifteen individuals engaged in a sit-in in protest of police brutality as part of Occupy Philadelphia. San Diego Police arrested forty-four protesters at Occupy San Diego, confiscating all personal belongings and all supplies and food that had been donated.[427]

Mind you, the compliance weapons described above and their use was aimed at nonviolent protesters such as 84-year-old Dorli Rainey. Rainey was pepper sprayed in the face and forced into compliance by the Seattle police.[428]

Of course, the great concern with compliance weapons is their chilling effect on free speech. Do they discourage citizens from peaceably assembling and petitioning their government for a redress of grievances—a right guaranteed by the First Amendment? Indeed, if one is liable to be pepper sprayed, tasered, tear gassed, or stunned with rubber bullets, why bother showing up at all? In such instances, the right to free speech—which is the core of our democracy—is rendered null and void.

Tasers

Tasers are now used by nearly all of the law enforcement agencies in the United States. Electroshock weapons designed to cause instant incapacitation by delivering a 50,000-volt shock, "tasers" are handheld electronic stun guns that fire barbed darts. The darts, which usually remain attached to the gun by wires, deliver the high voltage shock and can penetrate up to two inches of clothing or skin. The darts can strike the subject from a distance, or the taser can be applied directly to the skin. Although a taser shot is capable of jamming the central nervous system for up to 30 seconds, it can disable its victim for even longer. And because tasers can be aimed anywhere on the body, they can immobilize someone more easily than pepper spray, which must be sprayed in the face.

In some cases, the use of tasers can be lethal. In virtually all cases, they cause a significant degree of pain. Cops who have been shocked in the course of their training have described being tased as "the most profound pain," and "like getting punched 100 times in a row."[429]

Taser manufacturers and law enforcement agencies argue that tasers are a safer alternative to many conventional weapons typically used to restrain dangerous individuals. However, there is a growing body of evidence that suggests otherwise. A study recently published by the American Heart Association has determined that taser shocks applied to the chest can lead to cardiac arrest. According to cardiologist Byron Lee, "This is no longer arguable. This is a scientific fact."[430] In fact, since 2001, over 500 people have died after being stunned with tasers.[431] Also, in a 2008 report, Amnesty International reviewed hundreds of deaths following taser use and found that 90 percent of those who died after being struck with a taser were unarmed.[432]

Moreover, the potential for government abuse of this so-called "non-lethal" weapon is great, especially in the hands of domestic law enforcement who routinely use tasers as a substitute for low-level force weapons such as pepper spray or chemical spray. They have become a prevalent force tool, most often employed against individuals who do not pose a serious danger to themselves, the officers, or others, but who fail to immediately comply with officers' commands. In fact, a 2005 study compiled by Amnesty International reports that in instances where tasers are used, 80 percent of the time they are fired at unarmed suspects. In 36 percent of the cases, they are employed for verbal non-compliance, but only three percent of the time for cases involving "deadly assault."[433]

Tasering Women and Children

Sadly, the courts have essentially given police *carte blanche* authority when it comes to using tasers against American citizens. This is especially concerning in light of a growing trend in which police officers use tasers to force individuals into compliance in relatively non-threatening situations. In fact, rowdy schoolchildren, the elderly, and mentally ill individuals are increasingly finding themselves on the receiving end of these sometimes lethal electroshock devices.

Indeed, police looking for absolute deference to their authority are quick to utilize tasers. For example, there have been a number of incidents where suspects of minor crimes and even completely innocent people were electroshocked into compliance by cops. In Florida a 15-year-old girl was tasered and pepper sprayed after being taken off of a bus following a disturbance.[434] In Arizona, a run-away 9-year-old girl was tasered as she sat in the back seat of a police car with her hands cuffed behind her back.[435] In Oregon police tasered a blind and partially deaf 71-year-old multiple times in her own front yard.[436] In another instance a Florida woman, 12-weeks pregnant, was tasered after refusing to submit to a strip search at a jail. She spontaneously miscarried seven days later.[437] In Texas a 72-year-old great-grandmother was tasered after refusing to sign a speeding ticket.[438]

In Florida a 14-year-old schoolgirl was tasered for arguing with police officers after she and other students were put off a bus during a disturbance. She was stunned directly to the chest and then stunned twice from a distance before she was handcuffed. In Oregon a newspaper reported that officers used tasers on noncompliant people "after stopping them for nonviolent offenses, such as littering and jaywalking."[439] In Arizona a 13-year-old girl was tasered in a public library after she threw a book.[440] In Missouri an unarmed 66-year-old woman was tasered twice as she resisted being issued a ticket for honking her horn at a police car.[441] In another instance, an officer used a taser on a 9-year-old girl who had run away from a residential home for severely emotionally disturbed children. The child, who was already handcuffed and sitting in the back of a police car, was tasered for allegedly struggling as the officer attempted to put leg restraints on her.[442]

Margaret Kimbrell, a 75-year-old woman who suffers from arthritis and had six broken ribs, was given a 50,000-volt shock from a police taser and was forced to spend three hours behind bars. Her crime? Margaret had refused to leave a nursing home before she had the opportunity to visit a friend whose well-being she was concerned about. According to the police, Margaret posed a threat because she was waving her arms and threatening the staff. This was news to Margaret. "As weak as I am, how could I do that?" she asked.[443] Describing the pain of being tasered, this resident of Rock Hill, South Carolina, responded, "It was the worst pain. It felt like something going through my body. I thought I was dying. I said, 'Lord, let it be over.'"

Common sense and good judgment certainly seemed to be in short supply when a police run-in with 71-year-old Eunice Crowder resulted in the blind woman being pepper sprayed and tasered. City employees had shown up at Crowder's home to remove unsightly shrubs and trash from the handicapped woman's yard. However, shortly after city workers began taking her belongings from her yard, Crowder became concerned that a 90-year-old wagon had been placed in the truck to be hauled away with her other belongings. After voicing her concern about the wagon, which was a family heirloom, Crowder asked to be allowed to enter the truck to search for it. Despite the workers' refusal, the elderly woman insisted on searching the truck. The situation worsened when the police showed up to find Crowder with one foot on the curb and the other on the bumper of the trailer. When one of the officers stepped on her foot, Crowder, being blind, asked who it was. Moments later, one of the officers struck her on the head—which dislodged her prosthetic eye—kicked her in the back, and pepper-sprayed her in the face.[444]

While law enforcement advocates may suggest otherwise, these incongruous and excessive uses of force by the police are quickly becoming the rule, not the exception. A 2011 New York Civil Liberties Union report showed that of the eight police departments surveyed across the state, over 85 percent of taser uses occurred in cases where suspects were not armed. Incredibly, 40 percent of taser uses were aimed at the elderly, children, the mentally ill, or the severely intoxicated.[445] And despite claims that tasers de-escalate tense situations, a Michigan State

University study shows that suspects are more likely to be injured in incidences where police use stun guns (41% of the time), rather than when no stun gun is used (29% of the time).[446]

"I am pregnant!"

Then there is Malaika Brooks. Brooks, 33 years old and seven months pregnant, was driving her 11-year-old son to school on a November morning in 2004, when she was pulled over for driving 32 mph in a 20 mph school zone. Instructing her son to walk the rest of the way to school, Malaika handed over her driver's license to Officer Juan Ornelas for processing.[447] However, when instructed to sign the speeding ticket—which the government inexplicably requires, Malaika declared that she wished to contest the charge, insisting that she had not done anything wrong and fearing that signing the ticket would signify an admission of guilt.[448]

What happened next is a cautionary tale for anyone who still thinks that they can defy a police officer, even if it's simply to disagree about a speeding ticket. Rather than issuing a verbal warning to the clearly pregnant (and understandably emotional) woman, Officer Ornelas called for backup. Officer Donald Jones subsequently arrived and told Brooks to sign the ticket. Again she refused. The conversation became heated. The cops called in more backup. The next to arrive was Sergeant Steven Daman, who directed Brooks to sign the ticket, pointing out that if she failed to do so, she would be arrested and taken to jail. Again, she refused.

On orders from Sgt. Daman, Ornelas ordered the distraught Brooks to get out of the car, telling her she was "going to jail." She again refused, and the second cop, Jones, responded by pulling out his taser electroshock weapon, asking her if she knew what it was and warning her it would be used on her if she continued to resist.[449] Brooks told him "No," and then said, "I have to go to the bathroom, I am pregnant, I'm less than sixty days from having my baby."

Jones and Ornelas then proceeded to discuss how best to taser the pregnant woman and forcibly remove her from the car. One officer said, "Well, don't do it in her stomach; do it in her thigh." Opening the car door, Ornelas twisted Malaika Brook's arm behind her back. Desperate, Brooks held on tightly to the steering wheel, while Jones cycled the taser as a demonstration of its capacity to cause pain.

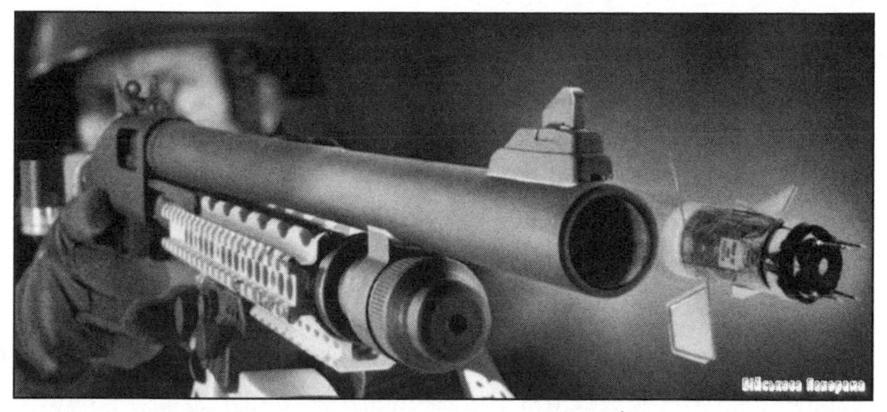

Taser Shotgun (Taser International)

With the taser in a "drive-stun" mode, Officer Jones then pressed the taser against Brooks' thigh while Ornelas held her hand behind her back. Brooks, in obvious pain, began to cry and honk her car horn—hoping someone would help. Thirty-six seconds later, Ornelas pressed it into her left arm. Six seconds later, he again stunned her, this time on the neck. After being tasered numerous times, Brooks' pregnant body eventually gave way. As Malaika fell over and out of the car, the officers dragged her onto the street, placing the pregnant woman face down on the pavement, handcuffing her and transporting her to jail.

While Malaika Brooks' ordeal with the police did not seem to negatively impact her unborn child—she gave birth to a healthy baby girl two months after the altercation—Malaika bears permanent burn scars on her body where she was tasered by police.[450]

As I noted earlier, the U.S. Supreme Court let stand an appeals court ruling that granted the police officers in Malaika Brooks' case immunity from prosecution. In other words, there appears to be very little protection from excessive police force.

Torture

Amnesty International has expressed concern that despite the far-reaching use of tasers, there has been no independent and impartial study of their use and effects. The growing employment of these weapons, as well as the number of associated deaths, presents serious questions.

Furthermore, the use of tasers in law enforcement raises a number of concerns for the protection of human rights. Portable, easy to use, and with the capacity to inflict severe pain at the push of a button without leaving substantial marks, tasers are open to even more abuse. Their use often violates standards set out under the United Nations Code of Conduct for Law Enforcement Officials, which requires that force be utilized as a last resort and that only the minimum amount necessary be used. In fact, in late 2007, the United Nations Committee Against Torture declared that the use of tasers constituted a form of torture.[451]

Yet despite all of the evidence that tasers are dangerous, taser technology continues to rapidly advance. One of the most recent advances in taser technology is the X12 Taser shotgun, which fires taser rounds at a distance of up to 100 feet, nearly 80 feet farther than a regular handheld taser.[452] It would not be a stretch to envision police using the X12 against protesters simply exercising their right to free speech and assembly under the First Amendment.

CHAPTER 20

The Goodbye Effect

"With but slight expenditures of force, an all-pervasive sense of fright may be produced in the 'invisible spheres' of life. An ounce of actual violence can yield a pound of terror."[453]

—Former presidential advisor BERTRAM GROSS

The corporate powers who work closely with the police and other government agents to develop the host of weapons used against the populace are steadily introducing new products—all, of course, purchased at taxpayer expense. The catalogue of "nonlethal" and lethal weapons that follow are now available to your local police to use in quieting the disquieted with the "Goodbye Effect." In other words, when you see the police, it's time to tremble and run for cover. But should that be our response to the police in a so-called "free country"?

The Barf Beamers

A non-lethal weapon with the potential to do untold damage is the previously mentioned "LED Incapacitator" (LEDI). Designed like a flashlight, this light saber (also dubbed a barf beamer and a puke saber) is intended to totally incapacitate the people at whom it is aimed by emitting multiple light frequencies and colors that confuse the brain, resulting in symptoms ranging from discomfort and disorientation to temporary blindness and nausea.

It has been suggested that LEDIs be installed in prisons so that riots can be stopped with the flip of a switch. Police vehicles with large versions mounted on top for riot control have also been proposed. But if LEDIs can be so easily employed on a mass scale and mounted on buildings, there is little that would stop police from dispersing even a mildly rowdy, but legal, political citizen protest and shutting down entire city blocks with virtually no resistance.

"Sergeant Pepper," UC Davis Pepper Spray Incident
(AP Photo/The Enterprise, Wayne Tilcock, File)

Devices such as LEDIs facilitate a non-dramatic, palatable use of force. Indeed, the Department of Homeland Security (DHS) has praised the LEDI device for its potential to peacefully apprehend border jumpers and resistant suspects and control riotous crowds. (DHS has also expressed interest in yet another non-lethal weapon in the form of security bracelets, a.k.a. "taser bracelets," which could be used to control crowds, quell protesters and inflict pain compliance on suspects from a distance.)[454]

Pepper Spray

In 1982 pepper spray (oleoresin capsicum or OC spray) was developed for use by the postal service to prevent attacks by dogs and other animals. Pepper spray is a mixture synthesized from capsaicin, a bitter compound found in hot peppers, that produces a burning sensation upon contact with the skin.[455] However, OC spray is highly concentrated, which makes it about three hundred times as strong as jalapeño peppers and five times as strong as commercially available pepper-spray blends.[456] The mixture is so extraordinarily painful as to force victims into compliance and submission. It has been reported that if left untreated, the burning can last between forty-five and sixty minutes and cause temporary blindness for about a half an hour.[457] Incredibly, Pepper Ball Technologies has now devised a paint ball-like weapon that shoots pepper spray in a "ball" form at a rate of 300 feet per second or 12 shots per second, attacking the victim's throat, nose and eyes with even greater force than the spray.[458]

Clearly, pepper spray is a potent tool in the arsenal of compliance weapons. Who could forget the stark photograph of the black-garbed policeman pepper spraying the University of California students in Berkeley as they sat on the ground in the lotus position in 2011? As part of the Occupy protests, these students were quietly, passively exercising their right to protest. However, "Sergeant Pepper," as this policeman became known, had other ideas.[459]

Sound Cannons

A more technologically advanced weapon in the toolkit of the American police force is the Long Range Acoustic Device (LRAD) or "sound cannon." Developed by the American Technology Corporation, these sound cannons have a range of three city blocks, or roughly 980 feet.[460] The sound waves emitted from the LRAD device are of a high frequency, which can trigger pain responses.[461] To compare the LRAD to everyday sounds, a normal conversation measures sixty decibels and a lawn mower registers at ninety.[462] Sound cannons are usually operated at a volume of 120 decibels, while the threshold of pain is about 130, depending on the person's tolerance level.[463] However, the LRAD's maximum volume override is 146 decibels, a level that can seriously impair the hearing of its victims.

Before being unveiled on the public in 2009, the LRAD was tested on pirates who attacked the cruise ship *Seabourn Spirit* off the coast of Somalia in 2005. It crippled the attackers, who were armed with machine guns and rocket-propelled grenades, and deterred their plan to overcome the *Seabourn Spirit*. Sound cannons were later used as a domestic weapon to disperse American citizens at the 2009 G-20 Summit.

Skin on Fire

Rumsfeld's Ray Gun, designed for use by the military and heavily promoted for use domestically in crowd-control situations, uses the Active Denial System (ADS), which dispenses brief, high-energy waves at an individual, resulting in a sensation of severe burning pain. As one reporter explained, the $51 million crowd-control device "rides atop a

Humvee, looks like a TV dish, and shoots energy waves 1/64 of an inch deep into the human skin."[464]

The ADS weapon directs electromagnetic radiation toward its targets at a frequency of 95 GHz. Upon contact with the skin, the energy in the waves turns to heat, causing the water molecules in the skin to heat to around 130 degrees Fahrenheit. Experiments were conducted on volunteer test subjects in 2003 and 2004 at Kirtland Air Force Base in Albuquerque, New Mexico. The results indicated that ADS causes pain within two to three seconds and becomes intolerable within five seconds, the intent being that the pain would be severe enough to cause a person to flee. As a test volunteer explained, "For the first millisecond, it just felt like the skin was warming up. Then it got warmer and warmer and felt like it was on fire ... As soon as you're away from that beam your skin returns to normal and there is no pain."[465]

The Air Force also explored the weapon's ability to control riots and unruly crowds by firing the ADS beam at volunteers acting as protesters or intruders. When the volunteers were zapped by the beam, they held their hands up and were given fifteen seconds to cool down before being targeted again. Volunteers were required to remove eye glasses, buttons, zippers and watches for fear that exposure to the beam could cause "hot spots" or severe burns. However, actual targets—such as average, ordinary American citizens—would certainly not be given the opportunity to remove such objects before being fired upon.

Although the military has been guarded about the radiation weapon's effect on humans, several medical professionals insist that ADS beams can cause severe long-term health problems, including corneal damage, cancer, and cataracts. In fact, Dominique Loye of the International Committee of the Red Cross notes that ADS can result in "new types of injuries we're not aware of and may not be capable of taking care of."[466] And as journalist Kelly Hearn points out, there are more questions than answers right now about how the weapon works, "what it does to the body and how it will be used in the streets of Basra and Baghdad or, one day, Boston."[467]

Reportedly on orders from the United States Justice Department, a version of ADS has been developed by the Raytheon Corporation for use by local police departments. Someday, according to a Raytheon spokesperson, ADS may be "miniaturized down to a hand-held device that could be carried in a purse or pocket and used for personal protection instead of something like Mace."[468]

Tear Gas

Tear gas, like the LRAD, can be very hazardous and harmful to innocent civilians, and wind can carry tear gas away from the intended center of action, putting innocent bystanders in harm's way. In March 2010 police used tear gas on University of Maryland students after their basketball team defeated Duke. The crowd took to the streets, ripped down traffic signs, and allegedly shook a bus on U.S. Route 1. Mounted police fired tear gas and sand bags to disperse the crowd, eventually resulting in bloodshed.[469]

During the April 2010 "Springfest," an annual party held off-campus at James Madison University in Harrisonburg, Virginia, police utilized various riot control practices when those enjoying the festivities became rowdy. Officers from six police agencies responded to the apparent disruption, and altercations took place between them and several of the 8,000 partiers.[470] After pepper spray and tear gas were deployed, the partiers dispersed. Once the gas and haze settled, over thirty arrests had been made.[471]

Some More 'Nice' Weapons

Police even have weapons that can shoot around corners. One such firearm, the "Israeli Corner Shot Weapon," uses a video monitor to track targets from around corners. This allows police officers to shoot safely at targets from a 90-degree angle while tracking them on the projector screen.[472] SWAT teams all across the country are hopeful about the advancements and new possibilities that this weapon brings. Captain Mike Shearer of Akron, Ohio, stated that this new weapon allows the police to "[e]xpose a weapon, expose a lethal threat, without exposing any part of your body . . . So it looks like a very nice weapon."[473]

Other weapons that have appeared in the arsenal of police units across the country are metal and wooden batons, riot guns, flashbang and smoke grenades, and sedative darts. The water cannon is another potent weapon that the police force has used, including on protesters during the Civil Rights Movement. The average water cannon has the ability to knock a person down from approximately one hundred yards away.[474]

Furthermore, some countries have gone as far as to dye the water and lace it with tear gas in order to wreak havoc on its victims. Police units in India have been known to dye the water, thus making it easier for law enforcement to recognize and target protesters as they flee the scene.[475]

In the past, water cannons have drawn their water from large natural bodies of water, fire hydrants, or even fire engines. Currently, however, water cannons are powered by kinetic pumps, which use a rotor propeller to shoot the water outward while simultaneously pressurizing it. A device called the deluge gun, which can be controlled remotely by a single person, allows greater control and precision for the cannon's target.[476]

The Trouble with Non-Lethal Weapons

There is a serious problem with "non-lethal, non-deadly" weapons: how they are used—or abused—largely depends on the individuals and agencies operating them. For example, as we have seen, many police forces around the world unabashedly use tasers as compliance weapons rather than as alternatives to deadly force. In these countries, tasers are more often used against passive resisters and stubborn individuals (i.e., people who talk back), while more deadly force is reserved for armed offenders. Consequently, abuses are on the rise and opposition to tasers is mounting worldwide, especially given the sharp increase in sudden deaths accompanying use of tasers.[477]

Also, we know very little about these non-lethal weapons. For instance, despite assurances from Homeland Security that LEDIs cannot do any real damage, the research is still out on the long-term effects of many of these non-lethal weapons. As with tasers, which have resulted in nearly 500 deaths over the past few years, LEDIs might cause greater than expected damage to individuals who are especially susceptible to their effects.

Moreover, non-lethal weapons such as LEDIs may not reduce the number of shootings by police. In Houston, Texas, for example, the introduction and routine use of tasers did not reduce the number of people shot, killed, or wounded by the police.[478] Nevertheless, while the use of non-lethal weapons such as tasers and LEDIs may not necessarily reduce the number of civilian casualties, they have been largely accepted as the humane alternative to deadly force because they make the use of force appear far less dramatic and violent than it has in the past.

Contrast, for instance, the image of police officers beating Rodney King with billy clubs as opposed to police officers continually shocking a person with a taser. Both are severe forms of abuse. However, because the act of pushing a button is far less dramatic and visually arresting than swinging a billy club, it can come across as much more humane to the general public. This, of course, draws much less media coverage and, thus, less bad public relations for the police.

Moreover, the use of tasers and other weapons of compliance empowers law enforcement officials to resort to non-lethal weapons in situations where previously no force would have been used at all, such as routine traffic stops or peaceful protests. And as force becomes easier and more common, with police neutralizing masses of people for the slightest disturbance and only facing relatively minor repercussions, constitutionally protected protests will be rendered useless.

No Revolt

There are also totalitarian ramifications to be considered. Governmental coercion is largely restrained by the fact that people will resist governmental violence that crosses a certain threshold. But when the threshold is subtle and justified under the rubric of being more humane or combating terrorism (as in requiring airline passengers to wear taser bracelets), it becomes more difficult to find the outrage necessary to oppose it.

Lest we forget, government domination is not usually accomplished by methods so dramatic that they spark a backlash from citizens. Thus, the real threat to freedom posed by such non-lethal weapons is a governmental system of coercion so well designed that it does not breed revolt.

CHAPTER 21

Attack of the Drones

"Although it is hard to predict where the drone infrastructure will grow, if other defense contracting projects are a reliable guide, the drone-ification of America will probably continue until there is a drone aerodrome in every state and a drone degree program to go with it."[479]—Richard Wheeler, *Wired*

Imagine a robot hovering overhead as you go about your day, driving to and from work, heading to the grocery store, or stopping by a friend's house. The robot records your every movement with a surveillance camera and streams the information to a government command center. If you make a wrong move, or even appear to be doing something suspicious, the police will respond quickly and you'll soon be under arrest. Worse, you might find yourself tasered into compliance by the robot floating on high. Even if you don't do anything suspicious, the information of your whereabouts, including what stores and offices you visit, what political rallies you attend, and what people you meet will be recorded, saved and easily accessed at a later date by the police and/or other government agents.

Coming Home to Roost

This is a frightening thought, but you don't have to imagine this scenario. Thanks to the introduction of drones into American airspace, we are only a few years away from the realization of this total surveillance and compliance society.

Drones—pilotless, remote controlled aircraft that have been used extensively in Iraq, Afghanistan, and Pakistan to assassinate suspected terrorists,[480] as well as innocent civilians[481]—have increasingly found favor with both military and law enforcement officials. "The more we have used them," stated Defense Secretary Robert Gates, "the more we have identified their potential in a broader and broader set of circumstances."[482] In fact, President Obama's 2012 military budget provided strong funding for drones with intelligence, surveillance, and reconnaissance capabilities, with $4.8 billion set aside just "to develop and procure additional Global Hawk Class (RQ-4), Predator Class (MQ 1/9), and other less expensive, low-altitude systems."[483]

Parrot Drone (Parrot SA)

Little surprise, then, that in early 2012 Congress passed and President Obama signed into law the FAA Reauthorization Act, which mandates that the Federal Aviation Administration (FAA) create a comprehensive program for the integration of drone technology into the national air space by 2015. By 2020 it is anticipated that there will be 30,000 drones crisscrossing the skies of America, all part of an industry that could be worth hundreds of millions of dollars per year.[484]

While there are undoubtedly legitimate uses for drone technology domestically, such as locating missing persons, domestic drones will be armed with "less-lethal" weaponry, including rubber bullets, bean bag guns, and tasers, while flying over political demonstrations, sporting events, and concert arenas. Eventually, these drones will be armed with the lethal weaponry that is currently being used overseas in Afghanistan and Pakistan.

The power of these machines is not to be underestimated. Many are equipped with cameras that provide a live video feed, as well as heat sensors and radar. Some are capable of peering at figures from 20,000 feet up and twenty-five miles away. They can also keep track of sixty-five persons of interest at once.[485] Some drones are capable of hijacking

Wi-Fi networks and intercepting electronic communications such as text messages.[486] The Army has developed drones with facial recognition software,[487] as well as drones that can complete a target-and-kill mission without any human instruction or interaction.[488]

Thus, with this single piece of legislation, Congress, in conjunction with the president, opened the floodgates to an entirely new era of surveillance and domestic police tactics—one in which no person is safe from the prying eyes of the government or the reach of its weapons. Yet the fact that these drones are coming home to roost (and fly) in domestic airspace should come as no surprise to those who have been paying attention. The U.S. government has a history of commandeering military technology for use against Americans. We saw this happen with tear gas, tasers, sound cannons, and assault vehicles, all of which were first used on the battlefield before being deployed against civilians at home.

The Hit Man

As President Obama learned first-hand, drones are the ultimate killing and spying machines. Indeed, the use of drones to target and kill insurgents became a centerpiece of the president's war on terror.

As the *New York Times* revealed in 2012,[489] President Obama, operating off a government "kill list," personally directed who should be targeted for death by military drones. Every few weeks, Obama and approximately a hundred members of his national security team gathered for their "Terror Tuesday" meetings in which they handpicked the next so-called national security "threat" to die by way of the American military/CIA drone program.[490] Obama signed off personally on about a third of the drone strikes.[491] (By the time he was awarded the Nobel Peace Prize in 2009, Obama had given the go-ahead to more drone strikes than Bush did during his entire presidency.[492] By the third year of his presidency, two times as many suspected

President Obama
(Official White House Photo by Pete Souza)

terrorists had been approved for killing by drone strikes than had been put in Guantanamo Bay during George W. Bush's presidency.[493])

It's not only suspected terrorists whose death warrants were personally signed by the president but innocent civilians geographically situated near a strike zone, as well, whether or not they have any ties to a suspected terrorist. As an anonymous government official on Obama's drone campaign observed, "They count the corpses and they're not really sure who they are."[494] In fact, Obama's first authorized drone attack in Yemen led to the deaths of fourteen women and twenty-one children, and only one al-Qaeda affiliate.[495]

Whatever one may say about the dubious merits of the President's kill list, there can be no doubt about the fact that President Obama managed to create a radical and chilling new power allowing future presidents to kill anyone at will. This includes American citizens whom the president might deem a threat to the nation's security. Indeed, in a decision he claimed was "an easy one,"[496] Obama killed two American citizens in this fashion: Anwar al-Awlaki, an American cleric living in Yemen who served as a propagandist for al-Qaeda, and his 16-year-old son.[497]

Entirely lacking in accountability[498] and legal justification as required by the Constitution, Obama's kill list takes to new heights Richard Nixon's brazen claim that "if the president does it, it's not illegal."[499] The ramifications are far-reaching, especially now that Obama has authorized the use of drones domestically.

Drone Ed

This is not a problem that's going to go away quickly or quietly. In fact, the FAA is facing mounting pressure from state governments and localities to issue flying rights for a range of unmanned aerial vehicles (UAVs) to carry out civilian and law-enforcement activities. As the Associated Press reports, "Tornado researchers want to send them into storms to gather data. Energy companies want to use them to monitor pipelines. State police hope to send them up to capture images of speeding cars' license plates. Local police envision using them to track fleeing suspects."[500]

Even universities are getting in on the drone action. As Richard Wheeler writing for *Wired* magazine points out:

> Federal education and stimulus money is being used to create nonmilitary drone education programs. The Department of Aviation at the University of North Dakota, located in Grand Forks and the operator of the test and training site at Grand Forks AFB, now offers the first Bachelors of Science program in Unmanned Aircraft Systems Operations. The Aviation Maintenance Technology program at Northland Community and Technical College, located in Thief River Falls, Minnesota just 40 miles east of Grand Forks, will soon offer courses in the repair of UAVs.[501]

The University of North Dakota is also offering a four-year degree in piloting drones in what is soon expected to be a $20 billion industry.

Up in the Sky

Unbeknownst to most Americans, remote-controlled aircraft have been employed domestically for years now. They were first used as a national security tool for patrolling America's borders and then as a means of monitoring citizens. For example, back in 2006, the Los Angeles County Sheriff's Department was testing out a SkySeer drone for use in police work. With a 6.5-foot wingspan, the lightweight SkySeer can be folded up like a kite and stored in a shoulder pack. At 250 feet, it can barely be seen with the naked eye.[502]

As another news story that same year reported, "one North Carolina county is using a UAV equipped with low-light and infrared cameras to keep watch on its citizens. The aircraft has been dispatched to monitor gatherings of motorcycle riders at the Gaston County fairgrounds from just a few hundred feet in the air—close enough to identify faces—and many more uses, such as the aerial detection of marijuana fields, are planned."[503]

Drone technology has advanced dramatically in the ensuing years, with surveillance drones getting smaller, more sophisticated and more lethal with each evolution. Modeling their prototype for a single-winged rotorcraft on the maple seed's unique design, aerospace engineering students at the University of Maryland have created the world's smallest controllable surveillance drones, capable of hovering to record conversations or movements of citizens.[504]

Nowhere to Hide

Thus far, the domestic use of drones has been primarily for surveillance purposes. Eventually, however, police departments and intelligence agencies will make drones a routine part of their operations. However, you can be sure they won't limit themselves to just surveillance.

Police today use whatever tools are at their disposal in order to anticipate and forestall crime. This means employing technology to attain total control. Technology, which functions without discrimination because it exists without discrimination, tends to be applied everywhere it can be applied. Thus the logical aim of technologically equipped police who operate as technicians must be control, containment, and eventually restriction of freedom. Unfortunately, to a drone, everyone is a suspect because drone technology makes no distinction between the law-abiding individual and the suspect. Everyone gets monitored, photographed, tracked, and targeted.

Parrot AR Drone (Micah Green/Dispatch Staff)

In this way, under the guise of keeping Americans safe and controlled, airborne drones will have to be equipped with an assortment of lethal and nonlethal weapons in order to effectuate control of citizens on the ground. The arsenal of nonlethal weapons will include LRADs, which are used to break up protests or riots by sending a piercing sound into crowds and can cause serious hearing damage; high-intensity strobe lights, which can cause dizziness, disorientation, and loss of balance and make it virtually impossible to run away; and tasers, which administer a powerful electric shock.

"Also available to police," writes journalist Paul Joseph Watson, "will be a drone that can fire tear gas as well as rubber pellets to disperse anyone still living under the delusion that they were born in a democratic country."[505] In fact, the French company Tecknisolar Seni has built a drone armed with a double-barreled 44 mm Flash-Ball gun. The one-kilo Flash-Ball resembles a large caliber handgun and fires so-called non-lethal rounds, including tear gas and rubber impact rounds to bring down a suspect. Despite being labeled a "non-lethal weapon," this, too, is not without its dangers.[506] As David Hambling writes for *Wired News*, "Like other impact rounds, the Flash-Ball is meant to be aimed at the body—firing from a remote, flying platform is likely to increase the risk of head injury."[507]

Drones are also outfitted with infrared cameras and radar[508] that can pierce through the darkness, allowing the police to keep track of anyone walking around, regardless of the nature of their business. Police drones are equipped with thermal imaging devices to see through walls.[509] There is absolutely nowhere to hide from these machines—even in your home.

As Congressmen Edward Markey and Joe Barton pointed out in a letter to the FAA:

> [S]tate and local governments, businesses, and private individuals are increasingly using unmanned aircraft in the U.S., including deployments for law enforcement operations. As technology advances and cost decreases—drones are already orders of magnitude less expensive to purchase and operate than piloted aircraft—the market for federal, state, and local government and commercial drones rapidly grows.
>
> Many drones are designed to carry surveillance equipment, including video cameras, infrared thermal imagers, radar, and wireless network "sniffers." The surveillance power of drones is amplified when the information from onboard sensors is used in conjunction with facial recognition, behavior analysis, license plate recognition, or any other system that can identify and track individuals as they go about their daily lives.[510]

American scientists have also created blueprints for nuclear powered drones which would increase air time from days to months. Potential problems are dire, such as a crashed drone becoming a dirty bomb or a source of nuclear propulsion for any terrorist groups that get their hands on it.[511]

However, while the lethal capabilities of these drones are troubling, especially when one factors in the possibility of them getting into the wrong hands or malfunctioning, the more pressing concern has to do with the drones' surveillance capabilities. As discussed earlier, with the help of nanotechnology, scientists have been able to create ever-smaller drones that mimic the behavior of birds and insects and are almost undetectable.[512] Despite their diminutive size, these drones are capable of capturing and relaying vast amounts of data and high-definition video footage. It's inevitable that as more local police agencies acquire these spy flies, their surveillance efforts will expand to include not only those suspected of criminal activity but anyone within range of the cameras.

Drone Errors, Risks and Vulnerabilities

Drones, however, are not foolproof. In fact, drones have a history of malfunctioning in midair. As David Zucchino reported in the *Los Angeles Times*, "The U.S. military often portrays its drone aircraft as high-tech marvels that can be operated seamlessly from thousands of miles away. But Pentagon accident reports reveal that the pilotless aircraft suffer from frequent system failures, computer glitches, and human error."[513] For example, the first drone sent to the Texas-Mexico border in the summer of 2010 experienced a communications failure that led to "pilot deviation."[514] Drones had to be temporarily grounded while technicians received more training. Fortunately, no one was hurt.

The U.S. military was on the verge of launching fighter jets and even entertained ideas about a possible shoot-down when an errant Navy drone veered into restricted airspace near Washington, D.C., in August 2010. The incident only served to reinforce concerns about drones let loose in American skies. "Do you let it fly over the national capital region? Let it run out of gas and hopefully crash in a farmer's field? Or do you take action and shoot it down?" said Navy Adm. James Winnefeld Jr., head of Northern Command. "You don't want to shoot it down over a populated area if you can avoid it."[515] Even so, Winnefeld is pushing to get more drones into the air, citing the need for a slower and lighter aircraft that could be used to monitor events such as outdoor sports games, political conventions, or inaugural activities.

Apart from the safety concerns, of which there are many, the widespread use of drones domestically also poses certain security and privacy risks. As one blogger notes, "One has to wonder if the cost of these high tech machines would be balanced by their potentially limited uses or if departments would be forced to expand the uses in order to even employ the drones. Like SWAT battering rams and armored vehicles, would departments feel compelled to use the drones more often than necessary simply to justify their cost?"[516]

There's also the problem of drones being hacked into and potentially hijacked. There have been a handful of high-profile crashes involving American drones abroad, including in Iran, the island nation of Seychelles,[517] and most recently in Somalia.[518] The Iranian government claimed they brought down the drone flying in their territory via a computer hack. This is two years after Iraqis were able to hack into the live feed of a few spy drones using "$26 off-the-shelf software."[519] And back in October 2011, the U.S. military admitted that their drone fleet had been infected by a "mysterious virus."[520] One can only imagine what a technically proficient hacker in America might be able to do with the wealth of information he could potentially take from these drones, not to mention what a terrorist could do with a fully-armed, remote-controlled airplane.

If there's one thing you *can* be sure of, it's that these drones *will* be equipped with weapons. In fact, the Pentagon actually wants some drones to be able to carry nuclear weapons.[521] The destruction brought about by a midair collision or sudden communications failure with a drone carrying weapons would be devastating.

Here to Stay

There are many constitutional concerns presented by drones recording Americans' daily activities, with the most obvious being what it means for the Fourth Amendment protection against unreasonable searches and seizures by government agents. While it will certainly give rise to a whole new dialogue about where to draw the line when it comes to the government's ability to monitor one's public versus private life, the courts have been notorious for their inability to keep pace with rapid advances in technology and its impact on our freedoms.

As with just about every freedom-leeching, technology-driven government policy inflicted on us by Congress and the White House in recent years, from whole-body scanners in airports to RFID chips in our passports and drivers licenses, the mass introduction of drones into domestic airspace has one main goal: to empower the corporate state by controlling the populace and enriching the military industrial complex. In the meantime, all you can do is keep your eyes on the skies. As Peter W. Singer, a military analyst for the Brookings Institution, recognizes, "There's no stopping this technology. Anybody who thinks they can put this genie back in the box—that's silliness."[522]

One thing is clear: while the idea of airborne drones policing America's streets may seem far-fetched, like something out of a sci-fi movie, it is now our new reality. It's just a matter of how soon you can expect them to be patrolling your own neighborhood. The crucial question, however, is whether Americans will be able to limit the government's use of such tools of surveillance and compliance or whether we will be caught in an electronic nightmare from which there is no escape.

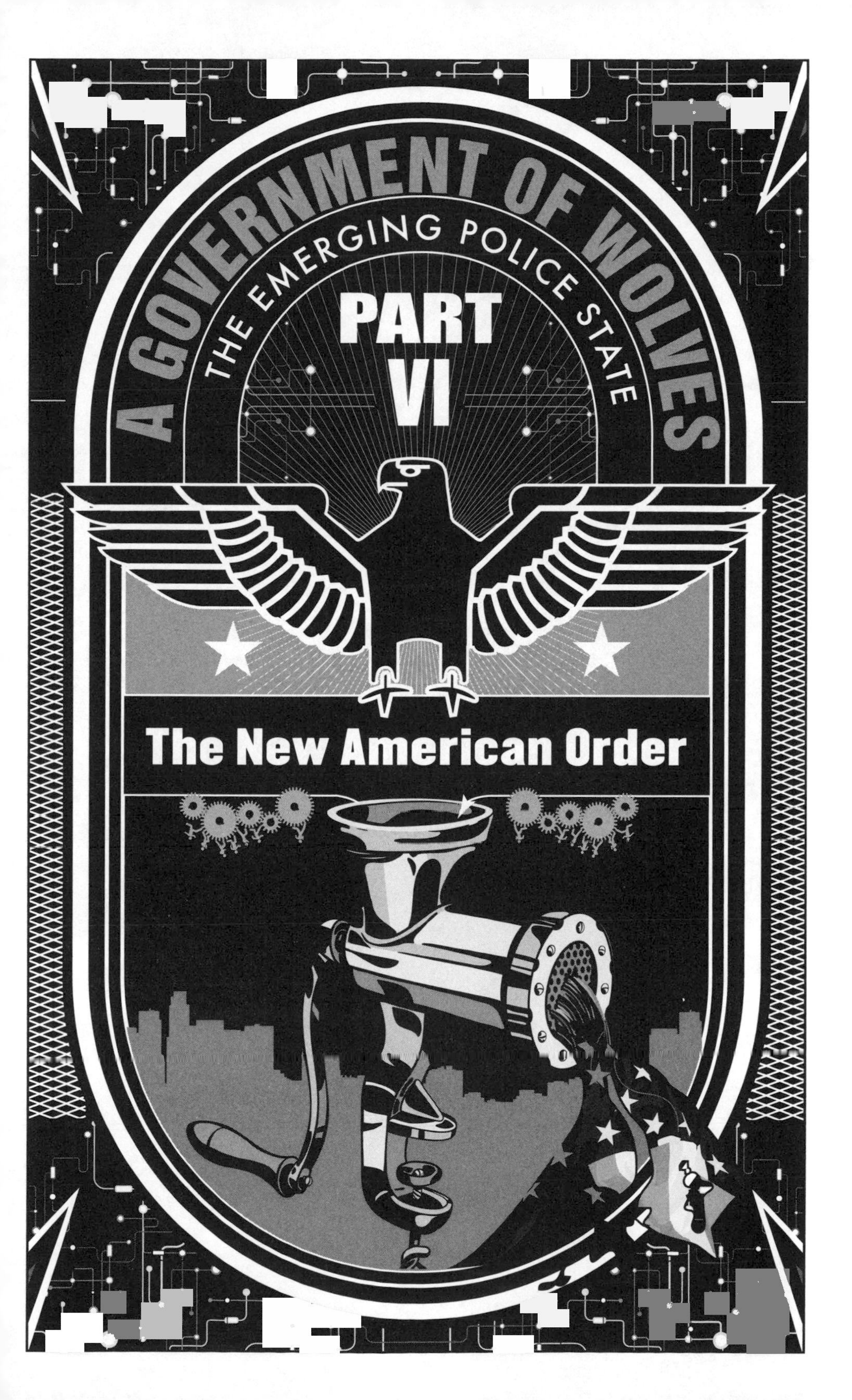
A GOVERNMENT OF WOLVES
THE EMERGING POLICE STATE
PART VI
The New American Order

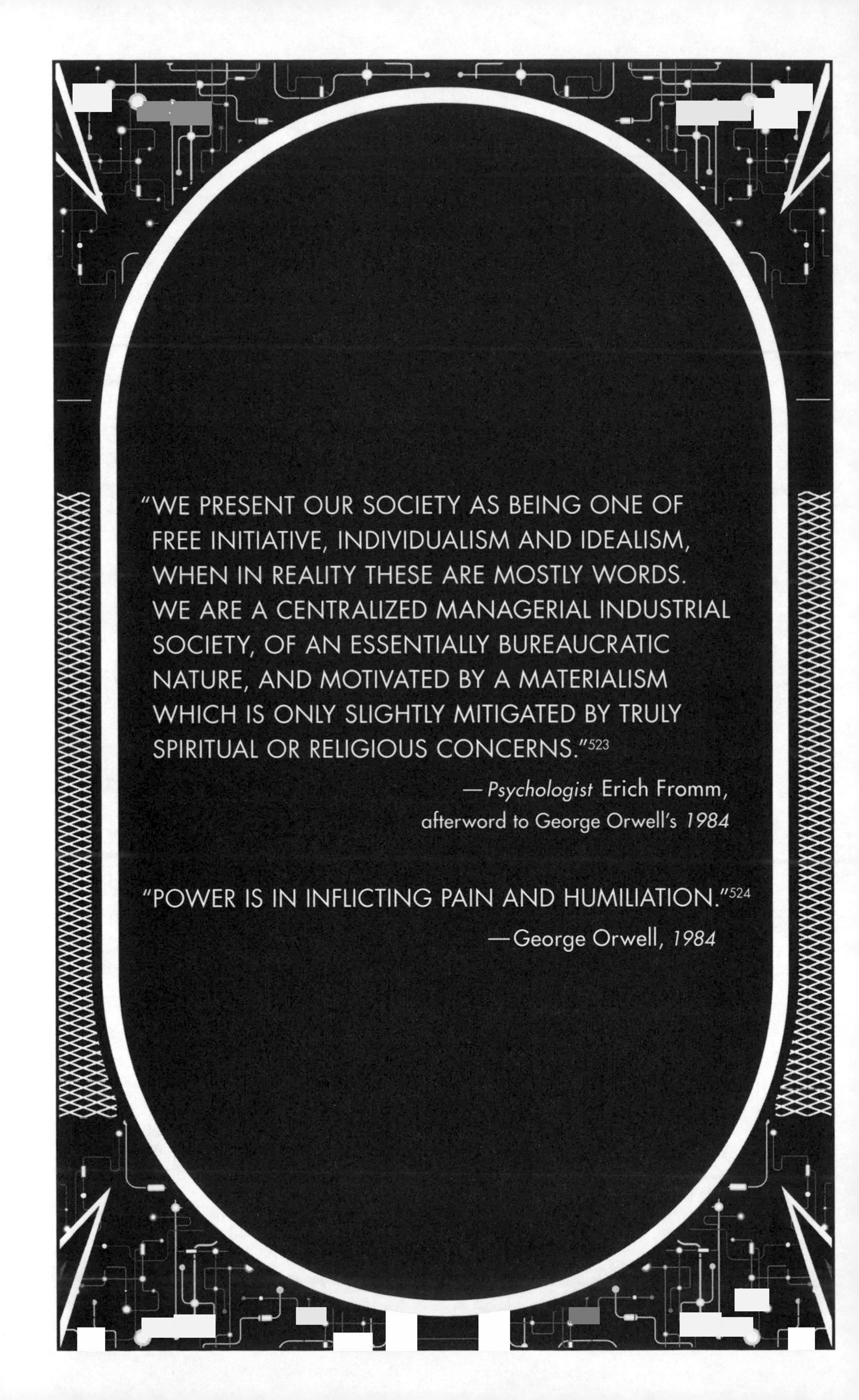
"WE PRESENT OUR SOCIETY AS BEING ONE OF FREE INITIATIVE, INDIVIDUALISM AND IDEALISM, WHEN IN REALITY THESE ARE MOSTLY WORDS. WE ARE A CENTRALIZED MANAGERIAL INDUSTRIAL SOCIETY, OF AN ESSENTIALLY BUREAUCRATIC NATURE, AND MOTIVATED BY A MATERIALISM WHICH IS ONLY SLIGHTLY MITIGATED BY TRULY SPIRITUAL OR RELIGIOUS CONCERNS."[523]
—*Psychologist* Erich Fromm,
afterword to George Orwell's *1984*
"POWER IS IN INFLICTING PAIN AND HUMILIATION."[524]
—George Orwell, *1984*

CHAPTER 22

Soylent Green is People!

"The liberty of a democracy is not safe if the people tolerate the growth of private power to a point where it becomes stronger than their democratic State itself. That, in its essence, is fascism—ownership of government by an individual, by a group, or any controlling private power."[525] —FRANKLIN D. ROOSEVELT

The one strand that weaves itself throughout all of the dystopian novels and films we have discussed thus far is the fact that the future will be ruled by a government that has fused with a corporate elite. "Orwell," as with other dystopian thinkers, writes sociologist Erich Fromm, "is simply implying that the new form of managerial industrialism, in which man builds machines which act like men and develops men who act like machines, is conducive to an era of dehumanization and complete alienation, in which men are transformed into things and become appendices to the process of production and consumption."[526]

Dehumanized people? How else do we explain the aggressive use of SWAT teams for minor crimes in American cities, the use of weapons of compliance on American citizens, the atrocities at Abu Ghraib, the President's kill lists, and the drone attacks that wipe out innocent civilians? Consider, too, how we have been reduced to mere consumers, carefully calculated parts of the GDP to be processed, packaged, and sold to the highest bidder.

This was all inevitable once "we the people" lost control of the government which now rules from the centralized bureaucracy in Washington, D.C. Gone are the local governmental units such as towns and counties which used to serve as our primary form of government. Now we are ruled from afar by a governmental elite which too often operates in secret formulating policies and laws.

Take, for example, the fact that the laws under which we are all regulated and sometimes prosecuted are no longer written by our so-called representatives. Such innumerable and often oppressive laws are written by such corporate membership organizations as the American Legislative Exchange Council (ALEC). These groups are merely the conduits that the megacorporations use to rule us.

Once an organic process of debate and citizen input, our government now operates as a mechanized bureaucracy, controlled by a corporate elite. The dangers inherent in such mechanical bureaucracies, as Richard Rubenstein tellingly illustrates in his book *The Cunning of History*, is that those caught within their snare are totally dehumanized and eventually eliminated and thrown out like so much human trash. Such was the case with the Nazi death camps, administered by corporations as profit-making ventures. In fact, one of "the chief functions of Auschwitz was to support a vast corporate enterprise involved in the manufacture of synthetic rubber" products for Europe.[527]

A similar approach is taken in the 1973 film *Soylent Green*. The year is 2022, and the world is suffering from pollution, overpopulation, depleted resources, poverty, dying oceans, and a miserably hot climate due to the greenhouse effect. Policeman Robert Thorn is dispatched to investigate the murder of a wealthy man who is intimately connected to the Soylent Corporation, whose newest product is Soylent Green, a green wafer advertised as "high energy plankton."

Through the twists and turns of trying to solve the murder while resisting the corporate state's attempt to shut down the investigation, Thorn learns the true secret of Soylent Green. It is made from human beings.

The warning, of course, is that the farther we move into a corporate-state vortex where the bottom line is greed, profit-making, and materialism, human beings will increasingly become more disposable commodities. At the same time, we are sold everything from toothpaste to politicians as products for consumption. This is fascism with a smile.

The point is that we are being conditioned to be slaves without knowing it. That way, we are easier to control. "A really efficient totalitarian state would be one in which the all-powerful executive of political bosses and their army of managers control a population of slaves who do not have to be coerced, because they love their servitude," writes

Aldous Huxley. "To make them love it is the task assigned, in present-day totalitarian states, to ministries of propaganda, newspaper editors and schoolteachers."[528]

All of this can come about without much coercion. As Dr. Robert Gellately, author of *Backing Hitler: Consent and Coercion in Nazi Germany, 1933-1944,* discovered about the German people in Nazi Germany, "There were relatively few secret police, and most were just processing the information coming in. I had found a shocking fact. It wasn't the secret police who were doing this wide-scale surveillance and hiding on every street corner. It was the ordinary German people who were informing on their neighbors."[529]

In fact, Gellately realized that those acting as the Gestapo's unsolicited agents and informing on their neighbors were motivated more by greed, jealousy, and petty differences than by any sense of patriotic duty. He found "cases of partners in business turning in associates to gain full ownership; jealous boyfriends informing on rival suitors; neighbors betraying entire families who chronically left shared bathrooms unclean or who occupied desirable apartments. And then there were those who informed because for the first time in their lives someone in authority would listen to them and value what they said."[530]

Thus, the key to bringing about an authoritarian regime that is geared to controlling, not governing, the citizenry is by selling it—propagandizing it, really—through the legislators, prisons, and the schools.

CHAPTER 23

Are We All Criminals Now?

"Such laws which enable government zealots to accuse almost anyone of committing three felonies in a day, do not just enable government misconduct, they incite prosecutors to intimidate decent people who never had culpable intentions. And to inflict punishments without crimes."[531]—Journalist GEORGE WILL

Farm Raid (Anna Vignet/The Daily Californian)

Is it possible that you are a felon? Or at least a criminal of some sort? This is the reality that more and more Americans are grappling with in the face of a government bureaucracy consumed with churning out laws, statutes, codes, and regulations that reinforce its powers and value systems and those of the police state and its corporate allies. All the while, the life is slowly being choked out of our individual freedoms. The aim, of course, is absolute control by way of thousands of regulations that dictate when, where, how, and with whom we live our lives.

Incredibly, Congress has been creating on average 55 new "crimes" per year,[532] bringing the total number of federal crimes on the books to more than 5,000, with as many as 300,000 regulatory crimes.[533] As journalist Radley Balko reports, "that doesn't include federal regulations, which are increasingly being enforced with criminal, not administrative, penalties. It also doesn't include the increasing leeway with which prosecutors can enforce broadly written federal conspiracy, racketeering, and money laundering laws. And this is before we even get to the states' criminal codes."[534]

Petty Criminals

In such a society, we are all petty criminals, guilty of violating some minor law. In fact, attorney Harvey Silvergate estimates that the average American now unknowingly commits three felonies a day, thanks to an overabundance of vague laws that render otherwise innocent activity illegal and an inclination on the part of prosecutors to reject the idea that there can't be a crime without criminal intent.[535] Consequently, we now find ourselves operating in a strange new world where small farmers who dare to make unpasteurized goat cheese and share it with members of their community are finding their farms raided,[536] while home gardeners face jail time for daring to cultivate their own varieties of orchids without having completed sufficient paperwork.[537]

This frightening state of affairs—where a person can actually be arrested and incarcerated for the most innocent and inane activities, including feeding a whale[538] and collecting rainwater on their own property[539] (these are actual court cases)—is due to what law scholars refer to as "overcriminalization," or the overt proliferation of criminal laws.

Welcome to the Nanny State

One of the major concerns in America today is the rise of the so-called "Nanny State," a British concept whereby the government legislates policies that attempt to limit or control human behavior. These laws, which we are told are good for us, are at times petty, and at other times bizarre because of the way they may interfere in our lives. For instance, Gary Harrington of Eagle Point, Oregon, was convicted of violating a 1925 state law by having "three illegal reservoirs" on his property. He allegedly diverted tributaries of the Big Butte River, which is considered public water, for his own use. Harrington says he had been using them to collect rainwater and runoff from melted snow on his own property. For this purported "crime," Harrington was sentenced to thirty days in jail.[540]

Such laws may be well-meaning, or may even have clear value to society. But what often happens is that such laws get stretched beyond the bounds of common sense. Assuming Harrington's claim to be true, his reservoirs would have been designed to make use of water he already had the right to use. But instead, he cannot save rainwater and snow for use in irrigation or drinking water.

Bizarre Laws and Lemonade Stands

These situations are more common than we think. More and more, sidewalk lemonade stands are being shut down for not having some required permit. Run by children, usually in front of their homes, these tiny stands sell lemonade or cookies for about a quarter per cup. In 2011, police in Coralville, Iowa, shut down three such stands set up during a bicycle race, citing a need to protect riders from health risks. The required permit would have cost $400.[541]

Criminalizing Lemonade Stands

"If the line is drawn to the point where a four-year-old eight blocks away can't sell a couple glasses of lemonade for 25 cents, then I think the line has been drawn at the wrong spot," said Dustin Krutsinger, whose daughter Abigail's stand was shut down after just half an hour of operation. She made $4 in sales during that time.[542]

Other bizarre laws of this nature include:

★ Minnetonka, Minnesota, has made it illegal for a vehicle to deposit mud or other substances onto streets and highways. It's considered a public nuisance, and the vehicle's owner is subject to a fine of up to $2,000.

★ During the summer of 2011, King County, Washington, mandated the use of life jackets for everybody "on or in a major river," regardless of the purpose for being there or the ability to swim. Violators faced an $86 fine.

★ Tennessee passed a law prohibiting schoolchildren from "exposing underwear or body parts in an 'indecent manner.'" Derisively called a "Saggy Pants" law, violators face a $250 fine or up to 160 hours of community service.

★ Maryland law requires parents to give summer camps consent for their children to use sunscreen, with or without assistance from counselors.

★ Hilton Head, South Carolina, banned the storage of trash in cars. A violation is punishable by a fine of up to $500 or a jail sentence of up to thirty days. The reason: it attracts rats.

★ As part of an effort to reduce greenhouse gas emissions and landfill use, San Francisco passed a law requiring residents and businesses to sort discarded materials into three different bins, depending on classification: recyclables, trash, and combustibles. Failure to properly sort results in a fine of $100-$500.

★ To protect hotel staff from injury, California introduced legislation that would ban the use of "flat sheets," in favor of fitted ones, as the bottom sheet on beds and require the use of "long-handled" tools to clean bathrooms.

★ Rockville, Maryland, made the use of foul language within earshot of others a crime punishable by a $100 fine and/or up to ninety days behind bars.[543]

Those are some of the more ridiculous statutes. In other areas, the "nanny state" may act in a coordinated fashion. Writing for *Forbes*, Dr. Paul Hsieh expressed concern about ongoing efforts to control the way we eat. He focused particular derision on New York City's restrictions on serving size and nutritional content over the past few years as part of a fight against obesity.

The nutrition police, however, are virtually everywhere. For example, in North Carolina, an inspector confiscated a child's homemade lunch, consisting of a "turkey and cheese sandwich, banana, potato chips, and apple juice," on the grounds that it lacked nutrition.[544] Massachusetts went so far as to ban bake sales, which are a traditional means of fund-raising for school groups.[545] The ban was later overturned.

In July 2012, New York City's board of health continued further restrictions on fattening foods. Despite its already having limited the use of salt and trans-fat, America's largest city might continue to tighten the metaphorical belt until it "dictates the caloric content of just about every food item sold outside the vegetable aisle."[546]

These policies are often described with positive intentions. One could even say they're meant to save the people from themselves. But what if the people don't want to be saved? Or they simply want the freedom to eat as they see fit?

There's always a proverbial "line" for when government goes too far. Sometimes we see it, more often we don't. We haven't reached that point yet, but I suspect it may come sooner than we think.

Criminalizing Free Speech

One of the key ingredients in a democracy is the right to freely speak our minds to those who represent us. In fact, it is one of the few effective tools we have left to combat government corruption and demand accountability. But now, even that right is being chipped away by statutes and court rulings which weaken our ability to speak freely. Activities which were once considered a major component of democratic life in America are now being criminalized.

For example, in a self-serving move aimed more at insulating government officials from discontent voters than protecting their hides, Congress overwhelmingly approved legislation that will keep the public not just at arms' length distance but a football field away by making it a federal crime to protest or assemble in the vicinity of protected government officials. The Trespass Bill (the Federal Restricted Buildings and Grounds Improvement Act of 2011) creates a roving "bubble" zone or perimeter around select government officials and dignitaries (anyone protected by the Secret Service), as well as any building or grounds "restricted in conjunction with an event designated as a special event of national significance."[547]

The bill's language is so overly broad as to put an end to free speech, political protest, and the right to peaceably assemble in all areas where government officials happen to be present. Rep. Justin Amash (R-MI) was one of only three members of the House of Representatives to vote against the legislation. As he explains:

> Current law makes it illegal to enter or remain in an area where certain government officials (more particularly, those with Secret Service protection) will be visiting temporarily if and only if the person knows it's illegal to enter the restricted area but does so anyway. The bill expands current law to make it a crime to enter or remain in an area where an official is visiting even if the person does not know it's illegal to be in that area and has no reason to suspect it's illegal.
>
> Some government officials may need extraordinary protection to ensure their safety. But criminalizing legitimate First Amendment activity—even if that activity is annoying to those government officials—violates our rights. I voted "no."[548]

Specifically, the bill, which was passed by a vote of 388 to 3, was signed into law by President Obama. It levies a fine and up to a year in prison against anyone found in violation, and if the person violating the statute is carrying a "dangerous weapon," the prison sentence is bumped up to no more than ten years. Thus, a person eating in a diner while a presidential candidate is trying to score political points with the locals could be arrested if government agents determine that he is acting "disorderly." And depending on who's making the assessment, anything can be considered disorderly, including someone exercising his right to free speech by muttering to himself about a government official. And if that person happens to have a pocketknife or nail clippers in his possession (or any other innocuous item that could be interpreted by the police as "dangerous"), he could face up to ten years in prison.

Given that the Secret Service not only protects the president but all past sitting presidents, members of Congress, foreign dignitaries, presidential candidates, and anyone whom the president determines needs protection, anywhere these officials happen to be becomes a zone where the First Amendment is effectively off-limits. The Secret Service is also in charge of securing National Special Security Events, which include events such as the G8 and NATO summits, the National Conventions of both major parties, and even the Super Bowl. Simply walking by one of these events places one in a zone of criminal trespass and thus makes him subject to arrest.

It's safe to say that what happened to Steven Howards will, under this law, become a common occurrence. Howards was at a Colorado shopping mall with his son in June 2006 when he learned that then-Vice President Dick Cheney and his Secret Service security detail were at the mall greeting the public. A Secret Service agent overheard Howards telling someone that he was going to approach Cheney, express his opposition to the war in Iraq, and ask him "how many kids he's killed today." Howards eventually approached Cheney and shared his view that Cheney's policies in Iraq "are disgusting." When Cheney turned and began to walk away, Howards brushed the Vice President's shoulder with his hand. The Secret Service subsequently arrested and jailed Howards, charging him with assaulting the Vice President. The assault charges were later dropped.[549]

Free Speech Zones

Unfettered free speech is vital to a functioning democracy. Unfortunately, the tendency on the part of government and law enforcement officials to purge dissent has largely undermined the First Amendment's safeguards for political free speech. The authoritarian mindset undergirding these roving bubble zones is no different from that which gave rise to "free speech zones," which are government-sanctioned areas located far away from government officials, into which activists and citizens are herded at political rallies and events. Both zones, however, have the same end result: dissent is muted or silenced altogether, and the centers of power are shielded from the citizen.

Free speech zones have become commonplace at political rallies and the national conventions of both major political parties. One of the most infamous free speech zones was erected at the 2004 Democratic National Convention in Boston. Not so much a zone of free expression as a cage, it was a space enclosed by chain link fences, Jersey walls, and razor wire.[550] Judge Douglas Woodlock, who toured the free speech cage before the convention, noted, "One cannot conceive of other elements put in place to make a space more of an affront to the idea of free expression than the designated demonstration zone."[551]

Bubble zones and free speech zones, in essence, destroy the very purpose of the First Amendment, which assures us of the right to peaceably assemble and petition the government for a redress of grievances. In other words, we, as citizens, have a constitutional right to address our

Corralling Protesters (CS Muncy)

government officials in a public manner so that they can hear our grievances or concerns. What these zones do, however, is create insulated barriers around public officials, thus keeping us out of sight and sound's reach of those who are supposed to represent us. Many prominent activists, from Occupiers and the Tea Party to antiwar protesters, and so on, are now herded like animals and cordoned off from the view of public officials. Obviously, these zones also serve a secondary purpose, which is to chill free speech by intimidating citizens into remaining silent.

Consider this: if these types of laws had been in effect during the Civil Rights movement, there would have been no March on Washington. Martin Luther King Jr. and his fellow activists would have been rendered criminals. And King's call for "militant nonviolent resistance" would have been silenced by police in riot gear.

What's Next?

What's next? There was a time in our nation's history when such an accounting of facts would have sparked immediate outrage. However, having bought into the idea that anything the government says and does is right, even when it is so clearly wrong, many Americans through their own compliance have become unwitting accomplices in the government's efforts to prosecute otherwise law-abiding citizens for unknowingly violating some statute in its vast trove of laws written by bureaucrats who operate above the law. Yet as author Nathan Burney so adeptly points out, "when crimes are too numerous to count . . . when you're punished, not because what you did was wrong, but simply because the law *says* so . . . when laws are too vague or overbroad . . . that's not justice."[552]

CHAPTER 24

The Criminalization of America's Schoolchildren

"[P]ublic school reform is now justified in the dehumanizing language of national security, which increasingly legitimates the transformation of schools into adjuncts of the surveillance and police state ... students are increasingly subjected to disciplinary apparatuses which limit their capacity for critical thinking, mold them into consumers, test them into submission, strip them of any sense of social responsibility and convince large numbers of poor minority students that they are better off under the jurisdiction of the criminal justice system than by being valued members of the public schools."[553]—PROFESSOR HENRY GIROUX

For those hoping to better understand how and why we arrived at this dismal point in our nation's history, where individual freedoms, privacy, and human dignity have been sacrificed to the gods of security, expediency, and corpocracy, look no farther than America's public schools.

Once looked to as the starting place for imparting principles of freedom to future generations, America's classrooms are becoming little more than breeding grounds for compliant citizens. In fact, as director Cevin Soling documents in his insightful, award-winning documentary *The War on Kids,*[554] the moment young people walk into school, they increasingly find themselves under constant surveillance: they are photographed, fingerprinted, scanned, x-rayed, sniffed, and snooped on. Between metal detectors at the entrances, drug-sniffing dogs in the hallways, and surveillance cameras in the classrooms and elsewhere, many of America's schools look more like prisons than learning facilities.

Add to this the epidemic of arresting schoolchildren and treating them as if they are dangerous criminals, and you have the makings of a perfect citizenry for the Orwellian society—one that can be easily cowed, controlled, and directed. In fact, what once was looked upon as classically childish behavior such as getting into food fights, playing tag, doodling, hugging, kicking, and throwing temper tantrums is now criminalized.

Arrested Development

Whereas in the past minor behavioral infractions at school such as shooting spitwads may have warranted a trip to the principal's office, in-school detention, or a phone call to one's parents, today they are elevated to the level of criminal behavior with all that implies. Consequently, young people are now being forcibly removed by police officers from the classroom, arrested, handcuffed, transported in the back of police squad cars, and placed in police holding cells until their frantic parents can get them out. For those unlucky enough to be targeted for such punishment, the experience will stay with them long after they are allowed back at school. In fact, it will stay with them for the rest of their lives in the form of a criminal record.

For example, in November 2011, a 14-year-old student in Brevard County, Florida, was suspended for hugging a female friend, an act which even the principal acknowledged as innocent.[555] A 9-year-old in Charlotte, North Carolina, was suspended for sexual harassment after a substitute teacher overheard the child tell another student that the teacher was "cute."[556] A 6-year-old in Georgia was arrested, handcuffed, and suspended for the remainder of the school year after throwing a temper tantrum in class.[557] A 6-year-old boy in San Francisco was accused of sexual assault following a game of tag on the playground.[558] A 6-year-old in Indiana was arrested, handcuffed, and charged with battery after kicking a school principal.[559]

Twelve-year-old Alexa Gonzalez was arrested and handcuffed for doodling on a desk.[560] Another student was expelled for speaking on a cell phone with his mother, to whom he hadn't spoken in a month because she was in Iraq on a military deployment.[561] Four high school students in Detroit were arrested and handcuffed for participating in a food fight and charged with a misdemeanor with the potential for a ninety-day jail sentence and a $500 fine.[562] A high school student in Indiana was expelled after sending a profanity-laced tweet through his Twitter account after school hours. The school had been conducting their own surveillance by tracking the tweeting habits of all students.[563]

Teens Suspended, Arrested After Food Fight (WXYZ)

The Lockdown in America's Public Schools

These are not isolated incidents. In 2010 some 300,000 Texas schoolchildren received misdemeanor tickets from police officials. One 12-year-old Texas girl had the police called on her after she sprayed perfume on herself during class.[564] In Albuquerque, New Mexico, over 90,000 kids were entered into the criminal justice system during the 2009-2010 school year, and over 500 of those were arrested at school.[565]

It is hard to believe that such things—children being handcuffed and carted off to jail for minor incidents—could take place in a so-called "free" country. However, since the introduction of police, high-tech surveillance systems, and zero tolerance policies into the schools, this is the reality with which nearly 50 million students in America's elementary and secondary public schools must contend. Many of these "say no to drugs/say no to violence"–type policies gained favor after the Columbine school shootings in 1999 and have continued to be adopted by school districts across the country. This, even in the wake of research indicating that zero tolerance neither makes schools safer nor discourages violence. "Ironically, the [Columbine] tragedy occurred as rates of school violence in general and shootings in particular were declining," writes author Annette Fuentes in *Lockdown High*.[566]

Zero Tolerance

Zero tolerance policies, the driving force behind the criminalization of schoolchildren, punish all offenses severely—no matter how minor. Disproportionately levied against minority students and students with emotional and behavioral disabilities,[567] these one-size-fits-all disciplinary procedures mandate suspension or expulsion for students who violate the rules, regardless of the student's intent or the nature of the violation.

Zero tolerance rules in many states also cover fighting, drug or alcohol use, and gang activity, as well as relatively minor offenses such as possessing over-the-counter medications and disrespect of authority. Nearly all American public schools have zero tolerance policies for firearms or other "weapons," and most have such policies for drugs and alcohol. In the wake of the Columbine school shootings, legislators and school boards further tightened their zero tolerance policies, creating what some critics call a national intolerance for childish behavior. As a result, these policies are now interpreted so broadly as to crack down on spit wads, Tweetie Bird key chains, and Certs breath mints—all of which constitute contraband of one kind or another. In some jurisdictions, carrying cough drops, wearing black lipstick, or dying your hair blue are expellable offenses.

Other examples: In May 2012 at Deltona High School in Florida, 17-year-old Michael Rudi had his inhaler taken from him by school officials during a search of his locker. Even though the inhaler was in its original packaging, complete with his name and directions for use, school officials decided to confiscate it because his mother had not signed "the proper form" allowing him to carry it. At some point, Michael began having trouble breathing, so school officials called his mother, Sue, but refused to give Michael his inhaler. Sue rushed to the school where she was taken to the nurse's office. The door was locked, and upon entering, they found the nurse numbly looking on as Michael lay on the ground, suffering a full-blown asthma attack. Michael claims that as he began passing out, the nurse locked the door. "It's like something out of a horror film. The person just sits there and watches you die," he said. "She sat there, looked at me and she did nothing." Officials with the Volusia County school district have stood by the nurse's decision.[568]

In September 2012, 8-year-old Konnor Vanatta was prevented from wearing his replica Denver Broncos football jersey with Peyton

Manning's number 18 on it because school officials claimed that the number 18 is associated with a local gang, the 18th street gang. Other numbers banned for gang associations are 13 and 14, as well as the reverse of all three, 81, 31, and 41. Pam Vanatta, Konnor's mother, pointed out the absurdity of the situation saying, "When they are counting and when they're learning their numbers, are they going to make them skip 14, 13, 41, 81, 18 when they are counting? It's getting ridiculous."[569]

In December 2011, 10-year-old Nicholas Taylor was severely disciplined for jokingly aiming a piece of pizza shaped like a gun at his classmates during lunch. For this childish behavior, Nicholas was relegated to the "silent" table for the rest of the semester, forced to meet with a school resource officer about gun safety, and threatened with suspension for any future infractions.[570]

A deaf 3-year-old preschooler in Nebraska was singled out by school administrators because one of the letters in his name, when signed, appeared to some as a gun being drawn in the air. Rather than letting him sign his name, a spokesman for the school district says they are "working with the parents to come to the best solution we can for the child."[571]

A high school valedictorian, heading to Oklahoma University on full scholarship, was denied her diploma because during her graduation speech, she said the word "hell." The school demanded that Kaitlin Nootbaar write them a formal apology in order to receive her diploma, which she refused to do.[572]

While expulsion and suspension used to be the worst punishment to be rendered against a child who had run afoul of the system, school officials have now upped the ante by routinely bringing the police into the picture. As Judith Browne Dianis, co-director of the Advancement Project, notes, "Media hysteria really created this groundswell of support for zero tolerance and folks being scared that it could happen at their school. Now, we have police officers in every school. He's not there to be law enforcement. He's there to lock up kids."[573]

Tracking Students

Increasing numbers of schools have even gone so far as to require students to drape Radio Frequency Identification (RFID) tags around their necks, which allow school officials to track every single step students take. So small that they are barely detectable to the human eye, RFID tags produce a radio signal by which the wearer's precise movements can be constantly monitored. For example, some 4,200 students at Jay High School and Jones Middle School in San Antonio, Texas, are convenient guinea pigs for the Student Locator Project, which required students to carry "smart" ID cards embedded with an RFID tracking chip.[574] Although these schools already boast 290 surveillance cameras,[575] the Northside School District ID program gave school officials the ability to track students' whereabouts at all times. School officials plan to expand the program to the district's 112 schools, with a student population of 100,000.[576] Students who refuse to take part in the ID program won't be able to access essential services like the cafeteria and library, nor will they be able to purchase tickets to extracurricular activities.[577]

Unfortunately, RFID tracking is actually the least invasive surveillance tactic being used in schools today. Chronically absent middle schoolers in Anaheim, California, for example, have been enrolled in a GPS tracking program. Journalist David Rosen explains:

> Each school day, the delinquent students get an automated 'wake-up' phone call reminding them that they need to get to school on time. In addition, five times a day they are required to enter a code that tracks their locations: as they leave for school, when they arrive at school, at lunchtime, when they leave school and at 8 pm. These students are also assigned an adult 'coach' who calls them at least three times a week to see how they are doing and help them find effective ways to make sure they get to school.[578]

Some schools in New York, New Jersey, and Missouri are tracking students labeled obese and overweight with wristwatches that record their heart rate, movement, and sleeping habits.[579] Schools in San Antonio even have chips in their lunch food trays, which allow administrators to track the eating habits of students.[580]

Schools in Michigan's second largest school district broadcast student activity caught by CCTV cameras on the walls of the hallways in real time, to let the students know they're being watched.[581] In 2003 a Tennessee middle school placed cameras in the school's locker rooms, capturing images of children changing before basketball practice. This practice was stuck down in 2008 by the U.S. Sixth Circuit Court of

Appeals, which ruled that students have an expectation of privacy in locker rooms.[582]

Some school districts have gone so far as to not even mention to students and parents that they are electronically tracking children. In 2010 it was revealed that a Pennsylvania school district had given students laptops installed with software that allowed school administrators to track their behavior at home. This revelation led to the threat of a class-action lawsuit, which resulted in the school district settling with irate students and parents for $600,000.[583]

Passive, Conditionable Objects

To return to what I was saying about schools being breeding grounds for compliant citizens, if Americans have come to view freedom as expedient and expendable, it is only because that's what they've been taught in the schools by government leaders and by the corporations who run the show. As psychologist Bruce Levine has noted, "Behaviorism and consumerism, two ideologies which achieved tremendous power in the twentieth century, are cut from the same cloth. The shopper, the student, the worker, and the voter are all seen by consumerism and behaviorism the same way: passive, conditionable objects."[584]

More and more Americans are finding themselves institutionalized from cradle to grave, from government-run daycares and public schools to nursing homes. In between, they are fed a constant, mind-numbing diet of pablum consisting of entertainment news, mediocre leadership, and technological gadgetry, which keeps them sated, distracted, and unwilling to challenge the status quo. All the while, in the name of the greater good and in exchange for the phantom promise of security, the government strips away our rights one by one—monitoring our conversations, chilling our expression, searching our bodies and our possessions, doing away with our due process rights, reversing the burden of proof, and rendering us suspects in a surveillance state.

Whether or not the powers-that-be, by their actions, are consciously attempting to create a compliant citizenry, the result is the same nevertheless for young and old alike. As journalist Hunter S. Thompson observed in *Kingdom of Fear: Loathsome Secrets of a Star-crossed Child in the Final Days of the American Century*:

Coming of age in a fascist police state will not be a barrel of fun for anybody, much less for people like me, who are not inclined to suffer Nazis gladly and feel only contempt for the cowardly flag-suckers who would gladly give up their outdated freedom to *live* for the mess of pottage they have been conned into believing will be freedom from fear. Ho ho ho. Let's not get carried away here. Freedom was yesterday in this country. Its value has been discounted. The only freedom we truly crave today is freedom from Dumbness. Nothing else matters.[585]

CHAPTER 25

The Prison Industrial Complex

"Mass incarceration on a scale almost unexampled in human history is a fundamental fact of our country today—perhaps the fundamental fact, as slavery was the fundamental fact of 1850. In truth, there are more black men in the grip of the criminal-justice system—in prison, on probation, or on parole—than were in slavery then. Over all, there are now more people under 'correctional supervision' in America—more than six million—than were in the Gulag Archipelago under Stalin at its height."[586]

—Journalist ADAM GOPNIK

GEO Group Editorial Cartoon by Khalil Bendib
(Copyright of Khalil Bendib, www.bendib.com, all rights reserved.)

In an age when freedom is fast becoming the exception rather than the rule, imprisoning Americans in private prisons run by mega-corporations has turned into a cash cow for big business. At one time, the American penal system operated under the idea that dangerous criminals needed to be put under lock and key in order to protect society. Today, as states attempt to save money by outsourcing prisons to private corporations, the flawed yet retributive American "system of justice" is being replaced by an even more flawed and insidious form of mass punishment based upon profit and expediency.

As author Adam Gopnik reports for the *New Yorker*:

> [A] growing number of American prisons are now contracted out as for-profit businesses to for-profit companies. The companies are paid by the state, and their profit depends on spending as little as possible on the prisoners and the prisons. It's hard to imagine any greater disconnect between public good and private profit: the interest of private prisons lies not in the obvious social good of having the minimum necessary number of inmates but in having as many as possible, housed as cheaply as possible.[587]

Jailing American for Profit

Consider this: despite the fact that violent crime in America has been on the decline,[588] the nation's incarceration rate has tripled since 1980.[589] Approximately 13 million people are introduced to American jails in any given year. Incredibly, more than 6 million people are under "correctional supervision" in America,[590] meaning that one in fifty Americans are working their way through the prison system, either as inmates, or while on parole or probation. According to the Federal Bureau of Prisons, the majority of those being held in federal prisons are convicted of drug offenses[591]—namely, marijuana. Presently, one out of every one hundred Americans is serving time behind bars.[592]

Little wonder, then, that public prisons are overcrowded.[593] Yet while providing security, housing, food, and medical care for six million Americans is a hardship for cash-strapped states, to profit-hungry corporations such as Corrections Corp of America (CCA) and GEO Group, the leaders in the partnership corrections industry, it's a $70 billion[594] gold mine. Thus, with an eye toward increasing its bottom line, CCA's goal is to buy and manage public prisons across the country at a substantial cost savings to the states. In exchange, and here's the kicker, the prisons have to contain at least 1,000 beds[595] and states have to agree to maintain a 90 percent occupancy rate in the privately run prisons for at least 20 years.[596]

The problem with this scenario, as Roger Werholtz, former Kansas secretary of corrections, recognizes is that while states may be tempted by the quick infusion of cash, they "would be obligated to maintain these (occupancy) rates and subtle pressure would be applied to make sentencing laws more severe with a clear intent to drive up the population."[597] Unfortunately, that's exactly what has happened. Among the laws aimed at increasing the prison population and growing the profit margins of special interest corporations like CCA are three-strike laws (mandating sentences of twenty-five years to life for multiple felony convictions) and "truth-in-sentencing" legislation (mandating that those sentenced to prison serve most or all of their time).[598] This, as we saw earlier, is the overcriminalization of America which means more prison inmates—for profit, that is.

And yes, in case you were wondering, part of the investment pitch for CCA and its cohort GEO Group includes the profits to be made in building "kindler, gentler" minimum-security facilities designed for detaining illegal immigrants, especially low-risk detainees like women and children. With immigration a persistent problem in the southwestern states, especially, and more than 250 such detention centers erected across the country, there is indeed money to be made.[599] For example, GEO's new facility in Karnes County, Texas, boasts a "608-bed facility still smelling of fresh paint and new carpet stretch[ing] across a 29-acre swath of farmland in rural South Texas. Rather than prison cells, jumpsuits, and barbed wire fencing, detainees here will sleep in eight-bed dormitory-style quarters, wearing more cozy attire like jeans and T-shirts. The facility's high walls enclose lush green courtyards with volleyball courts, an AstroTurfed soccer field, and basketball hoops, where detainees are free to roam throughout the day."[600]

"And this is where it gets creepy," observes reporter Joe Weisenthal for *Business Insider*, "because as an investor you're pulling for scenarios where more people are put in jail."[601] In making its pitch to potential investors, CCA points out that private prisons comprise a unique, recession-resistant investment opportunity, with more than 90 percent of the market up for grabs, little competition, high recidivism among prisoners, and the potential for "accelerated growth in inmate populations following the recession."[602] In other words, caging humans for profit is a sure bet, because the U.S. population is growing dramatically and the prison population will grow proportionally as well, and more prisoners equals more profits.

In this way, under the pretext of being tough on crime, state governments can fatten their coffers and fill the jail cells of their corporate benefactors. However, while a flourishing privatized prison system is a financial windfall for corporate investors, it bodes ill for any measures aimed at reforming prisoners and reducing crime. CCA understands this. As it has warned investors, efforts to decriminalize certain activities, such as drug use (principally possession of marijuana), could cut into their profits.[603] So too would measures aimed at reducing the prison system's disproportionately racist impact on minorities, given that the incarceration rate for blacks is seven times that of whites.[604] Immigrants are also heavily impacted, with roughly 2.5 million people having been through the immigration detention system since 2003.[605] As private prisons begin to dominate, the many troubling characteristics of our so-called criminal justice system today—racism, economic inequality, inadequate access to legal representation, and a lack of due process—will only become more acute.

Corruption Equals Criminals for Profit

Doubtless, a system already riddled by corruption will inevitably become more corrupt, as well. For example, consider the "kids for cash" scandal which rocked Luzerne County, Pennsylvania, in 2009. For ten years the Mid Atlantic Youth Service Corporation, which specializes in private prisons for juvenile offenders, paid two judges to jail youths and send them to private prison facilities. The judges, who made over $2.6 million in the scam,[606] had more than 5,000 kids come through their courtrooms and sent many of them to prison for petty crimes such as stealing DVDs from Wal-Mart and trespassing in vacant buildings.[607] When the scheme finally came to light, one judge was sentenced to 17.5 years in prison[608] and the other received 28 years,[609] but not before thousands of young lives had been ruined.

In this way, minor criminals, from drug users to petty thieves, are being handed over to corporations for lengthy prison sentences which do nothing to protect society or prevent recidivism. This is the culmination of an inverted justice system which has come to characterize the United States, a justice system based upon increasing the power and wealth of the corporate state.

No matter what the politicians or corporate heads might say, prison privatization is neither fiscally responsible nor in keeping with principles of justice. This perverse notion of how prisons should be run, that they should be full at all times, and full of minor criminals, is evil.

Corporate Takeover of America

Although big business and government have always had intimate relations, that relationship was at one time governed by a tacit understanding that the government's first priority was to protect the individual rights of its citizens, while corporations—private entities, separate from government—were free to concern themselves with making a profit. Unfortunately, the rise of the corporate state over the past seventy years (a development that both President Eisenhower and Martin Luther King Jr. warned against) has done away with democratic government as we have known it. In the process, the interests of megacorporations have been prioritized over those of the average citizen. Nowhere is this emphasis on corporate profit at the expense of the American citizenry more evident than in the American Legislative Exchange Council (ALEC).

A nonprofit membership organization which purports to uphold principles of "limited government, free markets, federalism and individual liberty,"[610] ALEC is comprised of state lawmakers and corporate representatives with a mutual interest in seeing legislation adopted at both the state and federal levels. ALEC was founded in 1973 and has approximately 2,000 state lawmakers among its members, or roughly a quarter of state legislators in the nation.[611] Unlike lobbying groups, however, ALEC is not required to disclose its relationship with legislators.

Although ALEC has been described as a conservative organization, the only credo—political or otherwise—subscribed to by that of its corporate members is materialism, which gives allegiance to no interest, political or otherwise, other than its own. Indeed, while ALEC keeps the names of its corporate members under tight wraps, its roster includes some of the biggest names in the corporate world.[612]

Arizona Police Enforce Racial Profiling Law (PressTV)

Whatever Happened to Representative Government?

In a nutshell, ALEC's formula for success relies on creating model legislation. Although ALEC's legislation crafting meetings are off limits to nonmembers,[613] the group's political might is well known. Roughly 1,000 ALEC bills are introduced in legislatures throughout the country each year, and about one-fifth become law.[614] The model legislation which ALEC produces and which state legislators, having paid a fee to access, can introduce to their own legislatures has been described as "ready-made, just add water, written in language that can withstand partisan debate and legal scrutiny."[615]

Not surprisingly, given the corporate bent of its membership, much of the model legislation created by ALEC involves privatizing government functions or creating policies which favor corporate profits over public interest. Incredibly, in Florida, legislation lowering the corporate tax rate was so closely worded to the ALEC model that it accidentally included the ALEC mission statement.[616]

In other words, although we elect our so-called representatives to write and debate the legislation which governs our lives, it is the corporate elite which now assumes that role. Of course, this means that representative government as we have known it is becoming extinct.

As you might expect, ALEC has been behind a number of controversial pieces of legislation that have become law.[617] For example, ALEC worked with the National Rifle Association in order to pass legislation in states across the country similar to Florida's "Stand Your Ground" law, which became the focal point of the Trayvon Martin shooting controversy. Twenty-five states now have similar laws.[618]

Bolstering the Police State

ALEC has also helped engineer a number of laws which bolster the aura of an emerging police state. For instance, ALEC has been the mastermind behind the strengthening or imposition of voter ID laws across the country.[619] In the past, these laws have been used to discriminate against specific demographic groups of voters.

One of ALEC's most infamous pieces of model legislation, one that has ushered in a police state in Arizona, formed the core of that state's controversial immigration law, which generally withstood a legal challenge before the U.S. Supreme Court. Among those members who helped draft the model legislation was CCA, the country's largest private prison company. CCA benefited greatly from ALEC's legislative efforts to privatize the prison industry. That model legislation morphed into SB 1070, a law which promotes racial profiling and allows police to randomly violate the Fourth Amendment by patting down, detaining, or arresting anyone they suspect might be an illegal immigrant, including American citizens. Two-thirds of the thirty-six immediate co-sponsors of the bill in the Arizona Senate were ALEC members or attendees at the legislation drafting meeting.[620]

Another one of ALEC's more egregious pieces of legislation, the Prison Industries Act (PIE), privatizes prison labor and directs any money earned by the prisoners towards expanding the prison industry, creating more prisoner work programs and paying corporations for setting them up. Prior to ALEC's intervention, that money was used to offset taxpayer expenses. Now it fattens corporate wallets. Some thirty states operate PIE programs based upon legislation derived from ALEC. Florida has forty-one prison industries, California has sixty, and there are roughly one hundred throughout the other states that employ prison labor.

Prison Labor

What some Americans may not have realized, however, is that these resulting prison labor industries, which rely on cheap, almost free labor, are doing as much to put the average American out of work as the outsourcing of jobs to China and India. "It's bad enough that our companies have to compete with exploited and forced labor in China. They shouldn't have to compete against prison labor here at home," noted Scott Paul, Executive Director of the Alliance for American Manufacturing.[621]

States influenced by ALEC are also seeking to replace public workers with prisoners who work not for pay but to get time off their sentences. Coupled with the trend towards privatized prisons—where, in exchange for corporations managing state prisons, states agree to maintain a 90 percent occupancy rate for at least twenty years—this expansion of the prison labor industry contributes to an environment in which there is a financial incentive for ensuring that more people are put and kept in jail.

Factories of Death

The historical parallels relating to the emergence of a corporate-driven prison industry are chillingly detailed in Richard Rubenstein's insightful book *The Cunning of History*.[622] Despite Nazi military commander Heinrich Himmler's infamous 1943 order calling for the total annihilation of the Jews, a directive replaced it that stated all able-bodied Jewish adults at Auschwitz be sent to hard labor camps instead of the crematorium.[623] The motive behind the change of plans: corporate profit. Many German corporations, including BASF, Bayer, Hoechst, and other major German chemical and pharmaceutical companies, invested huge sums in the construction of factories at death camps for the express purpose of utilizing the available and infinitely replenishable pool of death-camp slave labor—much of it to produce products for European countries.

Over the course of World War II, the German pharmaceutical corporation, Bayer A.G. of Leverkusen, made extensive use of death-camp inmates for their experiments on human beings. Bayer laboratories synthesized a new anti-typhus medicine and wanted it tested. The medicine came in two forms: tablet and powder. Bayer wanted to know which one had the fewest side effects. Bayer researchers were given permission to conduct their experiments on death camp inmates.[624]

Auschwitz Concentration Camp
(Keystone/Hulton Archive/Getty Images)

Medical experiments conducted by the Third Reich and its corporate enablers fell into two general categories: 1) use prisoners to conduct tests that would have been normal attempts at advancing medical knowledge had the subjects participated willingly, and 2) discover means to ensure German rule over Europe forever. The mass sterilization of Jews, Gypsies, and other undesirables by the Nazi regime fell into the latter category, and the death camps were the place to carry it out. In this nightmare vision, as Rubenstein realized, "the victims would have had as little control over their own destiny as cattle in a stockyard. In a society of total domination, helots could be killed, bred, or sterilized at will."[625]

This practice of using prisoners was not unique to Nazi Germany or other totalitarian regimes. No government holds a monopoly on the mentality that sees powerless human beings as unwilling or unsuspecting subjects of experiments on behalf of the "greater good." During the Cold War, the practice of using prisoners for medical experiments was very common in the United States as well.[626] In the notorious Tuskegee syphilis experiment, the U.S. government sought to study the natural progression of untreated syphilis by deceiving black prisoners into thinking they were receiving free health care. Those who received the placebo endured the full effects of the disease and/or death in the name of scientific progress.[627] This experiment only differed from those carried out by the Nazis in that the American prisoners were completely blind to what was being done to them whereas the Nazi victims had some idea of what was happening.

This psychopathic "modern" mentality, which places a higher priority on "solving an administratively defined problem" rather than focusing on its social consequences on human beings, characterized both the American and German experiments. Yet even though the numerous accounts of corporate complicity with the Third Reich are shocking and appalling, Rubenstein adamantly refutes the notion that the "corporate executives [were] possessed of some distinct quality of villainy."[628] Mass murder simply became part of business and a successful corporate venture.

Unless we ignore the socio-economic factors that facilitated the justification of massive killings, as Rubenstein recognizes, we cannot assume that it cannot happen elsewhere or in future times.[629] The lesson is clear: it is a stern warning for citizens and policy-makers today as the police state continues to spread its tendrils into everyday life with the assistance of better and more efficient technology in an attempt to profit from prison labor.

CHAPTER 26

The Psychology of Compliance

"Laws are rules made by people who govern by means of organized violence, for non-compliance with which the non-complier is subjected to blows, to loss of liberty, or even to being murdered."[630]—Author LEO TOLSTOY

Why did Nazi soldiers commit unspeakable atrocities at Hitler's request? Why do so many of us stand by silently when we witness bullying?

It appears that we, as humans, implicitly comply with authority. Furthermore, when in positions of authority, we innately act aggressively.

Thankfully, most of us will not have to confront a warlord or find ourselves in the position to seriously harm others. However, some groups in modern society, namely police and corrections officers, too often abuse their authority. Understanding why we create and allow hostility will enable us to create more effective safeguards against unnecessary violence.

The Experiments

In 1961 professor Stanley Milgram conducted an experiment at Yale University in which subjects were asked to administer an increasingly intense shock punishment to a friend or acquaintance[631] in another room whenever he or she answered a question wrong.[632] The test subjects believed they were causing another human being great harm, even though in reality they were not. Despite the fact that many subjects were visibly uncomfortable (nervously laughing, etc.) with giving painful shocks to another human being, twenty-six out of forty participants continued shocking people up to the highest (450-volt) level, labeled "XXX" on the machine. No subject stopped before giving a 300-volt shock, labeled "Intense Shock" despite the fact that the confederate in the next room expressed severe agony and health concerns. All of the subjects were voluntary participants. When a participant expressed an unwillingness to administer the next shock, experimenters prodded them to do so by asking "Please continue," or stating: "The experiment requires that you continue."[633]

A decade later, researchers conducting the Stanford Prison Experiment[634] randomly assigned participants to be either guards or prisoners in an intricate role play. With only the instruction to "maintain order" in the simulated prison, the "guards" began harassing and intimidating prisoners. "Prisoners" did attempt to rebel, but always returned to compliance quickly after an outburst, despite the fact that they were volunteers. Due to the extreme aggression of guards, the experiment was terminated after only five days (the original design would have held students for two weeks).

In the decades following these shocking studies, psychologists have asked, why do people (those in power or those subordinate to power) act aggressively? Organizations like the military or police force have been widely studied to answer this question. Today, theories of learned obedience are generally accepted.

For example, a SWAT member who believes a raid is unconstitutional will likely not defy orders from his superior because compliance was engendered in him during the training process. Norm Stamper, a former police chief, believes that the current "rank-and-file" organization of police departments results in "bureaucratic regulations [being emphasized] over conduct on the streets." [635] In war zones, soldiers are trained as subordinates and fulfill their superior's commands. Milgram's participants felt they were under the employ of the researchers and took the orders issued to them. Stamper argues that utilizing similar rigid power hierarchies in police departments leads to blind obedience. Researcher Eungkyoon Lee backs up Stamper's musings with empirical research. Lee found that trait compliance is highest in contexts that feature a well-defined authority figure and when the subject in question has a clearly inferior role.[636]

Pleasure in Violence?

Unfortunately, merely reorganizing systems of authority will not end excessive compliance. Individuals can, without orders from a superior, still act violently, as the Stanford Prison Experiment showed. Observational evidence, like the infamous smiles on the faces of American soldiers stationed at Abu Ghraib, has long suggested that it is human nature to take pleasure in violence.

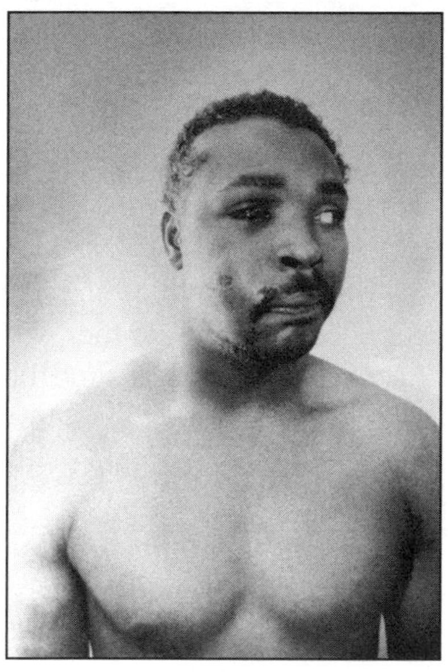

Rodney King (AP Photo)

Following the 1992 Rodney King incident, police brutality became a hot-button topic, especially as it relates to whether individuals who are predisposed to enjoy violence seek out positions as police officers. According to a study done by Brian Lawton, such self-selection into law enforcement does occur.[637] Making matters worse, "non-lethal" weapons such as tasers, pepper spray, and so on enable police to aggress with the push of a button, making the potential for overblown confrontations over minor incidents that much more likely. Case in point: the fact that seven-months-pregnant Malaika Brooks was tased three times[638] for refusing to sign a speeding ticket, while Keith Cockrell was shot with a taser for jaywalking.[639]

After the advent of automatic weapons, psychologists began examining whether or not modern weapons had their own independent effect on violent behavior. Researchers discovered that dehumanizing weapons like guns or tasers, which do not require the aggressor to make physical contact with his victim, are aggression-eliciting stimuli. One study found that simply showing an image of a gun to students caused them to clench their fists faster (a sign of aggressive effect) when presented with an aversive situation.[640] If a simple handgun can noticeably increase violent behavior, one can only imagine what impact the $500 million dollars' worth of weapons and armored vehicles (provided by the Pentagon to local police in states and municipalities across the country) have on already tense and potentially explosive situations.[641]

The Bystander Effect

While explanations have been proffered for the inclination towards violence on the part of law enforcement officials, what isn't immediately evident is why the American citizenry doesn't take a stand against such tactics. What, psychologically, is holding us back from staving off the emerging police state? Social psychologists believe the answer is centered on our group dynamics.

In 1964 dozens of onlookers witnessed the brutal murder of Kitty Genovese in Queens, New York, but no one called the police or took any other action to stop the crime.[642] This widely-reported case became the archetypal example of the "bystander effect" defined as people doing nothing in response to some injustice because they believe another witness will take responsibility for the situation.

An offshoot of the bystander effect—a desire to conform to the group—could also be responsible for the lack of outcry against the growing police state. We all want to fit in: if our peers aren't doing something, we probably won't either. A recreation of Milgram's shock experiments that involved allowing participants to watch one another administering shocks found that people were systematically more likely to "conform" to the group behavior (be it administering shocks or refusing to shock).[643] As a species, we learn by modeling the behavior of our peers and parents. Thus, it is not surprising that we put so much weight on the group norm. Indeed, doing what the group does can be an incredible tool when learning social standards, a new physical skill or how to cope with difficult emotions.

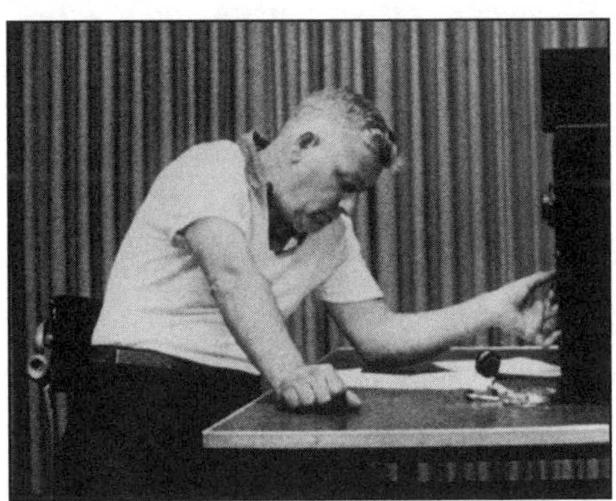

From the film *Obedience*
(© 1968 by Stanley Milgram; copyright renewed 1993 by Alexandra Milgram; distributed by Alexandra Milgram)

Zimbardo's Myth

Finally, consider that obedience to authority is not exclusively taught in militaristic contexts. Many parents attempt to foster trait compliance in their children. Commenting on Professor Milgram's experiment, Phillip Zimbardo—the mastermind of the Stanford Prison Experiment—noted that American society engenders obedience in its youth, at home and in school. Zimbardo argues that "obedience to authority requires each of us to first participate in the myth-making process of creating authority figures who then must legitimize their authority through the evidence of our submission to them."[644]

Zimbardo's "myth" is alive and well today. For example, a police officer may follow his commander out of deference to authority according to his training, or a citizen may follow an officer's order according to his or her moral teachings. In other words, we are raised to be obedient. Nowhere is this rigid adherence to rules and compliance better illustrated than in the schools with their zero tolerance policies, surveillance cameras, and other instruments of compliance.

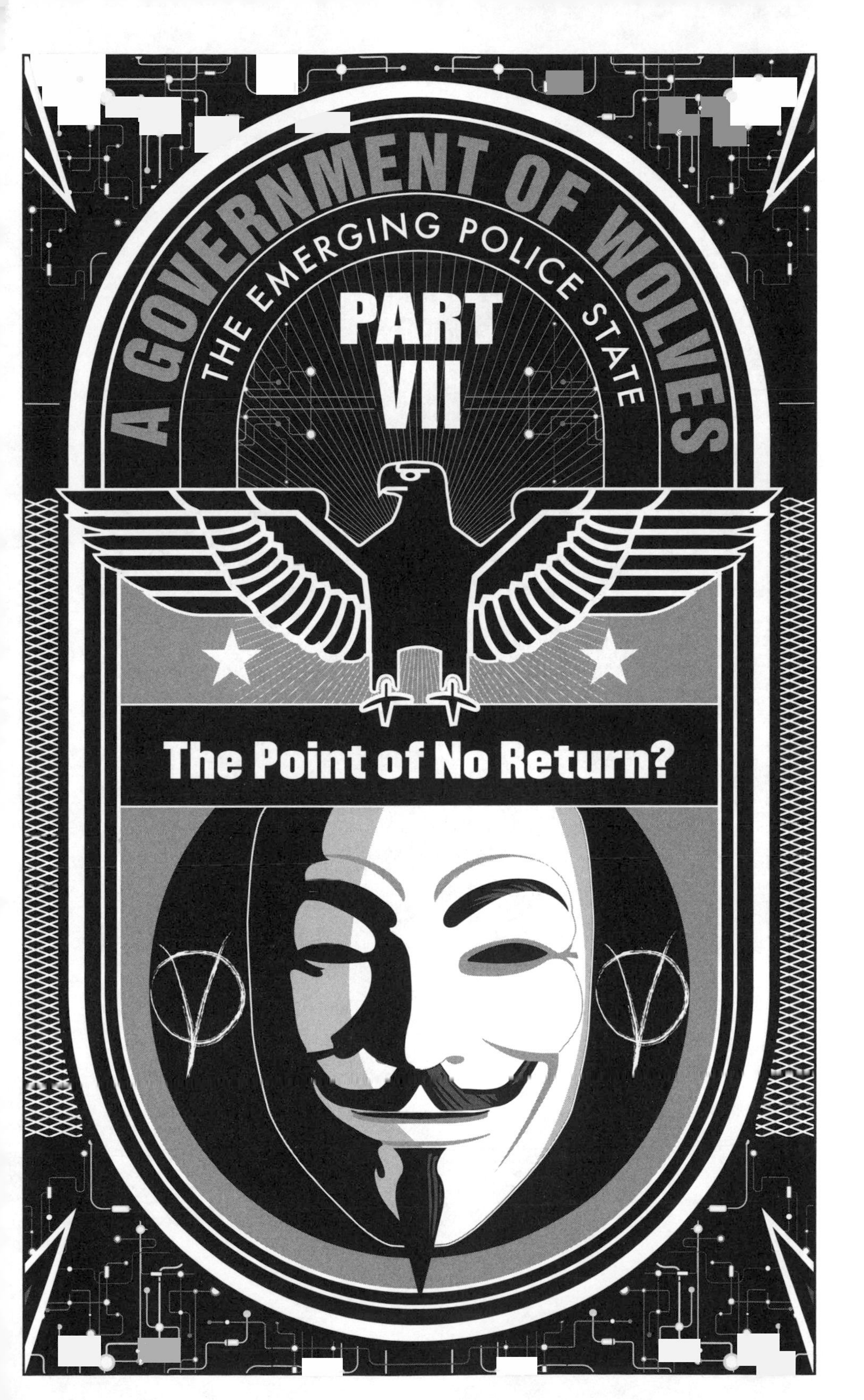
A GOVERNMENT OF WOLVES
THE EMERGING POLICE STATE
PART VII
The Point of No Return?

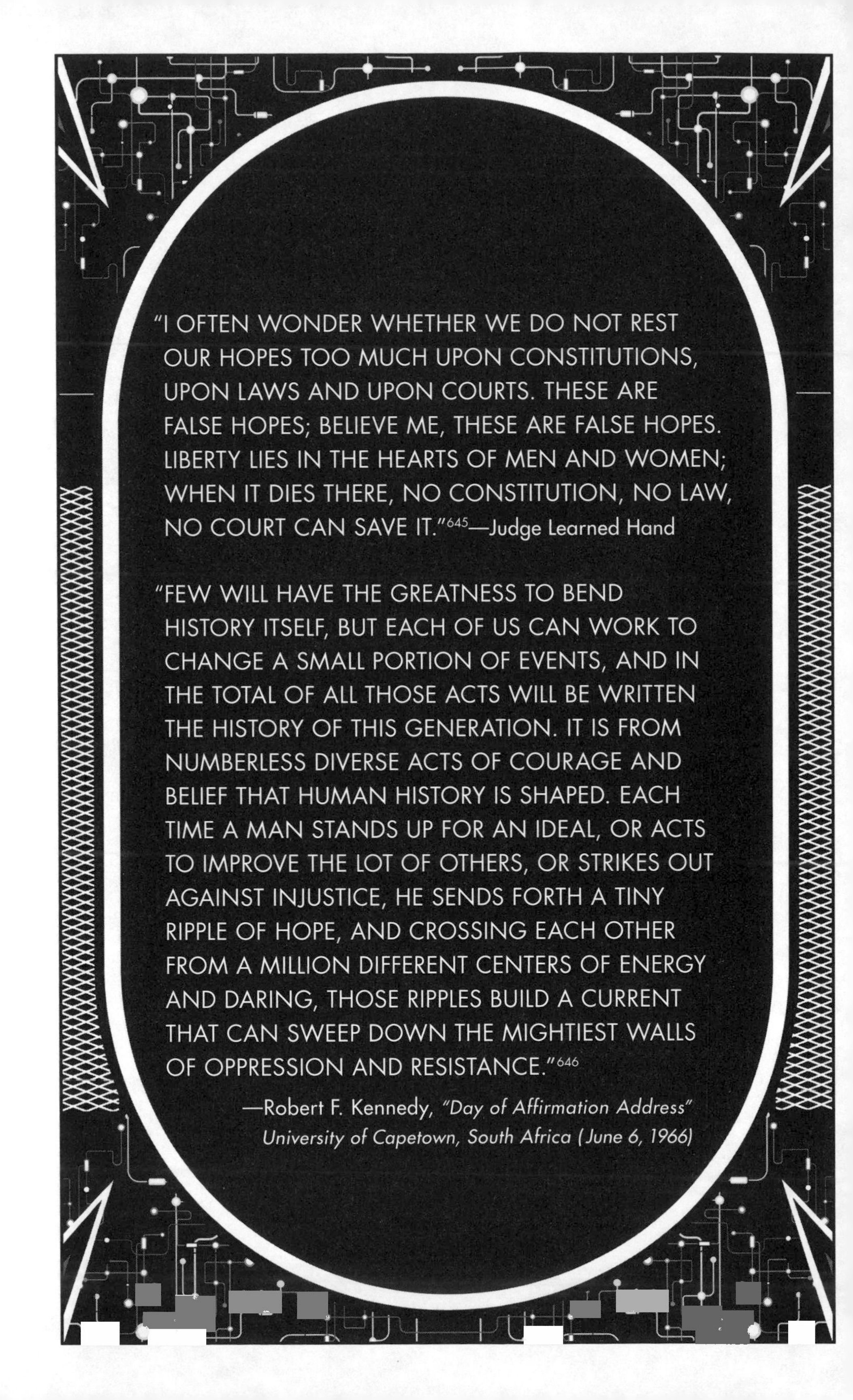
"I OFTEN WONDER WHETHER WE DO NOT REST OUR HOPES TOO MUCH UPON CONSTITUTIONS, UPON LAWS AND UPON COURTS. THESE ARE FALSE HOPES; BELIEVE ME, THESE ARE FALSE HOPES. LIBERTY LIES IN THE HEARTS OF MEN AND WOMEN; WHEN IT DIES THERE, NO CONSTITUTION, NO LAW, NO COURT CAN SAVE IT."[645]—Judge Learned Hand
"FEW WILL HAVE THE GREATNESS TO BEND HISTORY ITSELF, BUT EACH OF US CAN WORK TO CHANGE A SMALL PORTION OF EVENTS, AND IN THE TOTAL OF ALL THOSE ACTS WILL BE WRITTEN THE HISTORY OF THIS GENERATION. IT IS FROM NUMBERLESS DIVERSE ACTS OF COURAGE AND BELIEF THAT HUMAN HISTORY IS SHAPED. EACH TIME A MAN STANDS UP FOR AN IDEAL, OR ACTS TO IMPROVE THE LOT OF OTHERS, OR STRIKES OUT AGAINST INJUSTICE, HE SENDS FORTH A TINY RIPPLE OF HOPE, AND CROSSING EACH OTHER FROM A MILLION DIFFERENT CENTERS OF ENERGY AND DARING, THOSE RIPPLES BUILD A CURRENT THAT CAN SWEEP DOWN THE MIGHTIEST WALLS OF OPPRESSION AND RESISTANCE."[646]
—Robert F. Kennedy, *"Day of Affirmation Address"*
University of Capetown, South Africa (June 6, 1966)

CHAPTER 27

V for Vendetta

Good evening, London. Allow me first to apologize for this interruption. I do, like many of you, appreciate the comforts of every day routine—the security of the familiar, the tranquility of repetition. I enjoy them as much as any bloke. But in the spirit of commemoration, thereby those important events of the past usually associated with someone's death or the end of some awful bloody struggle, a celebration of a nice holiday, I thought we could mark this November the 5th, a day that is sadly no longer remembered, by taking some time out of our daily lives to sit down and have a little chat. There are of course those who do not want us to speak. I suspect even now, orders are being shouted into telephones, and men with guns will soon be on their way. Why? Because while the truncheon may be used in lieu of conversation, words will always retain their power. Words offer the means to meaning, and for those who will listen, the enunciation of truth. And the truth is, there is something terribly wrong with this country, isn't there? Cruelty and injustice, intolerance and oppression.

And where once you had the freedom to object, to think and speak as you saw fit, you now have censors and systems of surveillance coercing your conformity and soliciting your submission. How did this happen? Who's to blame? Well certainly there are those more responsible than others, and they will be held accountable, but again truth be told, if you're looking for the guilty, you need only look into a mirror. I know why you did it. I know you were afraid. Who wouldn't be? War, terror, disease.

There were a myriad of problems which conspired to corrupt your reason and rob you of your common sense. Fear got the best of you, and in your panic you turned to the now high chancellor, Adam Sutler. He promised you order, he promised you peace, and all he demanded in return was your silent, obedient consent. Last night I sought to end that silence. Last night I destroyed the Old Bailey, to remind this country of what it has forgotten. More than four hundred years ago a great citizen wished to embed the fifth of November forever in our memory. His hope was to remind the world that fairness, justice, and freedom are more than words, they are perspectives.

So if you've seen nothing, if the crimes of this government remain unknown to you then I would suggest you allow the fifth of November to pass unmarked. But if you see what I see, if you feel as I feel, and if you would seek as I seek, then I ask you to stand beside me one year from tonight, outside the gates of Parliament, and together we shall give them a fifth of November that shall never, ever be forgot.

—V FOR VENDETTA

The year is 2020 and the world is plagued by environmental plight. Great Britain is ruled by a totalitarian corporate state where concentration camps have been established to house political prisoners and others deemed to be enemies of the state. Executions of various undesirables are common, while other enemies of the state are made to "disappear." And, of course, the television networks are controlled by the government with the purpose of perpetuating the regime. Most of the population is hooked into an entertainment mode and are clueless.

V is a bold, charismatic freedom fighter who seeks revenge against the government officials who tortured him and disfigured his face. He urges the British people to rise up and resist the government. V tells them to meet him in one year outside the Houses of Parliament, which he promises to destroy. And as November 5 approaches, V's various resistance schemes cause chaos and the people begin waking up to the tyranny around them.

V organizes the distribution of thousands of Guy Fawkes masks, resulting in multitudes, all wearing the masks, marching on Parliament to watch the destruction of Big Ben and Parliament. Unfortunately, V does not make it to the finale. He is killed and dies in the arms of Evey, a young girl he befriended and whose eyes he opens to the reality of the world around her. Accompanied by the "1812 Overture," Parliament and Big Ben explode as thousands watch, including Evey. When asked to reveal the identity of V, Evey replies, "He was all of us."

With the film *V for Vendetta*, whose imagery borrows heavily from Nazi Germany's Third Reich and George Orwell's *1984*, we come full circle. The corporate state in *V* conducts mass surveillance on its citizens, helped along by closed-circuit televisions. Also, London is under yellow-coded curfew alerts, similar to the American government's color-coded Homeland Security Advisory System.

In speaking of the graphic novel upon which the film was based, the director James McTeighe said, "It really showed what can happen when society is ruled by government, rather than the government being run as a voice of the people. I don't think it's such a big leap to say things like that can happen when leaders stop listening to the people."[647]

Clearly, we have reached a point where our leaders have stopped listening to the American people. However, what will it take for the government to *start* listening to the people again?

We are—and have been for some time—the unwitting victims of a system so corrupt that those who stand up for the rule of law and aspire to transparency in government are in the minority. This corruption is so vast it spans all branches of government—from the power-hungry agencies under the executive branch and the corporate puppets within the legislative branch to a judiciary that is, more often than not, elitist and biased towards government entities and corporations.

We are ruled by an elite class of individuals who are completely out of touch with the travails of the average American. We are relatively expendable in the eyes of government—faceless numbers of individuals who serve one purpose, which is to keep the government machine running through our labor and our tax dollars. Those in power aren't losing any sleep over the indignities we are being made to suffer or the possible risks to our health. All they seem to care about are power and control.

Sadly, we've been made to suffer countless abuses since the 9/11 terrorist attacks. In the name of national security, we've been subjected to government agents wiretapping our phones, reading our mail, monitoring our emails, and carrying out warrantless "black bag" searches of our homes. Then we had to deal with surveillance cameras mounted on street corners and in traffic lights, weather satellites co-opted for use as spy cameras from space, and thermal sensory imaging devices that can detect heat and movement through the walls of our homes. Now we find ourselves subjected to cancer-causing full-body scanners in airports, and all the government can say is that it's "a really, really small amount relative to the security benefit you're going to get."[648]

"We the people" have not done the best job of holding our representatives accountable or standing up for our rights. But there must be a limit to our temerity. What will it take for Americans to finally say enough is enough? The First Amendment guarantees us the right to "assemble and petition the government for a redress of grievances." Nonviolent, public resistance is often the only recourse left to those who want to effect change in the cumbersome, often corrupt, bureaucratic governmental process.

The time to act is now if we are to make any meaningful move towards regaining our freedoms.

CHAPTER 28

Have We Reached the Point of No Return?

"I have begun the struggle and I can't turn back. I have reached the point of no return."[649]—MARTIN LUTHER KING JR.

Police Arresting Martin Luther King Jr. (© Bettmann/CORBIS)

The date was January 26, 1956. The white leadership had done everything possible to stem the boycott of their segregated bus system by the black citizens of Montgomery, Alabama. Inevitably, the city leaders resorted to what had always worked in the past: the use of police power.

It was in the afternoon, and the young minister of the Dexter Avenue Baptist Church was on his way home with two fellow church members. The acknowledged leader of the highly controversial boycott, he was put on notice to follow the traffic laws meticulously. There was no reason to make himself an easy target for arrest. But, as fate would have it, the police targeted the young minister, and he was arrested: "Get out King; you are under arrest for speeding thirty miles an hour in a twenty-five mile zone."

Thus begins Martin Luther King Jr.'s journey toward jail. The moment of truth had arrived for the young minister. Warned that he could be made to disappear by the authorities, fear began to grip King. As he writes:

> As we drove off, presumably to the city jail, a feeling of panic began to come over me. I had always had the impression that the jail was in the downtown section of Montgomery. Yet after riding for a while I noticed that we were going in a different direction. The more we rode the farther we were from the center of town. In a few minutes we turned into a dark and dingy street that I had never seen and headed under a desolate old bridge. By this time I was convinced that these men were carrying me to some faraway spot to dump me off. "But this couldn't be," I said to myself. "These men are officers of the law." Then I began to wonder whether they were driving me out to some waiting mob, planning to use the excuse later on that they had been overpowered. I found myself trembling within and without. Silently, I asked God to give me the strength to endure whatever came.[650]

This was at the height of segregation in the American system. It was a time when, if blacks got out of line, at a minimum they faced jail time. Only a month earlier, Rosa Parks, a seamstress, had refused to give up her seat on a Montgomery bus to a white man. This violation of the segregation law brought a swift arrest.

By this time, King was already seen as a troublemaker. Understanding that if you cut off the head, the movement dies, King began to panic as his ride with the police continued:

> By this time we were passing under the bridge. I was sure now that I was going to meet my fateful hour on the other side. But as I looked up I noticed a glaring light in the distance, and soon I saw the words "Montgomery City Jail." I was so relieved that it was some time before I realized the irony of my position: going to jail at that moment seemed like going to some safe haven![651]

As the jail doors slammed shut behind King, he felt a strong inner peace: "For the moment strange gusts of emotion swept through me like cold winds on an open prairie. For the first time in my life I had been thrown behind bars."[652]

Taking a Stand

Soon King's bail was posted and he was free to leave, but King's rendezvous with jail cells was just beginning. More importantly, the movement that began in Montgomery, Alabama, was moving beyond state borders. A nationwide movement was in process, making King even more of a target.

Several weeks later, King happened to be in Nashville, Tennessee, giving a lecture when he learned that he, with others, had been indicted by a grand jury for violating Montgomery's segregation laws. He immediately booked a flight home, stopping over to see his father in Atlanta. Martin Luther King Sr. recognized that a new scenario had developed. The threat was no longer jail time. It was death. "My father, so unafraid for himself," writes King, "had fallen into a constant state of terror for me and my family."

Earlier, King's home in Montgomery had been bombed and the police were watching his every move. After the bombing, King's mother had taken to bed under doctor's orders.

King's father brought some of Atlanta's leading citizens into his home to speak with his son about the dangers of returning to Montgomery. But King knew that often courage in the face of tyranny is all that the oppressed have at their disposal. It was time, as King said, to take a stand. As he told those assembled:

> My friends and associates are being arrested. It would be the height of cowardice for me to stay away. I would rather be in jail ten years than desert my people now. I have begun the struggle, and I can't turn back. I have reached the point of no return.[653]

Upon arrival in Montgomery, King headed for jail to discover that the others indicted with King had the day before surrendered for arrest. "A once fear-ridden people had been transformed. Those who had previously trembled before the law were now proud to be arrested for the cause of freedom."[654]

Nonviolent Resistance

Against incredible odds, the blacks of Montgomery not only won the right to be treated equally on the city's buses. Soon the movement took on amazing proportions which would compel a government that refused to hear their pleas to listen and heed their demands. But not a shot was fired by blacks of Montgomery.

Led by a man who believed in nonviolent resistance to government oppression, these brave people would soon transform the face of America—a man who believed that governments must listen to and heed our demands. If not, then it is within our power as a free people to press for change. And when government doesn't listen, then, in the words of King, we can engage in peaceful, nonviolent resistance.

CHAPTER 29

Know Your Rights or You Will Lose Them

"It astonishes me to find ... [that so many] of our countrymen ... should be contented to live under a system which leaves to their governors the power of taking from them the trial by jury in civil cases, freedom of religion, freedom of the press, freedom of commerce, the habeas corpus laws, and of yoking them with a standing army. This is a degeneracy in the principles of liberty ... which I [would not have expected for at least] four centuries."[655]—THOMAS JEFFERSON

Whether we can turn things around will depend on how many Americans are willing to learn their rights and take appropriate stands for freedom.

Militant Nonviolence

"Most citizens," writes author and journalist Nat Hentoff, "are largely uneducated about their own constitutional rights and liberties."[656]

The following true incident is a case in point for Hentoff's claim. A young attorney, preparing to address a small gathering about the need to protect freedom, especially in the schools, wrote the text of the First Amendment on a blackboard. After carefully reading the text, a woman in the audience approached the attorney, pointed to the First Amendment on the board and remarked, "My, the law is really changing. Is this new?" The woman was a retired schoolteacher.

For more than two hundred years, Americans have enjoyed the freedoms of speech, assembly, and religion, among others, without ever really studying the source of those liberties, found in the Bill of Rights.

Yet never has there been a time when knowing our rights has been more critical and safeguarding them more necessary.

Thus, it is vital that we gain a better understanding of what Thomas Jefferson described as "fetters against doing evil."[657] If not, I fear that with each passing day, what Jefferson called the "degeneracy" of "the principles of liberty" will grow worse until, half asleep, Americans will lose what our forefathers fought and died for.

Martin Luther King Jr. certainly understood the imperative to know your rights and then engage in expressive activity to further the cause of freedom. King knew very well that government is a reactive institution not a proactive one—that is, government reacts to "we the people" when we the people get active. As King wrote in an essay published shortly after he was assassinated:

> We need to put pressure on Congress to get things done. We will do this with First Amendment activity. If Congress is unresponsive, we'll have to escalate in order to keep the issue alive and before it. This action may take on disruptive dimensions, but not violent in the sense of destroying life or property: it will be militant nonviolence.[658]

The Bill of Rights

In other words, an active citizenry is all that stands between us and an authoritarian government. Education, thus, precedes action. It's time to become educated about your rights. A short summary of the first ten amendments shows how vital these freedoms are.

The First Amendment protects the freedom to assemble together and speak your mind and protest in peace without being bridled by the government. It also protects the freedom of the media, as well as the right to worship and pray without interference. In other words, Americans cannot be silenced by the government.

The Second Amendment guarantees "the right of the people to keep and bear arms." This is one of the most controversial provisions of the Bill of Rights. Indeed, there are those who claim that gun ownership in America should be restricted solely to the police and other government officials. In many countries, owning a firearm is a mere privilege, reserved for the rich and powerful. Self-protection, however, is not a privilege in America. It is an individual citizen right that the U.S. Supreme Court has recognized.

Protesters for Peace (Student movements and demonstrations (UA023.025.073), Special Collections Research Center, North Carolina State University Libraries.)

America was born during a time of martial law. British troops stationed themselves in homes and entered property without regard for the rights of the owners. That is why ***The Third Amendment*** prohibits the military from entering any citizen's home without "the consent of the owner." While Americans no longer have to fear the quartering of troops in their homes, the safeguards keeping the government—including the military—out of our homes are fast eroding. Increasingly, the threat of martial law being imposed is a clear and present danger.

There's a knock at the door. The police charge in and begin searching your home. They invade your privacy, rummaging through your belongings. You may think you're powerless to stop them, but you're not. ***The Fourth Amendment*** prohibits the government from searching your home without a warrant approved by a judge. But what about other kinds of invasions? Your telephone, mail, emails, computer, and medical records are now subject to governmental search. Even though they're all personal and private, they are increasingly at risk for unwarranted intrusion by government agents. The ominous rise of the surveillance state threatens the protections given us by this amendment.

You cannot be tried again after having been found innocent. The government cannot try you repeatedly for the same crime, hoping to get the result they want. It's one of the legal protections of ***The Fifth***

Amendment. Moreover, you cannot be forced to testify against yourself. You can "plead the Fifth." This means that if you are accused of committing a crime, it is up to the state to prove its case against you. You are innocent until proven guilty, and government authorities cannot deprive you of your life, your liberty, or your property without following strict legal codes of conduct.

The Sixth Amendment spells out the right to a "speedy and public trial." An accused person can confront the witnesses against him and demand to know the nature of the charge. The government cannot legally keep someone in jail for unspecified offenses. Moreover, unlike many other countries, Americans also have the right to be tried by a jury of ordinary citizens and to be represented by an attorney. Our fates in criminal proceedings are not decided by panels of judges or unaccountable politicians.

Property ownership is a fundamental right of free people. In a legal dispute over property, ***The Seventh Amendment*** guarantees citizens the right to a jury trial.

Like any other American citizen, those accused of being criminals have rights under the Constitution as well. In some countries, the government abuses what they see as disloyal or troublesome citizens by keeping them in jail indefinitely on trumped-up charges. If they cannot pay their bail, then they're not released. ***The Eighth Amendment*** is, thus, similar to the Sixth—it protects the rights of the accused. These are often the people most susceptible to abuse and who have the least resources to defend themselves. This amendment also forbids the use of cruel and unusual punishment.

The framers of our Constitution were so concerned about civil liberties that they wished to do everything conceivable to protect our future freedom. Some of the framers opposed a bill of rights because it might appear that these were the only rights the people possessed. ***The Ninth Amendment*** remedied that by providing that other rights not listed were nonetheless retained by the people. Our rights are inherently ours, and our government was created to protect them. The government does not, nor did it ever, have the power to grant us our rights. Popular sovereignty—the belief that the power to govern flows upward from the people rather than downward from the rulers—is clearly evident in this amendment and is a landmark of American freedom.

The framers established a federal system of government. This means that power is divided among local, state and national entities. ***The Tenth Amendment*** reminds the national government that the people and the states retain every authority that is not otherwise mentioned in the Constitution. Congress and the President have increasingly assumed more power than the Constitution grants them. However, it's up to the people and the state governments to make sure that they obey the law of the land.

"We the People"

Having stood the test of time, there is little doubt that the Bill of Rights is one of the greatest statements for freedom ever drafted and put into effect. In the end, however, it is the vigilance of "we the people" that will keep the freedoms we hold so dear alive. Therefore, know your rights, exercise them freely or you're going to lose them. If freedom is to survive in an environment where the government continues to ignore and oppress its citizens, then we will need to think and act like revolutionaries—nonviolent ones, that is.

CHAPTER 30

Compliant Lambs or Nonviolent Gadflies?

"We must see the need for nonviolent gadflies."[659]

—MARTIN LUTHER KING JR.

When it comes to the staggering loss of civil liberties, the Constitution hasn't changed. Rather, as we have seen, it is the American people who have changed.

Once a citizenry that generally fomented a rebellion and founded a country, Americans are no longer the people they once were. Americans today live in a glass dome, says author Nicholas von Hoffman, a kind of terrarium, cut off from both reality and the outside world. In his words, they are "bobbleheads in Bubbleland. They shop in bubbled malls, they live in gated communities, and they move from place to place breathing their own private air in bubble-mobiles known as SUVs."[660]

Like lambs to the slaughter, too many Americans march in lockstep with whatever the government dictates, believing that to be patriotism. And those who do get a bit rowdy in voicing their disagreement with government policies find themselves labeled "troublemakers" and made into easy targets for attack by the media, politicians, the government, and the police.

"Tension"

In the past, however, it has been the so-called troublemakers—those rowdy protesters who challenge the status quo—who have actually changed things for the better in America. When Birmingham, Alabama, became the epicenter of the civil rights struggle for African-Americans, Martin Luther King Jr. and others participated in peaceful protests such

Children's March Organized by Martin Luther King Jr. (Charles Moore / Black Star)

as mass marches and sit-ins. The police response was repression in the form of tear gas, dogs, fire hoses, and arrests, including that of King.

Yet as King acknowledged in his April 1963 "Letter from Birmingham Jail," demonstrations and objections to the status quo are sometimes necessary. Still, King was opposed to violent protests, preferring instead to encourage "tension." As he wrote: ". . . there is a type of constructive, nonviolent tension which is necessary for growth . . . we must see the need for nonviolent gadflies to create the kind of tension in society that will help men rise from the dark depths of prejudice and racism to the majestic heights of understanding and brotherhood."[661]

Civil Disobedience

King's philosophy was undergirded by civil disobedience. This means of nonviolent resistance was used to great effect by Mahatma Gandhi in his campaign for Indian independence from the British, in South Africa in the fight against apartheid, and, of course, by the civil rights movement, to name three examples. Civil disobedience was also used to great effect at the Boston Tea Party.

Protests can take the form of stopping traffic, sidewalk protests, sit-ins, and other non-verbal forms of expression. The key, however, is standing on principle without wavering. As author and agitator Henry David Thoreau wrote in his 1849 *Resistance to Civil Government, or Civil Disobedience*, inactivity by citizens can be more harmful to society than revolution:

> There are thousands who are *in opinion* opposed to slavery and to the war, who yet in effect do nothing to put an end to them; who, esteeming themselves children of Washington and Franklin, sit down with their hands in their pockets, and say that they know not what to do, and do nothing . . . They hesitate, and they regret, and sometimes they petition; but they do nothing in earnest and with effect. They will wait, well disposed, for others to remedy the evil, that they may no longer have it to regret.[662]

Thoreau goes on to note that for protest to be effective, it doesn't need to use force:

> If a thousand men were not to pay their tax bills this year, that would not be a bloody and violent measure, as it would be to pay them, and enable the State to commit violence and shed innocent blood. This is, in fact, the definition of a peaceable revolution.[663]

Moreover, civil disobedience, according to Professor Erich Fromm, is the definition of a "free" person:

> If a man can only obey and not disobey, he is a slave . . . Obedience to a person, institution or power (heteronomous obedience) is submission; it implies the abdication of my autonomy and the acceptance of a foreign will or judgment in place of my own. Obedience to my own reason or conviction (autonomous obedience) is not an act of submission but one of affirmation. My conviction and my judgment, if authentically mine, are part of me. If I follow them rather than the judgment of others, I am being myself . . .[664]

The Spirit of Resistance

Peaceable or not, the United States has a long history of revolutionary and reactionary behavior. Thomas Jefferson was one such rebel. "What country before ever existed a century and a half without a rebellion? And what country can preserve it's liberties if their rulers are not warned from time to time that their people preserve the spirit of resistance?" Jefferson wrote. "Let them take arms . . . What signify a few lives lost in a century or two? The tree of liberty must be refreshed from time to time with the blood of patriots and tyrants."[665]

The figurative message of Jefferson's words should be heeded by all. His words illustrate the importance of political action. Jefferson, like Thoreau and King, hated inaction and stasis. Each of these men believed that the status quo should be challenged when it was found lacking, and overturned when it yielded unjust results. Embracing that spirit today might lead to civil disobedience, but surely from time to time that is necessary. Without it, the civil rights movement would never have succeeded, the colonies of the United States would never have broken free from their British oppressor, and India might never have gained her independence.

Thomas Jefferson and those who followed took it as a rule of thumb that political progress stems from dissent. Under the First Amendment, people have a right to dissent. The great dissenters such as Martin Luther King Jr. were even willing to commit civil disobedience to force the government to assume its constitutional role.

But as author Howard Zinn points out all too well, "Civil disobedience is not our problem. Our problem is civil obedience."[666]

CHAPTER 31

What Kind of Revolutionary Will You Be?

"We know through painful experience that freedom is never voluntarily given up by the oppressor; it must be demanded by the oppressed."[667]—MARTIN LUTHER KING JR.

With the government's relentless assault on our pocketbooks and freedoms, the economic and fiscal picture for many Americans is bleak. The national debt is in the trillions. People are losing their homes and jobs and millions have fallen into poverty. At the same time, lucrative tax breaks exist for the corporate rich, while the average citizen is heavily taxed. The Constitution and civil liberties have been undermined at every step. And don't expect any of these developments to let up anytime soon.

Understandably, many are bewildered. But now is not the time to shrink from our responsibility as citizens. In fact, we should welcome the chance to regain control of a government out of control. And if there is to be any change, it is going to be brought about by us, "we the people," not the politicians. No president, no congressman, and no judge can do what you can.

There is no better time to act than the present. Fear, apathy, escapism, or reliance on some government official to save us will not carry the day. It is within our power as citizens to make a difference and seek corrective measures. That principle is the basis of the American governmental scheme.

Revolutionaries

We need to think like revolutionaries. Thus, there can be no room for timidity or lukewarm emotions. What we need is passion, dedication and courage. And to paraphrase Martin Luther King Jr., we have to demand change from the oppressors.

There are certain things that are common to every successful struggle. Here are a few suggestions:

1. **Get educated.** Without knowledge, very little can be accomplished. Thus, you must know your rights. Take time to read the Constitution. Study and understand history because the tales of those who seek power and those who resist it is an age-old one. Understand the vital issues of the day so that you can be cognizant of the threats to freedom.

2. **Get involved.** Become actively involved in community affairs, politics and legal battles. Think nationally, but act locally. If our freedoms are to be restored, taking action at that local level must be the starting point. Getting involved in local politics is one way to bring about change. Seek out every opportunity to voice your concerns, and demand that your government representatives account for their actions. Be relentless.

3. **Get organized.** You can overcome the governmental behemoth with enough cunning, skill, and organization. Play to your strengths and assets. Conduct strategy sessions with others to develop both the methods and ways to force change.

4. **Be creative.** Be bold and imaginative, for this is guerilla warfare—not to be fought with tanks and guns but through creative methods of dissent and nonviolent resistance. Creatively responding to circumstances will often be one of your few resources if you are to be an effective agent of change.

5. **Use the media.** Effective use of the media is essential. Attracting media coverage not only enhances and magnifies your efforts, it is a valuable education tool. It publicizes your message to a much wider audience. It is through the media—television, newspapers, internet sites, bloggers, and so on—that people find out about your growing resistance movement.

6. **Start brushfires for freedom.** Recognize that you don't have to go it alone. Engage those around you in discussions about issues of importance. Challenge them to be part of a national dialogue. One person at a city planning meeting with a protest sign is an irritant.

Andrea Hernandez and fellow protesters oppose RFID chips (Steve Hernandez)

Three individuals at the same meeting with the same sign are a movement. You will find that those in power fear and respect numbers.

7. Take action. Be prepared to mobilize at a moment's notice. It doesn't matter who you are, where you're located or what resources are at your disposal. What matters is that you recognize the problems and care enough to do something about them. Whether you're eight, twenty-eight, or eighty-eight, you have something unique to contribute. You don't have to be a hero. You just have to show up and be ready to take action.

8. Be forward-looking. Develop a vision for the future. Is what you're hoping to achieve enduring? Have you developed a plan to continue to educate others about the problems you're hoping to tackle and ensure that others will continue in your stead?

9. Develop fortitude. What is it that led to the successful protest movements of the past? Resolve and the refusal to be put off. When the time came, Martin Luther King Jr., for one, was willing to take to the streets for what he believed and even go to jail if necessary. King risked having an arrest record by committing acts of nonviolent civil disobedience. He was willing to sacrifice himself. But first, he had to develop the intestinal fortitude to give him the strength to stand and fight. If you decide that you don't have the requisite fortitude, find someone who does and back them.

10. Be selfless and sacrificial. Freedom is not free—there is always a price to be paid and a sacrifice to be made. If any movement is to be truly successful, it must be manned by individuals who seek a greater good and do not waver from their purposes.

11. Remain optimistic, and keep hope alive. Although our rights are increasingly coming under attack, we still have certain freedoms. We can still fight back. We have the right to dissent, to protest, and even to vigorously criticize or oppose the government and its laws.[668]

You Are the Change

The key to making a difference is in understanding that the first step begins with you. As Mahatma Gandhi said, "We need to be the change we wish to see in the world."[669]

Change, then, will only come from a citizenry willing to step beyond the propaganda of fear and sacrifice themselves for freedom. Of course, government agents armed to the teeth will be there to chill and/or suppress the freedom fighters. But let us stand with those courageous enough to place themselves on the front lines for freedom.

As Evey recognizes in *V for Vendetta*, the freedom fighter is "all of us." Otherwise, there is little or no hope left for us.

Acknowledgments

No one walks alone. Every step of the way, someone is there to help, and without such help from others, little would be accomplished.

Such was the assistance I received in researching and writing this book. First and foremost, I wish to thank my wife, Nisha, for her support, ideas, and editing, and Christopher Combs for creating the cover art and illustrations. Michael Khavari's research was invaluable, as was Carrick Owlett's assistance in procuring the images. Peggy Kelly, Lina Ragep, Ellie Miller, and Philip Timmerman were gracious about pitching in during the final stages of proofing. The following individuals, in addition to many others, also assisted with the mountains of research necessary for a book of this scope: Aaron Tao, Zachary Waksman, Jennifer Wilson, Melinda Ashe, Ricky Knicely, Jinyang Guo, Daniel Xu, Chelsea German, Brendan O'Connor, Austin Raynor, Allison Harnack, Ayushi Patidar, Dynne Sung, Hyun-Woo Shin, Trenton D. Boaldin, Than Cutler, and Charly Gilliam. Special thanks to Frank DeMarco and Bill Gladstone.

Finally, I would like to thank that tireless civil libertarian Nat Hentoff for the example he has established for those of us who have followed in his footsteps. Without voices like Nat's, freedom would simply be a word without content.

Notes

Part One: Is This America?

1 Bertram Gross, *Friendly Fascism: The New Face of Power in America* (South End Press, 1980), p. 3.

CHAPTER ONE

2 Abraham Lincoln, as restated from "The Perpetuation of Our Political Institutions: Address before the Young Men's Lyceum of Springfield, Illinois" (Jan. 27, 1838).

3 Associated Press, "Pregnant woman pepper sprayed at Occupy Seattle," *CBS News* (Nov. 16, 2011), http://www.cbsnews.com/8301-201_162-57325688/pregnant-woman-pepper-sprayed-at-occupy-seattle/.

4 David Edwards, "Pregnant Seattle protester miscarries after being kicked, pepper sprayed," *The Raw Story* (Nov. 22, 2011), http://www.rawstory.com/rs/2011/11/22/pregnant-seattle-protester-miscarries-after-being-kicked-pepper-sprayed/?utm_source=Raw+Story+Daily+Update&utm_campaign=bb1b72025b-11_22_1111_22_2011&utm_medium=email.

5 Malia Wollan, "Police Fire Tear Gas at Occupy Protesters in Oakland," *New York Times* (Oct. 26, 2011), http://thelede.blogs.nytimes.com/2011/10/26/police-said-to-fire-tear-gas-at-protesters-in-oakland-calif/.

6 Bertram Gross, *Friendly Fascism: The New Face of Power in America* (South End Press, 1980), p. 3.

7 *As quoted in* Bertram Gross, *Friendly Fascism: The New Face of Power in America* (South End Press, 1980), p. 6.

8 Chris Floyd, "Weather Report: The Hard Chill Begins to Bite," *Moscow Times* (Nov. 9, 2001), http://www.chris-floyd.com/index.php?option=com_content&task=view&id=433&Itemid=5.

9 Hermann Goering *as quoted in* Gustave Gilbert, *Nuremberg Diary* (Da Capo Press, 1995), p. 278.

10 Hannah Arendt, *The Origins of Totalitarianism* (Harcourt, 1968), p. 351.

11 "NYPD Stop-And-Frisks Increased 14 Percent In 2011; 87 Percent Of Those Stopped Black Or Hispanic," *Huffington Post* (Feb. 14, 2012), http://www.huffingtonpost.com/2012/02/14/nypd-stop-and-frisks-increased-2011_n_1277027.html.

12 "Councilman: NYPD's Stop And Frisk Rationalization Is 'Bullsh*t,'" *Gothamist* (Feb. 14, 2012), http://gothamist.com/2012/02/14/stop-and-frisk.php.

13 Herman Schwartz, "How the Supreme Court Came to Embrace Strip Searches for Trivial Offenses," *The Nation* (Aug. 16, 2012), http://www.thenation.com/article/169419/how-supreme-court-came-embrace-strip-searches-trivial-offenses#.

14 "Female US cop caught on tape giving two women body cavity search during routine traffic stop ... and 'using the SAME gloves on both,'" *Daily Mail* (Dec. 18, 2012), http://www.dailymail.co.uk/news/article-2250218/Angel-Ashley-Dobbs-suing-Texas-troopers-shocking-BODY-CAVITY-search-caught-tape.html#ixzz2HxDDYDoh.

15 Kevin Krause, "Texas trooper being sued in Irving body cavity search case has been suspended," *The Dallas Morning News* (Dec. 19, 2012), http://crimeblog.dallasnews.com/2012/12/irving-women-sue-state-troopers-in-federal-court-alleging-roadside-body-cavity-searches.html/.

16 Chris Sweeney, "Cops Strip Search Mom, "Forcibly" Pull Tampon Out of Her for Maybe Rolling Through Stop Sign," *Broward Palm Beach NewTimes* (Aug. 9, 2012), http://blogs.browardpalmbeach.com/pulp/2012/08/cops_strip_search_mom_pull_tam.php.

17 Gina Barton and John Diedrich, "4 Milwaukee police officers charged in strip-search case," *Milwaukee-Wisconsin Journal Sentinel* (Oct. 9, 2012), http://www.jsonline.com/news/crime/criminal-charges-against-police-in-strip-search-case-expected-today-gf5cb94-173312411.html.

18 Henry K. Lee, "Strip searches cost Oakland $4.6 million," *SF Gate* (Nov. 15, 2012), http://www.sfgate.com/crime/article/Strip-searches-cost-Oakland-4-6-million-4035103.php.

19 David Cohen, "Cops to draw blood at N. Shore checkpoint tonight," *WWL* (Dec. 13, 2012), http://www.wwl.com/Cops-to-draw-blood-at-N-Shore-checkpoint-tonight/15025595.

20 "NYPD, Feds Testing Gun-Scanning Technology, But Civil Liberties Groups Up In Arms," *CBS New York* (Jan. 17, 2012), http://newyork.cbslocal.com/2012/01/17/nypd-testing-gun-scanning-technology/.

21 Al Baker, "Police Working on Technology to Detect Concealed Guns," *New York Times* (Jan. 17, 2012), http://cityroom.blogs.nytimes.com/2012/01/17/police-working-on-technology-to-detect-concealed-guns/.

22 Michael Grabell, "Drive-by X-rays: Security screeners expanding radiation use," *Tucson Sentinel* (Feb. 1, 2012), http://www.tucsonsentinel.com/nationworld/report/020112_xrays/drive-by-x-rays-security-screeners-expanding-radiation-use/.

23 Matthew Kauffman, "Police Keeping Data From License Plate Scans; ACLU Files Privacy Protest," *Hartford Courant* (Feb. 21, 2012), http://www.courant.com/news/connecticut/hc-aclu-license-plate-scans-0222-20120221,0,5035715.story.

24 Chris North, "Police scanners allow for remote fingerprint identification," *Reporter Newspapers* (Feb. 23, 2012), http://www.reporternewspapers.net/2012/02/23/police-scanners-allow-for-remote-fingerprint-identification/.

CHAPTER TWO

25 Jon Wiener, *Come Together: John Lennon in His Time* (University of Illinois Press, 1990), p. 21.

26 Thomas Paine, *Common Sense* (1776), http://www.bartleby.com/133/3.html.

27 John Adams, *Novanglus Essays*, No. 7, http://en.wikisource.org/wiki/Novanglus_Essays/No._7.

28 Robert O'Harrow, *No Place to Hide* (Free Press, 2006), p. 4 of "Introduction."

29 Julia Scheeres, "Librarians Split on Sharing Info," *Wired* (Jan. 16, 2003), http://www.wired.com/politics/security/news/2003/01/57256.

30 "USA Patriot Improvement and Reauthorization Act of 2005."

31 Shannyn Moore, "Senate proves we should fear ourselves," *Anchorage Daily News* (Dec. 2, 2011), http://www.adn.com/2011/12/02/2201260/senate-proves-we-should-fear-ourselves.html.

32 Conor Friedersdorf, "Ceding Liberty to Terror: Senate Votes Against Due-Process Rights," *The Atlantic* (Dec. 2, 2011), http://www.theatlantic.com/politics/archive/2011/12/ceding-liberty-to-terror-senate-votes-against-due-process-rights/249388/.

33 Chris Hedges, Noam Chomsky, Daniel Ellsberg, and a few other journalists and activists sued President Obama over the provision of the NDAA allowing for the indefinite detention of American citizens. *See* Michael McAuliff, "Indefinite Detention Ban Stayed By Appeals Judge In NDAA Case," *The Huffington Post* (Sept. 18, 2012), http://www.huffingtonpost.com/2012/09/18/indefinite-detention-ban-_n_1893652.html.

34 Ashley Portero, "'Enemy Expatriation Act' Could Compound NDAA Threat to Citizen Rights," *International Business Times* (Jan. 24, 2012), http://www.ibtimes.com/articles/286940/20120124/enemy-expatriation-act-bypass-citizen-protections-ndaa.htm.

35 Tangerine Bolen, "What makes our NDAA lawsuit a struggle to save the US constitution," *The Guardian* (Aug. 10, 2012), http://www.guardian.co.uk/commentisfree/2012/aug/10/ndaa-lawsuit-struggle-us-constitution.

36 Thomas McAdam, “Sen. Rand Paul fights against martial law legislation,” *Louisville.com* (Nov. 30, 2011), http://www.louisville.com/content/sen-rand-paul-fights-against-martial-law-legislation-arena.

37 Radley Balko, “Paramilitary police don’t make us safer,” *Reason Reader* (Summer 2010), p. 6, http://reason.org/files/reasonreader-cutorbecut.pdf.

38 William Pitt’s speech in the House of Lords *according to* Henry Peter Brougham, *Historical Sketches of Statesmen Who Flourished in the Time of George III,* Vol. 1 (1839), p. 52.

39 *Barnes v. State of Indiana,* 946 N.E.2d 572 (Ind. 2011), http://www.nwitimes.com/news/state-and-regional/indiana/pdf_c82cdbb8-7ea0-5c55-bb00-2aa247134bbb.html.

40 *Kentucky v. King,* 131 S. Ct. 1849 (2011).

41 Editorial, “Standing Up to Unwarranted Police Power,” *New York Times* (May 24, 2011), http://www.nytimes.com/2011/05/25/opinion/25wed2.html.

42 *Reichle v. Howards,* 132 S. Ct. 2088 (U.S. 2012), http://www.supremecourt.gov/opinions/11pdf/11-262.pdf.

43 *Mattos v. Agarano,* 661 F.3d 433 (9th Cir. 2011).

44 *Florence v. Board of Chosen Freeholders of the County of Burlington,* 566 U.S. __ (2012), http://www.supremecourt.gov/opinions/11pdf/10-945.pdf.

45 *United States v. Jones,* 132 S. Ct. 945 (2012), http://www.supremecourt.gov/opinions/11pdf/10-1259.pdf.

46 *Citizens United v. Federal Election Commission,* 558 U.S. 310 (2010), http://www.supremecourt.gov/opinions/09pdf/08-205.pdf.

CHAPTER THREE

47 Hannah Arendt, *The Origins of Totalitarianism* (Harcourt, 1968), p. 460.

48 Naomi Wolf, “Fascist America in 10 Easy Steps,” *Guardian* (April 23, 2007), http://www.guardian.co.uk/world/2007/apr/24/usa.comment.

49 Anne Applebaum, *Gulag: A History* (Random House, 2004), http://www.siteground206.com/~anneappl/wordpress/wp-content/uploads/2008/11/gulag_ahistory_introduction.pdf.

50 “Psikhushka,” http://en.wikipedia.org/wiki/Psikhushka. Accessed on Sept. 10, 2012.

51 Anne Applebaum, *Gulag: A History* (Random House, 2004), http://www.siteground206.com/~anneappl/wordpress/wp-content/uploads/2008/11/gulag_ahistory_introduction.pdf.

52 Anne Applebaum, *Gulag: A History* (Random House, 2004), http://www.siteground206.com/~anneappl/wordpress/wp-content/uploads/2008/11/gulag_ahistory_introduction.pdf.

53 Harold Mandel, “China is locking up sane dissidents in mental hospitals,” *Examiner* (Aug. 23, 2012), http://www.examiner.com/article/china-is-locking-up-dissidents-mental-hospitals.

54 Cam Simpson and Gary Fields, “Veterans a Focus of FBI Extremist Probe,” *Wall Street Journal* (April 17, 2009), http://online.wsj.com/article/SB123992665198727459.html.

55 “Rightwing Extremism: Current Economic and Political Climate Fueling Resurgence in Radicalization and Recruitment,” U.S. Department of Homeland Security (April 7, 2009), www.fas.org/irp/eprint/rightwing.pdf.

56 Kevin Johnson, “Police get help with vets who are ticking bombs,” *USA Today* (Jan. 26, 2012), http://www.usatoday.com/news/washington/story/2012-01-24/police-training-combative-veterans/52794974/1.

57 Kevin Johnson, “Police get help with vets who are ticking bombs,” *USA Today* (Jan. 26, 2012), http://www.usatoday.com/news/washington/story/2012-01-24/police-training-combative-veterans/52794974/1.

58 Patrick Radden Keefe, “The Professional Paranoid,” *Slate* (Jan. 17, 2006), http://www.slate.com/articles/news_and_politics/politics/2006/01/the_professional_paranoid.html.

59 Jim Dwyer, “For Detained Whistle-Blower, a Hospital Bill, Not an Apology,” *New York Times* (March 15, 2012), http://www.nytimes.com/2012/03/16/nyregion/officer-adrian-schoolcraft-forcibly-hospitalized-got-no-apology-just-a-bill.html.

60 Hannah Arendt, *The Origins of Totalitarianism* (Harcourt, 1968), p. 447.

61 Hannah Arendt, *The Origins of Totalitarianism* (Harcourt, 1968), p. 449.

62 Hannah Arendt, *The Origins of Totalitarianism* (Harcourt, 1968), p. 449.

63 Hannah Arendt, *The Origins of Totalitarianism* (Harcourt, 1968), p. 451.

64 *As quoted in* Leonard Peikoff, *The Ominous Parallels: The End of Freedom in America* (Stein and Day, 1982), p. 7.

65 James Bamford, "The NSA Is Building the Country's Biggest Spy Center (Watch What You Say)," *Wired* (March 15, 2012), http://www.wired.com/threatlevel/2012/03/ff_nsadatacenter/all/.

66 Hannah Arendt, *The Origins of Totalitarianism* (Harcourt, 1968), p. 458.

Part Two: The Future Is Here

67 Donald Theall and Donald F. Theall, *The Virtual Marshall McLuhan* (McGill-Queen's Press - MQUP, 2001), p. 88.

CHAPTER FOUR

68 Roger Ebert, "Spielberg & Cruise & the movies," *Chicago Sun Times* (June 16, 2002), http://rogerebert.suntimes.com/apps/pbcs.dll/article?AID=/20020616/PEOPLE/66010302/1023.

69 Donald Theall and Donald F. Theall, *The Virtual Marshall McLuhan* (McGill-Queen's Press - MQUP, 2001), p. 88.

70 *As quoted in* "The Playboy Interview: Marshall McLuhan," *Playboy Magazine* (March 1969), http://www.nextnature.net/2009/12/the-playboy-interview-marshall-mcluhan/.

CHAPTER FIVE

71 *As quoted in* Laurence Sutin, *Divine Invasions: A Life of Philip K. Dick* (Harmony Books, 1989), pp. 188-89.

72 Bob Pool, "LAPD scoots into the future," *LA Times* (Nov. 10, 2007), http://articles.latimes.com/2007/nov/10/local/me-scooter10.

73 David Sirota, "Big Brother takes the wheel," *Salon* (Aug. 15, 2012), http://www.salon.com/2012/08/16/big_brother_takes_the_wheel/.

74 Peter Murray, "Google's Self-Driving Car Passes 300,000 Miles," *The Huffington Post* (Aug. 16, 2012), http://www.huffingtonpost.com/x-prize-foundation/googles-self-driving-car_b_1790781.html.

75 Paul Harris, "NYPD and Microsoft launch advanced citywide surveillance system," *The Guardian* (Aug. 8, 2012), http://www.guardian.co.uk/world/2012/aug/08/nypd-microsoft-surveillance-system.

76 "Google's eavesdropping technology: Going too far to sell ads?" *The Week* (March 23, 2012), http://theweek.com/article/index/226004/googles-eavesdropping-technology-going-too-far-to-sell-ads.

77 Austin Carr, "Iris Scanners Create the Most Secure City in the World. Welcome, Big Brother," *Fast Company* (Aug. 18, 2010), http://www.fastcompany.com/1683302/iris-scanners-create-most-secure-city-world-welcome-big-brother.

78 Zach Howard, "Police to begin iPhone iris scans amid privacy concerns," *Reuters* (July 20, 2011), http://www.reuters.com/article/2011/07/20/us-crime-identification-iris-idUSTRE76J4A120110720.

79 Ryan Gallagher, "Report: FBI Hopes To Launch Iris-Scan Database To Track Criminals," *Slate* (July 5, 2012), http://www.slate.com/blogs/future_tense/2012/07/05/iris_scan_database_for_the_fbi_.html.

80 John Villasenor, "Eye-Tracking Computers Will Read Your Thoughts," *Slate* (March 27, 2012), http://www.slate.com/articles/technology/future_tense/2012/03/eye_tracking_computer_programs_and_privacy_.html.

81 Sarah Freishtat, "Just a face in a crowd? Scans pick up ID, personal data," *The Washington Times* (July 26, 2012), http://www.washingtontimes.com/news/2012/jul/26/just-a-face-in-a-crowd-scans-pick-up-id-personal-d/.

82 Richard Gray, "Minority Report-style advertising billboards to target consumers," *The Telegraph* (Aug. 1, 2010), http://www.telegraph.co.uk/technology/news/7920057/Minority-Report-style-advertising-billboards-to-target-consumers.html.

83 Declan McCullagh, "Homeland Security moves forward with 'pre-crime' detection," *CNET* (Oct. 7, 2011), http://news.cnet.com/8301-31921_3-20117058-281/homeland-security-moves-forward-with-pre-crime-detection/.

84 Dan Nosowitz, "Mind-Reading Tech Reconstructs Videos From Brain Images," *Popular Science* (Sept. 22, 2011), http://www.popsci.com/science/article/2011-09/mind-reading-tech-reconstructs-videos-brain-images.

85 Peter Pachal, "IBM: Mind-Reading Machines Will Change Our Lives," *Mashable* (Dec. 21, 2011), http://mashable.com/2011/12/21/ibm-kevin-brown-mind-reading/.

86 Ian Sample, "Mind-reading program translates brain activity into words," *Guardian* (Jan. 31, 2012), http://www.guardian.co.uk/science/2012/jan/31/mind-reading-program-brain-words.

87 "Flashlight Weapon Makes Targets Throw Up," *FOX News* (Aug. 7, 2007), http://www.foxnews.com/story/0,2933,292271,00.html.

88 John Adams, "New 'Laser' Weapon Debuts in LA County Jail," *NBC Los Angeles* (Aug. 23, 2010), http://www.nbclosangeles.com/news/local/New-Laser-Weapon-Debuts-in-LA-County-Jail-101230974.html.

89 Gavin Thomas, "Sonic device deployed in London during Olympics," *BBC News* (May 21, 2012), http://www.bbc.co.uk/news/uk-england-london-18042528.

90 Allison Barrie, "June Beetles Conscripted Into Cyborg Army," *FOX News* (Jan. 5, 2012), http://www.foxnews.com/tech/2012/01/05/june-beetles-conscripted-into-cyborg-army/.

91 Rick Weiss, "Dragonfly or Insect Spy? Scientists at Work on Robobugs," *The Washington Post* (Oct. 9, 2007), http://www.washingtonpost.com/wp-dyn/content/article/2007/10/08/AR2007100801434.html.

92 Rick Weiss, "Dragonfly or Insect Spy? Scientists at Work on Robobugs," *The Washington Post* (Oct. 9, 2007), http://www.washingtonpost.com/wp-dyn/content/article/2007/10/08/AR2007100801434.html.

CHAPTER SIX

93 Neil Postman, *Amusing Ourselves to Death: Public Discourse in the Age of Show Business* (Penguin, 2006), p. xix.

94 Neil Postman, *Amusing Ourselves to Death: Public Discourse in the Age of Show Business* (Penguin, 1985), pp. 155-56.

95 Neil Postman, *Amusing Ourselves to Death: Public Discourse in the Age of Show Business* (Penguin, 1985), p. 163.

96 Neil Postman, *Amusing Ourselves to Death: Public Discourse in the Age of Show Business*, 20th Anniversary Edition (Penguin Group, [illegible]), p. 1[illegible]0.

Part Three: Welcome to the Police State

97 George Orwell, *1984* (Houghton Mifflin Harcourt, 1984).

98 Joel Miller, "The Problem with Drug Raids," *World Net Daily* (Sept. 15, 1999), http://www.wnd.com/1999/09/6289/.

CHAPTER SEVEN

99 *As quoted in* Bertram Gross, *Friendly Fascism: The New Face of Power in America* (South End Press, 1980), p. 294.

100 Milton Mayer, An excerpt from *They Thought They Were Free: The Germans, 1933–45* (University of Chicago Press, 1966), http://www.press.uchicago.edu/Misc/Chicago/511928.html.

101 Bertram Gross, *Friendly Fascism: The New Face of Power in America* (South End Press, 1980), p. 298.

CHAPTER EIGHT

102 David Shipler, "Free to Search and Seize," *New York Times* (June 22, 2011), http://www.nytimes.com/2011/06/23/opinion/23shipler.html?_r=1.

103 Speech by James Madison, *Constitutional Convention* (June 29, 1787).

104 Andrew Becker and G.W. Schulz, "Local police stockpile high-tech, combat-ready gear," *America's War Within* (Dec. 21, 2011), http://americaswarwithin.org/articles/2011/12/21/local-police-stockpile-high-tech-combat-ready-gear.

105 Andrew Becker and G.W. Schulz, "Local police stockpile high-tech, combat-ready gear," *America's War Within* (Dec. 21, 2011), http://americaswarwithin.org/articles/2011/12/21/local-police-stockpile-high-tech-combat-ready-gear.

106 Lorenzo Franceschi-Bicchierai, "Small-Town Cops Pile Up on Useless Military Gear," *Wired* (June 26, 2012), http://www.wired.com/dangerroom/2012/06/cops-military-gear/all/.

107 Paul C. Roberts, "The Empire Turns Its Guns on the Citizenry," *Prison Planet* (Jan. 24, 2007), http://www.prisonplanet.com/articles/january2007/240107_b_Empire.htm.

108 Benjamin Carlson, "Battlefield Main Street," *The Daily* (Dec. 5, 2011), http://www.thedaily.com/page/2011/12/05/120511-news-militarized-police-1-6/.

109 Benjamin Carlson, "Battlefield Main Street," *The Daily* (Dec. 5, 2011), http://www.thedaily.com/page/2011/12/05/120511-news-militarized-police-1-6/.

110 Andrew Becker and G.W. Schulz, "Local police stockpile high-tech, combat-ready gear," *America's War Within* (Dec. 21, 2011), http://americaswarwithin.org/articles/2011/12/21/local-police-stockpile-high-tech-combat-ready-gear.

111 Andrew Becker and G.W. Schulz, "Local police stockpile high-tech, combat-ready gear," *America's War Within* (Dec. 21, 2011), http://americaswarwithin.org/articles/2011/12/21/local-police-stockpile-high-tech-combat-ready-gear.

112 Andrew Becker and G.W. Schulz, "Local police stockpile high-tech, combat-ready gear," *America's War Within* (Dec. 21, 2011), http://americaswarwithin.org/articles/2011/12/21/local-police-stockpile-high-tech-combat-ready-gear.

113 Andrew Becker and G.W. Schulz, "Local police stockpile high-tech, combat-ready gear," *America's War Within* (Dec. 21, 2011), http://americaswarwithin.org/articles/2011/12/21/local-police-stockpile-high-tech-combat-ready-gear.

114 Benjamin Carlson, "Battlefield Main Street," *The Daily* (Dec. 5, 2011), http://www.thedaily.com/page/2011/12/05/120511-news-militarized-police-1-6/.

115 Benjamin Carlson, "Battlefield Main Street," *The Daily* (Dec. 5, 2011), http://www.thedaily.com/page/2011/12/05/120511-news-militarized-police-1-6/.

116 Benjamin Carlson, "Battlefield Main Street," *The Daily* (Dec. 5, 2011), http://www.thedaily.com/page/2011/12/05/120511-news-militarized-police-1-6/.

117 "Battlefield US: Pentagon arms police departments with free heavy weaponry," *RT* (Dec. 7, 2011), http://rt.com/usa/news/police-weaponry-military-pentagon-205/.

118 Benjamin Carlson, "Battlefield Main Street," *The Daily* (Dec. 5, 2011), http://www.thedaily.com/page/2011/12/05/120511-news-militarized-police-1-6/.

119 "Drones cleared for domestic use across the US," *RT* (Nov. 29, 2011), http://rt.com/usa/news/us-drones-border-patrol-489/.

120 "Drones cleared for domestic use across the US," *RT* (Nov. 29, 2011), http://rt.com/usa/news/us-drones-border-patrol-489/.

121 Glenn Greenwald, "The growing menace of domestic drones," *Salon* (Dec. 12, 2011), http://www.salon.com/2011/12/12/the_growing_menace_of_domestic_drones/singleton/.

122 Glenn Greenwald, "The growing menace of domestic drones," *Salon* (Dec. 12, 2011), http://www.salon.com/2011/12/12/the_growing_menace_of_domestic_drones/singleton/.

123 "Federal Law Enforcement Statistics," Bureau of Justice Statistics, http://www.ojp.usdoj.gov/bjs/fedle.htm.

124 The Department of Education caused public confusion in 2010 when it purchased 27 riot shotguns *as cited in* Valerie Strauss, "Education Department Buying 27 Shotguns," *The Washington Post* (March 11, 2010), http://voices.washingtonpost.com/answer-sheet/education-secretary-duncan/ed-department-buying-27-shotgu.html. The Wright raid presumably indicates the intended use of those weapons.

125 Radley Balko, "Overkill: The Rise of Paramilitary Police Raids in America," Cato Institute (July 17, 2006), http://www.cato.org/pubs/wtpapers/balko_whitepaper_2006.pdf, p. 13.

126 "What is the Inspector General's (IG) mission?" Council of the Inspectors General on Integrity and Efficiency, http://www.ignet.gov/igs/faq1.html#mission.

127 Federal Offices of Inspectors General (OIGs), http://en.wikipedia.org/wiki/Inspector_General#United_States.

128 The official press release issued by the Office of Inspector General is available here: http://www2.ed.gov/about/offices/list/oig/oigstatement.pdf.

129 Matt Welch, "Dept. of Education SWAT Raid Update: Not for a Student Loan, DoE Says," *Reason Hit and Run Blog* (June 8, 2011), http://reason.com/blog/2011/06/08/dept-of-education-swat-team-up.

130 Leigh Paynter, "DOE Raids Stockton Home as Part of Fraud Investigation," *ABC News10* (June 8, 2011), http://www.news10.net/news/article/141207/2/DOE-raids-Stockton-home-as-part-of-fraud-investigation.

131 Matt Welch, "Dept. of Education SWAT Raid Update: Not for a Student Loan, DoE Says," *Reason Hit and Run Blog* (June 8, 2011), http://reason.com/blog/2011/06/08/dept-of-education-swat-team-up.

132 Leigh Paynter, "DOE Raids Stockton Home as Part of Fraud Investigation," *ABC News10* (June 8, 2011), http://www.news10.net/news/article/141207/2/DOE-raids-Stockton-home-as-part-of-fraud-investigation.

133 Eloise Lee and Robert Johnson, "The Department of Homeland Security Is Buying 450 Million New Bullets," *Business Insider* (March 28, 2012), http://www.businessinsider.com/us-immigration-agents-are-loading-up-on-as-many-as-450-million-new-rounds-of-ammo-2012-3.

134 Paul Joseph Watson, "DHS To Purchase Another 750 Million Rounds Of Ammo," *Prison Planet* (Aug. 13, 2012), http://www.prisonplanet.com/dhs-to-purchase-another-750-million-rounds-of-ammo.html.

135 "Request for Quote for Ammunition," *Federal Business Opportunities*, https://www.fbo.gov/index?s=opportunity&mode=form&id=6c39a2a9f00a10187a1432388a3301e5&tab=core&_cview=0&fb_source=message.

136 Paul Joseph Watson, "Social Security Administration To Purchase 174 Thousand Rounds Of Hollow Point Bullets," *Infowars* (Aug. 15, 2012), http://www.infowars.com/social-security-administration-to-purchase-174-thousand-rounds-of-hollow-point-bullets/.

137 Millard K. Ives, "Training excercise startles locals," *The Daily Commercial* (Jan. 4, 2012), http://www.dailycommercial.com/News/LakeCounty/010412shield.

138 "13--Ammunition and Shooting Targets," *Federal Business Opportunities*, https://www.fbo.gov/index?s=opportunity&mode=form&tab=core&id=bfd95987a1ad9a6dfb22bca4a1915 0cb&_cview=0.

139 Paul Joseph Watson, "National Weather Service Follows DHS In Huge Ammo Purchase," *Infowars* (Aug. 14, 2012), http://www.infowars.com/national-weather-service-follows-dhs-in-huge-ammo-purchase/.

140 Jason Samenow, "National Weather Service 'ammunition' solicitation triggers confusion," *The Washington Post* (Aug. 14, 2012), http://www.washingtonpost.com/blogs/capital-weather-gang/post/national-weather-service-ammunition-solicitation-triggers-confusion/2012/08/14/3dc6b67e-e62a-11e1-936a-b801f1abab19_blog.html.

CHAPTER NINE

141 John Vining, "'A Terrible Mistake': SWAT Teams in the US," *The Epoch Journal* (June 1, 2009), http://epochjournal.org/2009/06/01/the-story-of-swat-teams-in-the-us/.

142 Peter Kraska and Victor Kappeler, "Militarizing American Police: The Rise and Normalization of Paramilitary Units," *Social Problems*, Vol. 44, No. 1 (Feb. 1997), p. 4., available on JSTOR, http://www.jstor.org/pss/3096870.

143 Peter Kraska and Victor Kappeler, "Militarizing American Police: The Rise and Normalization of Paramilitary Units," *Social Problems*, Vol. 44, No. 1 (Feb. 1997), available on JSTOR, http://www.jstor.org/pss/3096870.

144 Radley Balko, "Overkill: The Rise of Paramilitary Police Raids in America," Cato Institute (July 17, 2006), http://www.cato.org/pubs/wtpapers/balko_whitepaper_2006.pdf.

145 Radley Balko, "Overkill: The Rise of Paramilitary Police Raids in America," Cato Institute (July 17, 2006), http://www.cato.org/pubs/wtpapers/balko_whitepaper_2006.pdf.

146 Radley Balko, "Overkill: The Rise of Paramilitary Police Raids in America," Cato Institute (July 17, 2006), http://www.cato.org/pubs/wtpapers/balko_whitepaper_2006.pdf.

147 Radley Balko, "4.5 SWAT Raids Per Day," *Reason Magazine* (March 1, 2010), http://reason.com/archives/2010/03/01/45-swat-raids-per-day.

148 Radley Balko, "4.5 SWAT Raids Per Day," *Reason Magazine* (March 1, 2010), http://reason.com/archives/2010/03/01/45-swat-raids-per-day.

149 Radley Balko, "4.5 SWAT Raids Per Day," *Reason Magazine* (March 1, 2010), http://reason.com/archives/2010/03/01/45-swat-raids-per-day.

150 Peter Kraska and Victor Kappeler, "Militarizing American Police: The Rise and Normalization of Paramilitary Units," *Social Problems*, Vol. 44, No. 1 (Feb. 1997), p. 3, available on JSTOR, http://www.jstor.org/pss/3096870.

151 Diane Cecilia Webster, "Warrior Cops: The Ominous Growth of Paramilitarism in American Police Departments," Cato Institute (Aug. 26, 1999), http://www.cato.org/pubs/briefs/bp50.

152 Peter Kraska and Victor Kappeler, "Militarizing American Police: The Rise and Normalization of Paramilitary Units," *Social Problems*, Vol. 44, No. 1 (Feb. 1997), available on JSTOR, http://www.jstor.org/pss/3096870.

153 Diane Cecilia Webster, "Warrior Cops: The Ominous Growth of Paramilitarism in American Police Departments," Cato Institute (Aug. 26, 1999), http://www.cato.org/pubs/briefs/bp50.pdf.

154 Radley Balko, "Overkill: The Rise of Paramilitary Police Raids in America," Cato Institute (July 17, 2006), http://www.cato.org/pubs/wtpapers/balko_whitepaper_2006.pdf.

155 Radley Balko, "More Militarized than the Military," *Reason Hit and Run Blog* (May 14, 2010), http://reason.com/blog/2010/05/14/more-militarized-than-the-mili.

156 Radley Balko, "Overkill: The Rise of Paramilitary Police Raids in America," Cato Institute (July 17, 2006), http://www.cato.org/pubs/wtpapers/balko_whitepaper_2006.pdf.

157 Meghann Cuniff, "State Patrol Officer Shoots Pregnant Woman During Spokane Drug Raid," *The News Tribune* (Sept. 25, 2010), http://www.thenewstribune.com/2010/09/25/1356027/state-patrol-officer-shoots-pregnant.html.

158 Radley Balko, "Death by SWAT," *Reason Magazine* (Jan. 2009), http://reason.com/archives/2008/12/05/death-by-swat.

159 The Cato Institute provides a useful map, prepared by Radley Balko, of botched raids nationwide at http://www.cato.org/raidmap/.

160 Radley Balko, "Another Isolated Incident," *Reason Hit and Run Blog* (June 23, 2009), http://reason.com/blog/2009/06/23/another-isolated-incident.

161 Radley Balko, "Another Isolated Incident," *Reason Hit and Run Blog* (Dec. 11, 2008), http://reason.com/blog/2008/12/11/another-isolated-incident.

162 Radley Balko, "Another Isolated Incident," *Reason Hit and Run Blog* (Jan. 30, 2009), http://reason.com/blog/2009/01/30/another-isolated-incident.

163 Radley Balko, "Overkill: The Rise of Paramilitary Police Raids in America," Cato Institute (July 17, 2006), http://www.cato.org/pubs/wtpapers/balko_whitepaper_2006.pdf.

164 Tom Finnegan, "Wrong-house Bust Brings Suit," *Honolulu Star-Bulletin* (Jan. 12, 2006), http://archives.starbulletin.com/2006/01/12/news/story08.html.

165 Radley Balko, "Overkill: The Rise of Paramilitary Police Raids in America," Cato Institute (July 17, 2006), http://www.cato.org/pubs/wtpapers/balko_whitepaper_2006.pdf.

166 Phuong Cat Le and Hector Castro, "Police are too quick to grab for Taser's power, say critics," *Seattle Post-Intelligencer* (Nov. 30, 2004), http://seattlepi.nwsource.com/local/201700_taser30.html.

167 John Vining, "'A Terrible Mistake': SWAT Teams in the US," *The Epoch Journal* (June 1, 2009), http://epochjournal.org/2009/06/01/the-story-of-swat-teams-in-the-us/.

168 Radley Balko, "Drug War Police Tactics Endanger Innocent Citizens," *FOX News* (July 21, 2006), http://www.cato.org/pub_display.php?pub_id=6552/.

169 Radley Balko, "Overkill: The Rise of Paramilitary Police Raids in America," Cato Institute (July 17, 2006), http://www.cato.org/pubs/wtpapers/balko_whitepaper_2006.pdf.

170 Radley Balko, "Your Friendly Paramilitary Police Raid Post," *Reason Hit and Run Blog* (Jan. 12, 2009), http://reason.com/blog/2009/01/12/your-friendly-paramilitary-pol.

171 Ted Conover, "A Snitch's Dilemma," *New York Times* (June 29, 2012), http://www.nytimes.com/2012/07/01/magazine/alex-white-professional-snitch.html?pagewanted=all.

172 Randall Chase, "Del. city settles in shooting of former Marine," *Marine Corps Times* (Dec. 10, 2010), http://www.marinecorpstimes.com/news/2010/12/ap-marine-city-family-settle-in-shooting-death-121010/.

173 Shaila K. Dewan, "City to Pay $1.6 Million in Fatal, Mistaken Raid," *New York Times* (Oct. 29, 2003), http://www.nytimes.com/2003/10/29/nyregion/city-to-pay-1.6-million-in-fatal-mistaken-raid.html.

174 Robert Bauman, "Exclusive Justice," *Reason* (May 1995), http://reason.com/archives/1995/05/01/exclusive-justice.

175 Joel Miller, "The Problem with Drug Raids," *World Net Daily* (Sept. 15, 1999), http://www.wnd.com/1999/09/6289/.

176 Caroline Black, "Police Raid that Killed Child Was 'Flawed,' Says Lawyer; Filming for TV Got Officers 'Excited,'" *CBS News* (May 17, 2010), http://www.cbsnews.com/8301-504083_162-20005157-504083.html.

177 Radley Balko, "Overkill: The Rise of Paramilitary Police Raids in America," Cato Institute (July 17, 2006), http://www.cato.org/pubs/wtpapers/balko_whitepaper_2006.pdf.

178 Radley Balko, "Overkill: The Rise of Paramilitary Police Raids in America," Cato Institute (July 17, 2006), http://www.cato.org/pubs/wtpapers/balko_whitepaper_2006.pdf.

179 Radley Balko, "Overkill: The Rise of Paramilitary Police Raids in America," Cato Institute (July 17, 2006), http://www.cato.org/pubs/wtpapers/balko_whitepaper_2006.pdf.

180 Radley Balko, "Jose Guerena Killed: Cops Shoot Former Marine in Botched Pot Raid," *The Huffington Post* (May 25, 2011), http://www.huffingtonpost.com/2011/05/25/jose-guerena-arizona-_n_867020.html.

181 Radley Balko, "Jose Guerena Killed: Cops Shoot Former Marine in Botched Pot Raid," *The Huffington Post* (May 25, 2011), http://www.huffingtonpost.com/2011/05/25/jose-guerena-arizona-_n_867020.html.

182 Ellen Tumposky, "Arizona SWAT Team Defends Shooting Iraq Vet 60 Times," *ABC News* (May 20, 2011), http://abcnews.go.com/US/tucson-swat-team-defends-shooting-iraq-marine-veteran/story?id=13640112.

183 Barbara Grijalva, "Double murder takes parents of two young Tucson girls," *Tucson News Now* (April 5, 2010), http://www.tucsonnewsnow.com/story/12225088/double-murder-takes-parents-of-two-young-tucson-girls?redirected=true.

184 Ellen Tumposky, "Arizona SWAT Team Defends Shooting Iraq Vet 60 Times," *ABC News* (May 20, 2011), http://abcnews.go.com/US/tucson-swat-team-defends-shooting-iraq-marine-veteran/story?id=13640112.

185 Fernanda Echavarri, "SWAT Team Fired 71 Shots in Raid," *Arizona Daily Star* (May 11, 2011) ,http://azstarnet.com/news/local/crime/article_d7d979d4-f4fb-5603-af76-0bef206f8301.html.

186 http://pimasheriff.org/files/1013/0463/5381/OIS050511.pdf

187 Radley Balko, "Jose Guerena Killed: Cops Shoot Former Marine in Botched Pot Raid," *The Huffington Post* (May 25, 2011), http://www.huffingtonpost.com/2011/05/25/jose-guerena-arizona-_n_867020.html.

188 Radley Balko, "Jose Guerena Killed: Cops Shoot Former Marine in Botched Pot Raid," *The Huffington Post* (May 25, 2011), http://www.huffingtonpost.com/2011/05/25/jose-guerena-arizona-_n_867020.html.

189 Peter Kraska and Victor Kappeler, "Militarizing American Police: The Rise and Normalization of Paramilitary Units," *Social Problems*, Vol. 44, No. 1 (Feb. 1997), p. 7, available on JSTOR at http://www.jstor.org/pss/3096870.

190 "Martin and Leona Goldberg," *Government Abuse Information* (March 31, 2004), http://governmentabuse.info/reports/view/1825.

191 Jerry Markon, "Violent crime in U.S. on the decline," *The Washington Post* (May 25, 2010), http://www.washingtonpost.com/wp-dyn/content/article/2010/05/24/AR2010052402210.html.

192 Ronald Bailey, "How Scared of Terrorism Should You Be?" *Reason* (Sept. 6, 2011), http://reason.com/archives/2011/09/06/how-scared-of-terrorism-should.

193 Radley Balko, "A Decade After 9/11, Police Departments Are Increasingly Militarized," *The Huffington Post* (Nov. 12, 2011), http://www.huffingtonpost.com/2011/09/12/police-militarization-9-11-september-11_n_955508.html.

194 Stephen Gutwillig, "America needs strategy to exit its longest war," *Daily News* (June 16, 2011), http://www.dailynews.com/opinions/ci_18294627.

195 Radley Balko, "The Drug War Goes to the Dogs," *Reason* (April 5, 2006), http://www.cato.org/pub_display.php?pub_id=6339%3Cbr%20/%3E%3Cbr%20/%3ESee.

196 Uniform Crime Reports, Federal Bureau of Investigation and http://www.drugsense.org/cms/wodclock.

197 Uniform Crime Reports, Federal Bureau of Investigation and http://www.drugsense.org/cms/wodclock.

198 Federal Bureau of Investigation. "Crime in the United States," Federal Bureau of Investigation (1991), http://en.wikipedia.org/wiki/War_on_Drugs#cite_ref-50.

199 Radley Balko, "The Drug War Goes to the Dogs," *Reason* (April 5, 2006), http://www.cato.org/pub_display.php?pub_id=6339%3Cbr%20/%3E%3Cbr%20/%3ESee.

200 John Vining, "'A Terrible Mistake': SWAT Teams in the US," *The Epoch Journal* (June 1, 2009), http://epochjournal.org/2009/06/01/the-story-of-swat-teams-in-the-us/.

201 Paul Armentano, "Alcohol Lobby Now Openly Spending Against CA's Legal Pot Initiative in Alliance with Police Industrial Complex," *Alternet* (Sept. 17, 2010), http://www.alternet.org/story/148213/alcohol_lobby_now_openly_spending_against_ca's_legal_pot_initiative_in_alliance_with_police_industrial_complex.

202 Eric Blumenson and Eva Nilsen, "Policing for Profit: The Drug War's Hidden Economic Agenda," *University of Chicago Law Review* (65 U. Chi. L. Rev. 35 (1998)), http://lawreview.uchicago.edu/issues/archive/v65/winter/nilsen.html. Quote taken from abstract as cited on http://www.fear.org/chicago.html.

CHAPTER TEN

203 Marcus Baram, "Fear Pays: Chertoff, Ex-Security Officials Slammed for Cashing in on Government Experience," *Huffington Post* (Nov. 23, 2010), http://www.huffingtonpost.com/2010/11/23/fear_pays_chertoff_n_787711.html.

204 Jennifer Abel, "The Fightback Against TSA Tyranny Begins," *Guardian* (March 10, 2011), http://www.guardian.co.uk/commentisfree/cifamerica/2011/mar/10/transport-usdomesticpolicy.

205 CNN Wire Staff, "TSA stands by officers after pat-down of elderly woman in Florida," *CNN* (June 28, 2011), http://www.cnn.com/2011/US/06/26/florida.tsa.incident/.

206 Laura Riparbelli, "TSA Screenings Outrage Some Airline Passengers," *ABC World News* (July 16, 2011), http://abcnews.go.com/US/airport-security-measures-prompt-outrage-elderly-children/story?id=14081084#.

207 Associated Press, "Transportation Security Administration defends pat-down of Isabella Brademeyer, 4, in Kansas," *CBS News* (April 26, 2012), http://www.cbsnews.com/8301-201_162-57421681/transportation-security-administration-defends-pat-down-of-isabella-brademeyer-4-in-kansas/.

208 Tara Servatius, "TSA Now Storming Public Places 8,000 Times a Year," *American Thinker* (June 20, 2011), http://www.americanthinker.com/2011/06/tsa_now_storming_public_places_8000_times_a_tear.html.

209 "Screening of Passengers at Savannah Amtrak Station," *TSA Blog* (Feb. 26, 2011), http://blog.tsa.gov/2011/02/screening-of-passengers-at-savannah.html.

210 Tara Servatius, "TSA Now Storming Public Places 8,000 Times a Year," *American Thinker* (June 20, 2011), http://www.americanthinker.com/2011/06/tsa_now_storming_public_places_8000_times_a_tear.html.

211 "TSA Security Checkpoints Coming to a 'Soft" Spot Near You," taken from CBS News, accessed at Youtube, http://www.youtube.com/watch?v=p2p6f4Asnm0&feature=player_detailpage.

212 "TSA Security Checkpoints Coming to a 'Soft' Spot Near You," *CBS News* (May 4, 2011), http://theintelhub.com/2011/05/04/tsa-security-checkpoints-coming-to-a-soft-spot-near-you/.

213 Jim Harper, "'VIPR Stands for 'Visible Intermodal Prevention and Response'..." *Cato@Liberty* (Oct. 27, 2009), http://www.cato at liberty.org/vipr-stands-for-visible-intermodal-prevention-and-response/.

214 "DHS, TSA, and Tampa Bay Police Set Up Nazi Style Checkpoints at Bus Stations!" *ABC Action News* (Nov. 29, 2010), http://theintelhub.com/2010/11/29/police-state-2010-dhs-tsa-and-tampa-bay-police-set-up-nazi-style-checkpoints-at-bus-stations/.

215 Jeffrey Leib, "TSA Tests Capability of Nuclear-Detection Devices at DIA," *The Denver Post* (Dec. 18, 2009), http://www.denverpost.com/ci_14022529.

216 Sara Goo, "Marshals to Patrol Land, Sea Transport," *The Washington Post* (Dec. 14, 2005), http://www.washingtonpost.com/wp-dyn/content/article/2005/12/13/AR2005121301709.html.

217 "Building Security Force Multipliers," Transportation Security Administration, http://www.tsa.gov/what_we_do/tsnm/mass_transit/force_multipliers.shtm.

218 Cynthia Hodges, "The Surreal World of U.S. Homeland Security," *Examiner* (June 21, 2011), http://www.examiner.com/homeland-security-in-chicago/the-surreal-world-of-u-s-homeland-security.

219 Tara Servatius, "TSA Now Storming Public Places 8,000 Times a Year," *American Thinker* (June 20, 2011), http://www.americanthinker.com/2011/06/tsa_now_storming_public_places_8000_times_a_tear.html.

220 Alex Newman, "TSA Searches Expand as Opposition Mounts," *New American* (June 22, 2011), http://www.thenewamerican.com/usnews/constitution/7957-tsa-searches-expand-as-opposition-mounts.

221 John Pistole, "Testimony Before U.S. Senate Committee on Commerce, Science and Transportation," *TSA* (June 14, 2011), http://www.tsa.gov/assets/pdf/061411_testimony_905338_tsa_pistole_rail_transit_security.pdf.

222 Fran Golden, "Why Did TSA Pat Down Kids, Adults Getting Off Train?" *AOL Travel* (Feb. 28, 2011), http://news.travel.aol.com/2011/02/28/why-did-tsa-pat-down-kids-adults-getting-off-train/.

223 Don Phillips, "Trains Exclusive: Amtrak Police Chief Bars Transportation Security Administration from Some Security Operations," *Trains* (March 3, 2011), http://cs.trains.com/TRCCS/forums/p/188504/2059127.aspx.

224 Don Phillips, "Trains Exclusive: Amtrak Police Chief Bars Transportation Security Administration from Some Security Operations," *Trains* (March 3, 2011), http://cs.trains.com/TRCCS/forums/p/188504/2059127.aspx.

225 Fran Golden, "Why Did TSA Pat Down Kids, Adults Getting Off Train?" *AOL Travel* (Feb. 28, 2011), http://news.travel.aol.com/2011/02/28/why-did-tsa-pat-down-kids-adults-getting-off-train/.

226 Fran Golden, "Why Did TSA Pat Down Kids, Adults Getting Off Train?" *AOL Travel* (Feb. 28, 2011), http://news.travel.aol.com/2011/02/28/why-did-tsa-pat-down-kids-adults-getting-off-train/.

227 Don Phillips, "Trains Exclusive: Amtrak Police Chief Bars Transportation Security Administration from Some Security Operations," *Trains* (March 3, 2011), http://cs.trains.com/TRCCS/forums/p/188504/2059127.aspx.

228 Heather Mills, "TSA to Oversee Searches at Santa Fe Prom," *KOB* (May 20, 2011), http://www.kob.com/article/stories/S2122102.shtml.

229 "Authorities Conduct Random Inspections at Port of Brownsville," *KRGV* (June 7, 2011), http://rgvreview.com/?p=7783.

230 Cynthia Hodges, "The Surreal World of U.S. Homeland Security," *Examiner* (June 21, 2011), http://www.examiner.com/homeland-security-in-chicago/the-surreal-world-of-u-s-homeland-security.

231 Cynthia Hodges, "The Surreal World of U.S. Homeland Security," *Examiner* (June 21, 2011), http://www.examiner.com/homeland-security-in-chicago/the-surreal-world-of-u-s-homeland-security.

232 Tara Servatius, "TSA Now Storming Public Places 8,000 Times a Year," *American Thinker* (June 20, 2011), http://www.americanthinker.com/2011/06/tsa_now_storming_public_places_8000_times_a_tear.html.

233 Tara Servatius, "TSA Now Storming Public Places 8,000 Times a Year," *American Thinker* (June 20, 2011), http://www.americanthinker.com/2011/06/tsa_now_storming_public_places_8000_times_a_tear.html.

234 Kathy Lynn Gray, "Law Agencies Collaborate in Anti-terrorism Training," *Columbus Dispatch* (June 15, 2011), http://www.dispatch.com/live/content/local_news/stories/2011/06/15/law-agencies-collaborate-in-anti-terrorism-training.html.

235 "TSA Conducting Security Exercise," *The Marietta Times* (June 15, 2011), http://www.mariettatimes.com/page/content.detail/id/536701/TSA-conducting-security-exercise-.html?nav=5002.

236 Kathy Lynn Gray, "Law Agencies Collaborate in Anti-terrorism Training," *The Columbus Dispatch* (June 15, 2011), http://www.dispatch.com/live/content/local_news/stories/2011/06/15/law-agencies-collaborate-in-anti-terrorism-training.html.

237 Tara Servatius, "TSA Now Storming Public Places 8,000 Times a Year," *American Thinker* (June 20, 2011), http://www.americanthinker.com/2011/06/tsa_now_storming_public_places_8000_times_a_tear.html.

238 http://www.youtube.com/watch?v=JdeTvsDY1ik&feature=player_embedded#!

239 Josiah Ryan, "DHS-affiliated SWAT team stages unannounced military-style raid on public university's campus," *Campus Reform* (Sept. 13, 2012), http://www.campusreform.org/blog/?ID=4359.

240 Jim Harper, "'VIPR Stands for 'Visible Intermodal Prevention and Response'...'" *Cato@ Liberty* (Oct. 27, 2009), http://www.cato-at-liberty.org/vipr-stands-for-visible-intermodal-prevention-and-response/.

241 James Bovard, "Dominate. Intimidate. Control." *Reason* (Feb. 2004), http://reason.com/archives/2004/02/01/dominate-intimidate-control/3.

242 "DHS, TSA, and Tampa Bay Police Set Up Nazi Style Checkpoints at Bus Stations!" *ABC Action News* (Nov. 29, 2010), http://theintelhub.com/2010/11/29/police-state-2010-dhs-tsa-and-tampa-bay-police-set-up-nazi-style-checkpoints-at-bus-stations/.

243 "DHS, TSA, and Tampa Bay Police Set Up Nazi Style Checkpoints at Bus Stations!" *ABC Action News* (Nov. 29, 2010), http://theintelhub.com/2010/11/29/police-state-2010-dhs-tsa-and-tampa-bay-police-set-up-nazi-style-checkpoints-at-bus-stations/.

244 Mike Ahlers and Jeanne Meserve, "TSA Security Looks at People Who Complain About... TSA Security," *CNN* (April 15, 2011), http://www.cnn.com/2011/TRAVEL/04/15/tsa.screeners.complain/index.html?hpt=C1.

245 James Bovard, "Dominate. Intimidate. Control," *Reason Magazine* (Feb. 2004), http://reason.com/archives/2004/02/01/dominate-intimidate-control.

246 "Military Training Exercises to Take Place In and Around Boston," *City of Boston* (July 25, 2011), http://www.cityofboston.gov/news/Default.aspx?id=5212.

247 Lidia Dinkova, "Military helicopter exercise startles downtown Brickell residents," *Sun Sentinel* (April 20, 2011), http://articles.sun-sentinel.com/2011-04-20/news/mh-miami-brickell-helicopter-scare-20110420-4_1_helicopters-choppers-drill.

248 Max Brantley, "Public notice possible, but not done on LR night exercise," *Arkansas Times* (Nov. 21, 2011), http://www.arktimes.com/ArkansasBlog/archives/2011/11/21/public-notice-was-promised-on-military-training-in-lr.

249 Dan Bacher, "LA Police Department Conducts Joint Exercises with the Military," *Truthout* (Jan. 28, 2012), http://www.truth-out.org/la-police-department-conducts-joint-exercises-military/1327767532.

CHAPTER ELEVEN

250 "Bloomberg: 'I have my own army,'" *RT* (Nov. 30, 2011), http://rt.com/usa/news/bloomberg-nypd-army-york-599/.

251 "Fighting terrorism in New York City," *CBS 60 Minutes* (Sept. 25, 2011), http://www.cbsnews.com/2100-18560_162-20111059.html?pageNum=2&tag=contentMain;contentBody.

252 Reid Pillifant, "The Gentleman Commissioner," *Capital New York* (Sept. 7, 2011), http://www.capitalnewyork.com/article/culture/2011/09/3271979/gentleman-commissioner-why-nypd-controversies-never-seem-touch-ray-k.

253 Adam Goldman and Matt Apuzzo, "Post-9/11, NYPD targets ethnic communities, partners with CIA," *MSNBC* (Aug. 24, 2011), http://www.msnbc.msn.com/id/44255142/ns/us_news-security/t/post--nypd-targets-ethnic-communities-partners-cia/#.T1TeP4eivkp.

254 Jen Doll, "Ray Kelly: the NYPD Could Take Down an Aircraft if Necessary," *Village Voice* (Sept. 26, 2011), http://blogs.villagevoice.com/runninscared/2011/09/nypd_commission.php.

255 Jen Doll, "Ray Kelly: the NYPD Could Take Down an Aircraft if Necessary," *Village Voice* (Sept. 26, 2011), http://blogs.villagevoice.com/runninscared/2011/09/nypd_commission.php.

256 Jen Doll, "Ray Kelly: the NYPD Could Take Down an Aircraft if Necessary," *Village Voice* (Sept. 26, 2011), http://blogs.villagevoice.com/runninscared/2011/09/nypd_commission.php.

257 "Fighting terrorism in New York City," *CBS 60 Minutes* (Sept. 25, 2011), http://www.cbsnews.com/2100-18560_162-20111059.html?pageNum=2&tag=contentMain;contentBody.

258 "NYPD, Feds Testing Gun-Scanning Technology, But Civil Liberties Groups Up In Arms," *CBS New York* (Jan. 17, 2012), http://newyork.cbslocal.com/2012/01/17/nypd-testing-gun-scanning-technology/.

259 Paul Harris, "NYPD and Microsoft Launch Surveillance System," *Reader Supported News* (Aug. 9, 2012), http://readersupportednews.org/news-section2/345-justice/12850-focus-nypd-and-microsoft-launch-surveillance-system.

260 "NYPD Unveils Crime- And Terror-Fighting 'Domain Awareness System,'" *CBS New York* (Aug. 8, 2012), http://newyork.cbslocal.com/2012/08/08/nypd-unveils-crime-and-terror-fighting-domain-awareness-system/.

261 "Fighting terrorism in New York City," *CBS 60 Minutes* (Sept. 25, 2011), http://www.cbsnews.com/2100-18560_162-20111059.html?pageNum=2&tag=contentMain;contentBody.

262 Michael Endler, "NYPD, Microsoft Push Big Data Policing Into Spotlight," *Information Week* (Aug. 20, 2012), http://www.informationweek.com/security/privacy/nypd-microsoft-push-big-data-policing-in/240005838.

263 Paul Harris, "NYPD and Microsoft Launch Surveillance System," *Reader Supported News* (Aug. 9, 2012), http://readersupportednews.org/news-section2/345-justice/12850-focus-nypd-and-microsoft-launch-surveillance-system.

264 "Stop-and-Frisk Campaign: About the Issue," NYCLU, http://www.nyclu.org/issues/racial-justice/stop-and-frisk-practices. Accessed on October 5, 2012.

265 "Stop-and-Frisk Campaign: About the Issue," NYCLU, http://www.nyclu.org/issues/racial-justice/stop-and-frisk-practices. Accessed on October 17, 2012.

266 Associated Press, "Justice Dept. to review NYPD over Muslim spying," *CBS News* (Feb. 28, 2012), http://www.cbsnews.com/8301-201_162-57387258/justice-dept-to-review-nypd-over-muslim-spying/.

267 Jill Colvin, "NYPD Spying on Muslim Communities with Help of CIA, Report Says," *DNA Info* (Aug. 24, 2011), http://www.dnainfo.com/20110824/manhattan/nypd-spying-on-muslim-communities-with-help-of-cia-report-says#ixzz1a3JDoBIO.

268 Adam Goldman and Matt Apuzzo, "Post-9/11, NYPD targets ethnic communities, partners with CIA," *MSNBC* (Aug. 24, 2011), http://www.msnbc.msn.com/id/44255142/ns/us_news-security/t/post--nypd-targets-ethnic-communities-partners-cia/#.T1TeP4eivkp.

269 Geoffrey Gray, "Boss Kelly," *New York* (May 16, 2010), http://nymag.com/news/crimelaw/66025/index5.html.

270 Editorial, "Police and the Press," *New York Times* (Nov. 25, 2011), http://www.nytimes.com/2011/11/26/opinion/police-and-the-press.html.

271 Jeff Stein, "NYPD intelligence detectives go their own way," *The Washington Post* (Nov. 10, 2010), http://voices.washingtonpost.com/spy-talk/2010/11/nypds_foreign_cops_play_outsid.html.

Part Four: The Electronic Concentration Camp

272 Marshall McLuhan, *Understanding Media: the Extensions of Man* (Mentor, 1964), p. 56.

CHAPTER TWELVE

273 Marshall McLuhan, *Understanding Media: the Extensions of Man* (Mentor, 1964), p. 56.

274 Steve Swires, "John Carpenter and the Invasion of the Yuppie Snatchers," *Starlog*, pp. 37–40; 43, http://en.wikipedia.org/wiki/They_live#cite_note-Swires.2C_Steve-0.

CHAPTER THIRTEEN

275 Anthony Summers, *Official and Confidential: The Secret Life of J. Edgar Hoover* (Open Road Media, 2012), Section 5, Chapter 15.

276 Dana Priest and William M. Arkin, "Monitoring America," *The Washington Post* (Dec. 20, 2010), http://projects.washingtonpost.com/top-secret-america/articles/monitoring-america/1/.

277 "Obama's 2012 budget: agency by agency," *Federal Times* (Feb. 15, 2011), http://www.federaltimes.com/article/20110215/AGENCY01/102150302/.

278 Ronald Kessler, *The Bureau: The Secret History of the FBI* (Macmillan, 2003), p. 157.

279 James Bovard, *Terrorism and Tyranny: Trampling Freedom, Justice, and Peace to Rid the World of Evil* (Palgrave Macmillan, 2004), p. 150.

280 Adam Fairclough, *Martin Luther King Jr.* (University of Georgia Press, 1995), p. 96.

281 Allan M. Jallon, "A break-in to end all break-ins," *Los Angeles Times* (March 8, 2006), http://articles.latimes.com/2006/mar/08/opinion/oe-jalon8.

282 Transcript, "Gimme Some Truth: The FBI Files of John Lennon," *Democracy Now* (May 25, 2000), http://www.democracynow.org/2000/5/25/gimme_some_truth_the_fbi_files.

283 "Patterns of Misconduct: FBI Intelligence Violations from 2001 – 2008," Electronic Freedom Foundation (Feb. 23, 2011), https://www.eff.org/wp/patterns-misconduct-fbi-intelligence-violations.

284 Barton Gellman, "The FBI's Secret Scrutiny," *The Washington Post* (Nov. 6, 2005), http://www.washingtonpost.com/wp-dyn/content/article/2005/11/05/AR2005110501366.html.

285 Dan Eggen, "FBI Papers Indicate Intelligence Violations," *The Washington Post* (Oct. 24, 2005), http://www.washingtonpost.com/wp-dyn/content/article/2005/10/23/AR2005102301352.html.

286 Colin Moynihan and Scott Shane, "For Anarchist, Details of Life as F.B.I. Target," *New York Times* (May 28, 2011), http://www.nytimes.com/2011/05/29/us/29surveillance.html?_r=1&pagewanted=all.

287 Peter Wallsten, "Activists Cry Foul over FBI Probe," *Washington Post* (June 13, 2011), http://www.washingtonpost.com/politics/activists-cry-foul-over-fbi-probe/2011/06/09/AGPRskTH_story.html.

288 Andy Grimm and Cynthia Dizikes, "FBI raids anti-war activists' homes," *Chicago Tribune* (Sept. 24, 2010), http://articles.chicagotribune.com/2010-09-24/news/ct-met-fbi-terrorism-investigation-20100924_1_fbi-agents-anti-war-activists-federal-agents.

289 Colin Moynihan and Scott Shane, "For Anarchist, Details of Life as F.B.I. Target," *New York Times* (May 28, 2011), http://www.nytimes.com/2011/05/29/us/29surveillance.html?_r=1&pagewanted=all.

290 Colin Moynihan and Scott Shane, "For Anarchist, Details of Life as F.B.I. Target," *New York Times* (May 28, 2011), http://www.nytimes.com/2011/05/29/us/29surveillance.html?_r=1&pagewanted=all.

291 Editorial, "A Reminder for the F.B.I.," *New York Times* (Sept. 26, 2010), http://www.nytimes.com/2010/09/27/opinion/27mon2.html?scp=1&sq=a%20reminder%20for%20the%20f.b.i.&st=cse.

292 The Thomas Merton Center, "Projects" Page, http://thomasmertoncenter.org/projects/.

293 Editorial, "A Reminder for the F.B.I.," *New York Times* (Sept. 26, 2010), http://www.nytimes.com/2010/09/27/opinion/27mon2.html?scp=1&sq=a%20reminder%20for%20the%20f.b.i.&st=cse.

294 Office of Inspector General, "A Review of the FBI's Investigations of Certain Domestic Advocacy Groups," (Sept. 20, 2010) p. 42, http://documents.nytimes.com/justice-department-inspector-general-report.

295 Charlie Savage, "Loosening of F.B.I. Rules Stirs Privacy Concerns," *New York Times* (Oct. 28, 2009), http://www.nytimes.com/2009/10/29/us/29manual.html.

296 Charlie Savage, "Loosening of F.B.I. Rules Stirs Privacy Concerns," *New York Time* (Oct. 28, 2009), http://www.nytimes.com/2009/10/29/us/29manual.html.

297 Charlie Savage, "F.B.I. Casts Wide Net Under Relaxed Rules for Terror Inquiries, Data Show," *New York Times* (March 26, 2011), http://www.nytimes.com/2011/03/27/us/27fbi.html?ref=surveillanceofcitizensbygovernment.

298 Editorial, "Backward at the F.B.I.," *New York Times* (June 18, 2011), http://www.nytimes.com/2011/06/19/opinion/19sun1.html?_r=1.

299 Editorial, "Backward at the F.B.I.," *New York Times* (June 18, 2011), http://www.nytimes.com/2011/06/19/opinion/19sun1.html?_r=1.

300 "I call it the law of the instrument, and it may be formulated as follows: Give a small boy a hammer, and he will find that everything he encounters needs pounding."— Abraham Kaplan, *The Conduct of Inquiry: Methodology for Behavioral Science* (1964).

CHAPTER FOURTEEN

301 Alex Kozinski, dissent in *United States v. Juan Pineda-Moreno*, 617 F.3d 1120 (9th Cir. 2010), http://www.ca9.uscourts.gov/datastore/opinions/2010/08/12/08-30385.pdf.

302 "GPS Program Funding," http://www.gps.gov/policy/funding/. Accessed on October 5, 2012.

303 *United States v. Jones*, 132 S. Ct. 945 (2012), http://www.supremecourt.gov/opinions/11pdf/10-1259.pdf.

304 "Federal Appeals Court Rules Against GPS Tracking," *The Newspaper* (Nov. 26, 2010), http://www.thenewspaper.com/news/33/3333.asp.

305 "Federal Appeals Court Rules Against GPS Tracking," *The Newspaper* (Nov. 26, 2010), http://www.thenewspaper.com/news/33/3333.asp.

306 John W. Whitehead, "U.S. v. Jones: Where Privacy, Technology and the Constitution Collide," *Huffington Post* (Oct. 10, 2011), http://www.huffingtonpost.com/john-w-whitehead/us-v-jones-where-privacy-_b_1003812.html.

307 *United States v. Jones*, 132 S. Ct. 945 (2012), http://www.supremecourt.gov/opinions/11pdf/10-1259.pdf.

308 *United States v. Jones*, 132 S. Ct. 945 (2012), http://www.supremecourt.gov/opinions/11pdf/10-1259.pdf.

309 Eric Lichtblau, "Police Are Using Phone Tracking as a Routine Tool," *New York Times* (March 31, 2012), http://www.nytimes.com/2012/04/01/us/police-tracking-of-cellphones-raises-privacy-fears.html?_r=2&nl=todaysheadlines&emc=edit_th_20120401.

310 Eric W. Dolan, "Appeals court: Police can track cell phones without warrant," *Raw Story* (Aug. 14, 2012), http://www.rawstory.com/rs/2012/08/14/appeals-court-police-can-track-cell-phones-without-warrant/.

311 Christopher Soghoian, "Why Google Won't Protect You From Big Brother," *Tedx* (2012), Lecture, http://www.youtube.com/watch?v=esA9RFO1Pcw&feature=youtu.be.

312 Jennifer Valentino-Devries, "Feds Shift Tracking Defense," *Wall Street Journal* (Nov. 2, 2011), http://online.wsj.com/article/SB10001424052970204621904577014363024341028.html.

313 Paul Izzo, "Cell Phone Tracking Case Raises Constitutional Law Questions," *Sharon Patch* (Nov. 22, 2011), http://sharon.patch.com/articles/cell-phone-tracking-case-raises-constitutional-law-questions.

314 Eric Lichtblau, "More Demands on Cell Carriers in Surveillance," *New York Times* (July 8, 2012), http://www.nytimes.com/2012/07/09/us/cell-carriers-see-uptick-in-requests-to-aid-surveillance.html?_r=1.

315 Eric Lichtblau, "More Demands on Cell Carriers in Surveillance," *New York Times* (July 8, 2012), http://www.nytimes.com/2012/07/09/us/cell-carriers-see-uptick-in-requests-to-aid-surveillance.html?_r=1.

316 Eric Lichtblau, "More Demands on Cell Carriers in Surveillance," *New York Times* (July 8, 2012), http://www.nytimes.com/2012/07/09/us/cell-carriers-see-uptick-in-requests-to-aid-surveillance.html?_r=1.

317 Athima Chansanchai, "ACLU: Police track cellphones, too," *NBC News*, http://www.nbcnews.com/technology/technolog/aclu-police-track-cellphones-too-625114.

318 Eric Lichtblau, "More Demands on Cell Carriers in Surveillance," *New York Times* (July 8, 2012), http://www.nytimes.com/2012/07/09/us/cell-carriers-see-uptick-in-requests-to-aid-surveillance.html?_r=1.

319 Eric Lichtblau, "Police Are Using Phone Tracking as a Routine Tool," *New York Times* (March 31, 2012), http://www.nytimes.com/2012/04/01/us/police-tracking-of-cellphones-raises-privacy-fears.html?_r=2&nl=todaysheadlines&emc=edit_th_20120401.

320 Timothy B. Lee, "Documents show cops making up the rules on mobile surveillance," *Ars Technica* (April 3, 2012), http://arstechnica.com/tech-policy/2012/04/documents-show-cops-making-up-the-rules-on-mobile-surveillance/.

321 Kim Zetter, "Justice Department Sues Telecom for Challenging National Security Letter," *Wired* (July 18, 2012), http://www.wired.com/threatlevel/2012/07/doj-sues-telecom-over-nsl/.

322 David Rosen, "America's Spy State: How the Telecoms Sell Out Your Privacy," *Reader Supported News* (June 2, 2012), http://readersupportednews.org/opinion2/294-159/11729-americas-spy-state-how-the-telecoms-sell-out-your-privacy.

323 William Faulkner, *Requiem for a Nun* (1951), Act 1, sc. 3.

324 David Talbot, "A Phone that Knows Where You're Going," *Technology Review* (July 9, 2012), http://www.technologyreview.com/news/428441/a-phone-that-knows-where-youre-going/.

325 Pratap Chatterjee, "The New Cyber-Industrial Complex Spying on Us," *Reader Supported News* (Dec. 4, 2011), http://readersupportednews.org/opinion2/275-42/8734-focus-the-new-cyber-industrial-complex-spying-on-us.

326 The phrase "chilling effect" made its Supreme Court debut in *Gibson v. Florida Legis. Investigation Comm.*, 372 U.S. 539, 556-57 (1963).

327 Alex Kozinski, dissent in *United States v. Juan Pineda-Moreno*, 617 F.3d 1120 (9th Cir. 2010), http://www.ca9.uscourts.gov/datastore/opinions/2010/08/12/08-30385.pdf.

CHAPTER FIFTEEN

328 George Orwell, *1984* (Plume, 1983), p. 2.

329 Gary Stoller, "Homeland security generates multibillion dollar business," *USA Today* (Sept. 10, 2006), http://usatoday30.usatoday.com/money/industries/2006-09-10-security-industry_x.htm.

330 Robert O'Harrow, *No Place to Hide* (Free Press, 2005), p. 9.

331 Jeffrey Rosen, "A Cautionary Tale for a New Age of Surveillance," *New York Times* (Oct. 7, 2001), http://www.nytimes.com/2001/10/07/magazine/07SURVEILLANCE.html?ex=1346212800&en=2d546360047ae54d&ei=5070.

332 Noam Biale, "Expert Findings on Surveillance Cameras," ACLU, http://www.aclu.org/images/asset_upload_file708_35775.pdf.

333 "Surveillance society keeps an eye out," *The Ottawa Citizen* (Sept. 3, 2006), http://www.canada.com/ottawacitizen/news/story.html?id=8a36b5db-9dc7-4e1c-b796-d6ef0834170a.

334 Bruce Finley, "Terror Watch Uses Local Eyes," *Denver Post* (June 29, 2008), http://www.denverpost.com/commented/ci_9732641.

335 "DHS Secretary Napolitano, Missouri Governor Nixon Address Annual National Fusion Center Conference," U.S. Department of Homeland Security (March 11, 2009), http://www.dhs.gov/news/2009/03/11/secretary-napolitano-missouri-governor-address-fusion-center-conference.

336 "Who's Spying in Your Neighborhood?" http://www.aclu.org/whos-spying-your-neighborhood-map. Accessed July 8, 2011.

337 "Declassified Docs Reveal Military Operative Spied on WA Peace Groups, Activist Friends Stunned," *Democracy Now* (July 28, 2009), http://www.democracynow.org/2009/7/28/broadcast_exclusive_declassified_docs_reveal_military.

338 "ACLU Says Fusion Centers Remain Problematic," American Civil Liberties Union (April 17, 2008), http://www.aclu.org/national-security-technology-and-liberty/aclu-says-fusion-centers-remain-problematic.

339 "Privacy Impact Assessment for the Department of Homeland Security State, Local, and Regional Fusion Center Initiative," Department of Homeland Security (Dec. 11, 2008), http://www.dhs.gov/xlibrary/assets/privacy/privacy_pia_ia_slrfci.pdf.

340 "Privacy Impact Assessment for the Department of Homeland Security State, Local, and Regional Fusion Center Initiative," Department of Homeland Security (Dec. 11, 2008), http://www.dhs.gov/xlibrary/assets/privacy/privacy_pia_ia_slrfci.pdf.

341 Joseph Straw, "Smashing Intelligence Stovepipes," *Security Management*, http://www.securitymanagement.com/article/smashing-intelligence-stovepipes?page=0%2C1.

342 Michael Isikoff, "Homeland Security 'fusion' centers spy on citizens, produce 'shoddy' work, report says," *NBC News* (Oct. 2, 2012), http://openchannel.nbcnews.com/_news/2012/10/02/14187433-homeland-security-fusion-centers-spy-on-citizens-produce-shoddy-work-report-says?lite.

343 Robert O'Harrow, "DHS 'fusion centers' portrayed as pools of ineptitude, civil liberties intrusions," *The Washington Post* (Oct. 2, 2012), http://www.washingtonpost.com/investigations/dhs-fusion-centers-portrayed-as-pools-of-ineptitude-and-civil-liberties-intrusions/2012/10/02/10014440-0cb1-11e2-bd1a-b868e65d57eb_story.html.

344 Matthew Harwood, "Problems at Fusion Centers Tied to Poor Training," *Security Management* (Oct. 5, 2012), http://www.securitymanagement.com/news/problems-fusion-centers-tied-poor-training-0010525.

345 Michael Isikoff, "Homeland Security 'fusion' centers spy on citizens, produce 'shoddy' work, report says," *NBC News* (Oct. 2, 2012), http://openchannel.nbcnews.com/_news/2012/10/02/14187433-homeland-security-fusion-centers-spy-on-citizens-produce-shoddy-work-report-says?lite.

346 Robert O'Harrow, "DHS 'fusion centers' portrayed as pools of ineptitude, civil liberties intrusions," *The Washington Post* (Oct. 2, 2012), http://www.washingtonpost.com/investigations/dhs-fusion-centers-portrayed-as-pools-of-ineptitude-and-civil-liberties-intrusions/2012/10/02/10014440-0cb1-11e2-bd1a-b868e65d57eb_story.html.

347 Jesse Walker, "Fusion Centers: Expensive, Practically Useless, and Bad for Your Liberty," *Reason* (Oct. 2, 2012), http://reason.com/blog/2012/10/03/fusion-centers-expensive-practically-use.

348 Matthew Harwood, "Problems at Fusion Centers Tied to Poor Training," *Security Management* (Oct. 5, 2012), http://www.securitymanagement.com/news/problems-fusion-centers-tied-poor-training-0010525.

349 "Indicators and Warnings," http://www.tlo.org/portal/indicators.htm (accessed July 1, 2011).

350 "Indicators and Warnings," http://www.tlo.org/portal/indicators.htm (accessed July 1, 2011).

351 David Rittgers, "We're All Terrorists Now," Cato Institute (Feb. 2, 2011), http://www.cato-at-liberty.org/we%E2%80%99re-all-terrorists-now/.

352 Stephen C. Webster, "Fusion center declares nation's oldest universities possible terror threat," *Raw Story* (April 6, 2009), http://rawstory.com/news/2008/Virginia_terror_assessment_targets_enormous_crosssection_0406.html.

353 James Bamford, "The NSA Is Building the Country's Biggest Spy Center (Watch What You Say)," *Wired* (March 15, 2012), http://www.wired.com/threatlevel/2012/03/ff_nsadatacenter/all/1.

354 James Bamford, "The NSA Is Building the Country's Biggest Spy Center (Watch What You Say)," *Wired* (March 15, 2012), http://www.wired.com/threatlevel/2012/03/ff_nsadatacenter/all/1.

355 James Bamford, "The NSA Is Building the Country's Biggest Spy Center (Watch What You Say)," *Wired* (March 15, 2012), http://www.wired.com/threatlevel/2012/03/ff_nsadatacenter/all/1.

356 James Bamford, "The NSA Is Building the Country's Biggest Spy Center (Watch What You Say)," *Wired* (March 15, 2012), http://www.wired.com/threatlevel/2012/03/ff_nsadatacenter/all/1.

357 James Bamford, "The NSA Is Building the Country's Biggest Spy Center (Watch What You Say)," *Wired* (March 15, 2012), http://www.wired.com/threatlevel/2012/03/ff_nsadatacenter/all/1.

358 James Bamford, "The NSA Is Building the Country's Biggest Spy Center (Watch What You Say)," *Wired* (March 15, 2012), http://www.wired.com/threatlevel/2012/03/ff_nsadatacenter/all/1.

359 James Bamford, "The NSA Is Building the Country's Biggest Spy Center (Watch What You Say)," *Wired* (March 15, 2012), http://www.wired.com/threatlevel/2012/03/ff_nsadatacenter/all/1.

360 Jane Mayer, "The Secret Sharer," *New Yorker* (May 23, 2011), http://www.newyorker.com/reporting/2011/05/23/110523fa_fact_mayer?currentPage=all.

361 Jane Mayer, "The Secret Sharer," *New Yorker* (May 23, 2011), http://www.newyorker.com/reporting/2011/05/23/110523fa_fact_mayer?currentPage=all.

362 James Bamford, "The NSA Is Building the Country's Biggest Spy Center (Watch What You Say)," *Wired* (March 15, 2012), http://www.wired.com/threatlevel/2012/03/ff_nsadatacenter/all/1.

363 James Bamford, "The NSA Is Building the Country's Biggest Spy Center (Watch What You Say)," *Wired* (March 15, 2012), http://www.wired.com/threatlevel/2012/03/ff_nsadatacenter/all/1.

364 James Bamford, "The NSA Is Building the Country's Biggest Spy Center (Watch What You Say)," *Wired* (March 15, 2012), http://www.wired.com/threatlevel/2012/03/ff_nsadatacenter/all/1.

365 *As quoted in* David Burnham, *The Rise of the Computer State* (Random House, 1983), p. 47, 48.

CHAPTER SIXTEEN

366 U.S. Supreme Court Justice William O. Douglas dissenting in *Osborn v. United States*, 385 U.S. 323 (1966).

367 Jessica Bennett, "Smile! You're on Hidden Camera," *Newsweek* (Nov. 20, 2007), http://www.newsweek.com/id/71506/output/print.

368 Bruce Horovitz, "Smile! You're on a Redflex camera," *USA Today* (July 5, 2006), http://usatoday30.usatoday.com/tech/news/2006-07-04-redflex-usat_x.htm.

369 Christine Vendel, "High-tech wow for police is a privacy worry for some," *Kansas City Star* (Aug. 2, 2010), http://www.elsag.com/detail.asp?i=280.

370 Andy Greenberg, "Full-Body Scan Technology Deployed In Street-Roving Vans," *Forbes* (Aug. 24, 2010), http://www.forbes.com/sites/andygreenberg/2010/08/24/full-body-scan-technology-deployed-in-street-roving-vans/.

371 Jason Milley, "DoD to use iris scans, fingerprints for building security," *Federal News Radio* (April 6, 2012), http://www.federalnewsradio.com/?nid=396&sid=2817314.

372 Steve Johnson, "Does rise of biometrics mean a future without anonymity?" *Mercury News* (Sept. 17, 2012), http://www.mercurynews.com/business/ci_21557578/unlocking-future-faces-heartbeats-and-maybe-even-body.

373 Michael Endler, "FBI's Facial Recognition Program: Better Security Through Biometrics," *Information Week* (Sept. 11, 2012), http://www.informationweek.com/government/security/fbis-facial-recognition-program-better-s/240007101?pgno=2.

374 Steve Johnson, "Does rise of biometrics mean a future without anonymity?" *Mercury News,* (Sept. 17, 2012), http://www.mercurynews.com/business/ci_21557578/unlocking-future-faces-heartbeats-and-maybe-even-body.

375 Steve Johnson, "Does rise of biometrics mean a future without anonymity?" *Mercury News* (Sept. 17, 2012), http://www.mercurynews.com/business/ci_21557578/unlocking-future-faces-heartbeats-and-maybe-even-body.

376 Thomas Claburn, "Facebook: We Fumbled Face Recognition Roll-Out," *Information Week* (June 8, 2011), http://www.informationweek.com/security/privacy/facebook-we-fumbled-face-recognition-rol/230500058.

377 Austin Carr, "Iris Scanners Create the Most Secure City in the World. Welcome, Big Brother," *Fast Company* (Aug. 18, 2010), http://www.fastcompany.com/1683302/iris-scanners-create-most-secure-city-world-welcome-big-brother.

378 Austin Carr, "Iris Scanners Create the Most Secure City in the World. Welcome, Big Brother," *Fast Company* (Aug. 18, 2010), http://www.fastcompany.com/1683302/iris-scanners-create-most-secure-city-world-welcome-big-brother.

379 "Sheriff's department to demo new eye scanners," *Columbia Daily Tribune* (Oct. 27, 2010), http://www.columbiatribune.com/news/2010/oct/27/sheriffs-department-to-demo-new-eye-scanners/.

380 Howard Portnoy, "Big Brother alert: U.S. police preparing to use facial recognition iPhone," *Examiner* (July 15, 2011), http://www.examiner.com/article/big-brother-alert-u-s-police-preparing-to-use-facial-recognition-iphone.

381 "Overview," *AOptix Technologies,* http://www.aoptix.com/about-us/overview. Accessed June 5, 2012.

382 Sara Reardon, "FBI launches $1 billion face recognition project," *New Scientist* (Sept. 7, 2012), http://www.newscientist.com/article/mg21528804.200-fbi-launches-1-billion-face-recognition-project.html.

383 Tana Ganeva, "5 Things You Should Know About the FBI's Massive New Biometric Database," *Alternet* (Jan. 8, 2012), http://www.alternet.org/story/153664/5_things_you_*should*_know_about_the_fbi%27s_massive_new_biometric_database.

384 Joseph J. Atick, "Face Recognition in the Era of the Cloud and Social Media: Is it Time to Hit the Panic Button?" *findBiometrics* (Oct. 19, 2011), http://www.findbiometrics.com/articles/i/9335/.

385 Ryan Gallagher, "Internet Activists: The Software Program TrapWire Is Not a Global Conspiracy To Photograph Your Face," *Slate* (Aug. 13, 2012), http://www.slate.com/blogs/future_tense/2012/08/13/trapwire_internet_rumors_about_the_surveillance_software_aren_t_based_in_reality_.html.

386 Jesus Diaz, "FBI's Sinister New $1 Billion Project Will Track Everyone By Their Face," *Gizmodo* (Sept. 10, 2012), http://gizmodo.com/5941926/fbis-sinister-new-1-billion-project-will-track-everyone-by-their-face.

387 Ellen Nakashima and Craig Whitlock, "With Air Force's Gorgon Drone 'we can see everything,'" *The Washington Post* (Jan. 2, 2011), http://www.washingtonpost.com/wp-dyn/content/article/2011/01/01/AR2011010102690.html.

388 Tana Ganeva, "Why Is the Government Collecting Your Biometric Data?" *Reader Supported News* (June 26, 2012), http://truth-out.org/news/item/9989-why-is-the-government-collecting-your-biometric-data.

389 Zach Howard, "Police to begin iPhone iris scans amid privacy concerns," *Reuters* (July 20, 2011), http://www.reuters.com/article/2011/07/20/us-crime-identification-iris-idUSTRE76J4A120110720.

390 Scott Lemieux, "Are Police Building a Massive DNA Database?" *Reader Supported News* (March 25, 2012), http://readersupportednews.org/opinion2/304-justice/10624-are-police-building-a-massive-dna-database.

391 Jason Milley, "DoD to use iris scans, fingerprints for building security," *Federal News Radio* (April 6, 2012), http://www.federalnewsradio.com/?nid=396&sid=2817314.

392 Salvador Rodriguez, "Facedeals checks you in with facial-recognition cameras," *The Los Angeles Times* (Aug. 10, 2012), http://www.latimes.com/business/technology/la-fi-tn-facedeals-facebook-facial-recognition-20120810,0,2763521.story.

393 "Mannequins collect data on shoppers via facial-recognition software," *The Washington Post*, (Nov. 22, 2012), http://www.washingtonpost.com/business/economymannequins-collect-data-on-shoppers-via-facial-recognition-software/2012/11/22/0751b992-3425-11e2-9cfa-e41bac906cc9_story.html.

394 "Mannequins collect data on shoppers via facial-recognition software," *The Washington Post*, (Nov. 22, 2012), http://www.washingtonpost.com/business/economy/mannequins-collect-data-on-shoppers-via-facial-recognition-software/2012/11/22/0751b992-3425-11e2-9cfa-e41bac906cc9_story.html.

395 "Mannequins collect data on shoppers via facial-recognition software," *The Washington Post*, (Nov. 22, 2012), http://www.washingtonpost.com/business/economy/mannequins-collect-data-on-shoppers-via-facial-recognition-software/2012/11/22/0751b992-3425-11e2-9cfa-e41bac906cc9_story.html.

396 Tana Ganeva, "5 Things You Should Know About the FBI's Massive New Biometric Database," *Alternet* (Jan. 8, 2012), http://www.alternet.org/story/153664/5_things_you_should_know_about_the_fbi%27s_massive_new_biometric_database.

397 Rebecca Bowe, "Red Flag On Biometrics: Iris Scanners Can Be Tricked," *Electronic Frontier Foundation* (July 27, 2012), https://www.eff.org/deeplinks/2012/07/red-flag-biometrics-iris-scanner-vulnerability-revealed.

398 Tom Pritchard, "The Anonymous Guide to Hiding From Facial Recognition, or the Long Arm of the Law," *Gizmodo* (Aug. 23, 2012), http://www.gizmodo.co.uk/2012/08/the-anonymous-guide-to-hiding-from-facial-recognition-or-the-long-arm-of-the-law/.

399 Walter Cronkite, "Preface," from the 1984 edition of *1984* by George Orwell, http://www.newspeakdictionary.com/go-pre.html.

Part Five: America the Battlefield

400 James Madison in a speech before the Constitutional Convention (1787-06-29), from Max Farrand's *Records of the Federal Convention of 1787*, vol. I [1] (1911), p. 465.

CHAPTER SEVENTEEN

401 Aldous Huxley, *Brave New World* (Bantam, 1968), p. xii.

402 Qiuping Gu, M.D., Ph.D.; Charles F. Dillon, M.D., Ph.D.; and Vicki L. Burt, Sc.M., R.N., "Prescription Drug Use Continues to Increase: U.S. Prescription Drug Data for 2007-2008," *Centers for Disease Control and Prevention* (Sept. 2010).

403 David Gutierrez, "Prescription Drugs Kill 300 Percent More Americans Than Illegal Drugs," *Truthout* (Nov. 10, 2008), http://archive.truthout.org/111208HA.

CHAPTER EIGHTEEN

404 Howard Zinn, *The Zinn Reader: Second Edition* (Seven Stories Press, 2009), p. 158.

405 Dean Reynolds, "1000s protest the Chicago NATO summit," *CBS News* (May 20, 2012), http://www.cbsnews.com/8301-18563_162-57437946/1000s-protest-the-chicago-nato-summit/.

406 Steven Yaccino, "Protesters and Police Clash at NATO Meeting; 2 Held on Terrorism Charges," *New York Times* (May 20, 2012), http://www.nytimes.com/2012/05/21/us/two-held-on-terrorism-charges-at-nato-meeting.html?pagewanted=all.

407 Andrew Stern, "Chicago braces for violence at NATO summit," *Reuters* (May 15, 2012), http://www.reuters.com/article/2012/05/15/us-nato-summit-security-idUSBRE84E1KR20120515.

408 "Fighter Jets In Skies Over Chicago On Friday Morning Before NATO Summit," *CBS Chicago* (May 17, 2012), http://chicago.cbslocal.com/2012/05/17/fighter-jets-in-skies-over-chicago-on-friday-morning-before-nato-summit/.

409 Yana Kunichoff, "The NATO Raids and Arrests: This Is What Jail Solidarity Looks Like," *Truthout* (May 19, 2012), http://truth-out.org/news/item/9251-this-is-what-jail-solidarity-looks-like.

410 "USA: Excessive and lethal force?" Amnesty International (Nov. 29, 2004), http://www.amnestyusa.org/node/55449?page=show.

411 Carlos Miller, "Texas cop uses Taser on 72-year-old great grandmother," *Pixiq* (June 2, 2009), http://www.pixiq.com/article/texas-deputy-uses-taser-on-72-year-old-great-grandmother.

412 "Flashlight Weapon Makes Targets Throw Up," *FoxNews* (Aug. 7, 2007), http://www.foxnews.com/story/0,2933,292271,00.html.

413 "Silent Guardian™ Protection System," *Raytheon Company*, http://www.raytheon.com/capabilities/products/silent_guardian/. Accessed on Apr. 25, 2012.

414 Matthew Holehouse, "Police to test laser that 'blinds rioters,'" *Telegraph* (Dec. 11, 2011), http://www.telegraph.co.uk/news/uknews/crime/8949060/Police-to-test-laser-that-blinds-rioters.html.

415 "LRAD/Product Overview," LRAD Corporation, http://www.lradx.com/site/content/view/15/110/. Accessed on April 30, 2012.

416 Eric H. Chudler, "Sensory Apparatus," University of Washington (April 30, 2012), http://faculty.washington.edu/chudler/facts.html#sensory.

417 Matthew Weaver, "G20 protestors blasted by sonic cannon: US police spark outrage by using wartime acoustic weapon to disperse G20 protestors in Pittsburgh," *Guardian* (Sept. 25, 2009), http://www.guardian.co.uk/world/blog/2009/sep/25/sonic-cannon-g20-pittsburgh.

418 Rich Lord, "Professor sues city over use of siren aimed at protestors," *Post-Gazette* (Sept. 22, 2011), http://www.post-gazette.com/stories/local/neighborhoods-city/professor-sues-city-over-use-of-siren-aimed-at-protesters-315763/.

419 Ben Gruber, "Critics raise the alarm over U.S. police drone plans," *Reuters* (Jan. 11, 2012), http://www.reuters.com/video/2012/01/11/critics-raise-the-alarm-over-us-police-d?videoId=228416406.

420 Josh Bell, "VIDEO: See What Armed Domestic Drones Look Like," American Civil Liberties Union (March 13 2012), http://www.aclu.org/blog/technology-and-liberty-national-security/video-see-what-armed-domestic-drones-look.

421 Jefferson Morley, "Drones for 'urban warfare,'" *Salon* (April 24, 2012), http://www.salon.com/2012/04/24/drones_for_urban_warfare/singleton/.

422 Jefferson Morley, "The drones are coming – to America," *Salon* (April 10, 2012), http://www.salon.com/2012/04/10/the_drones_are_coming_to_america/singleton/.

CHAPTER NINETEEN

423 Daniel Kurtzman, "Learning to love Big Brother: George W. Bush channels George Orwell," *San Francisco Chronicle* (July 28, 2002), http://www.sfgate.com/opinion/article/Learning-to-love-Big-Brother-George-W-Bush-2790661.php.

424 Matt Deluca and Christina Boyle, "Wall Street protesters cuffed, pepper-sprayed during 'inequality' march," *NY Daily News* (Sept. 24, 2011), http://articles.nydailynews.com/2011-09-24/news/30219815_1_pepper-spray-protesters-unarmed-man.

425 Chris Francescani and Michelle Nichols, "Generators taken from NY anti-Wall St protesters," *Reuters* (Oct. 28, 2011), http://www.reuters.com/article/2011/10/28/usa-wallstreet-protests-idUSN1E79R1T620111028.

426 Adam Gabbatt, "Scott Olsen injuries prompt review as Occupy Oakland protests continue," *Guardian* (Oct. 26, 2011), http://www.guardian.co.uk/world/2011/oct/26/scott-olsen-occupy-oakland-review.

427 Melissa Bell, "Dorli Rainey, 84, the new face of the Occupy protests," *The Washington Post* (Nov. 17, 2011), http://www.washingtonpost.com/blogs/blogpost/post/dorli-rainey-84-the-new-face-of-the-occupy-protests/2011/11/17/gIQAeEXKUN_blog.html.

428 Dashiell Bennett, "84-Year-Old Woman Becomes the Pepper-Sprayed Face of Occupy Seattle," *Atlantic Wire* (Nov. 16, 2011), http://www.theatlanticwire.com/national/2011/11/84-year-old-woman-becomes-pepper-sprayed-face-occupy-seattle/45035/#.

429 "USA: Excessive and lethal force? Amnesty International's concerns about deaths and ill-treatment involving police use of Tasers," Amnesty International (Nov. 29, 2004), http://www.amnestyusa.org/node/55449?page=show.

430 Erica Goode, "Tasers Pose Risks to Heart, a Study Warns," *New York Times* (April 30, 2012), http://www.nytimes.com/2012/05/01/health/research/taser-shot-to-the-chest-can-kill-a-study-warns.html?_r=2.

431 Nick Penzenstadler, "Appleton cops use Tasers fewer times in recent years." *Post Crescent* (May 7, 2012), http://www.postcrescent.com/article/20120507/APC0101/305070076/Police-use-Tasers-fewer-times-recent-years-story-videos-.

432 David Morgan, "U.N.: Tasers Are a Form of Torture," *CBSNews* (Feb. 11, 2009), http://www.cbsnews.com/2100-201_162-3537803.html.

433 "Excessive and Lethal Force: Deaths and Ill-Treatment Involving Police Use of Tasers," Amnesty International (Nov. 30, 2004), http://web.amnesty.org/library/index/engamr511392004.

434 "USA: Excessive and lethal force? Amnesty International's concerns about deaths and ill-treatment involving police use of Tasers," Amnesty International (Nov. 29, 2004), http://www.amnestyusa.org/node/55449?page=show.

435 "USA: Excessive and lethal force? Amnesty International's concerns about deaths and ill-treatment involving police use of Tasers," Amnesty International (Nov. 29, 2004), http://www.amnestyusa.org/node/55449?page=show.

436 "USA: Excessive and lethal force? Amnesty International's concerns about deaths and ill-treatment involving police use of Tasers," Amnesty International (Nov. 29, 2004), http://www.amnestyusa.org/node/55449?page=show.

437 "USA: Excessive and lethal force? Amnesty International's concerns about deaths and ill-treatment involving police use of Tasers," Amnesty International (Nov. 29, 2004), http://www.amnestyusa.org/node/55449?page=show.

438 Carlos Miller, "Texas cop uses Taser on 72-year-old great grandmother," *Pixiq* (June 2, 2009), http://www.pixiq.com/article/texas-deputy-uses-taser-on-72-year-old-great-grandmother

439 Nick Budnick, "Shocking Differences," *Williamette Week* (Feb. 18, 2004), http://www.wweek.com/portland/article-2950-shocking_differences.html.

440 "Meet the new shock jocks," *Guardian* (Aug. 18, 2005), http://www.guardian.co.uk/theguardian/2005/aug/19/guardianweekly.guardianweekly12.

441 Alex Berenson, "As Police Use of Tasers Rises, Questions Over Safety Increase," *New York Times* (June 18, 2004), http://www.nytimes.com/2004/07/18/national/18TASER.html?ei=5090&en=2c9c37c0dfaef9a6&ex=1247803200&partner=rssuserland&pagewanted=print&position=.

442 Phuong Cat Le and Hector Castro, "Police are too quick to grab for Taser's power, say critics," *Seattle Post-Intelligencer* (Nov. 30, 2004), http://seattlepi.nwsource.com/local/201700_taser30.html.

443 Matt Garfield, "Police Taser 75-year-old at nursing home," *The Herald* (Oct. 20, 2004), http://www.infowars.com/print/ps/taser_oldwoman.htm.

444 "Excessive and Lethal Force: Deaths and Ill-Treatment Involving Police Use of Tasers," Amnesty International (Nov. 30, 2004), http://web.amnesty.org/library/index/engamr511392004.

445 Corey Stoughton, "Get a grip on Taser overuse," *Times Union* (May 6, 2012), http://www.timesunion.com/opinion/article/Get-a-grip-on-Taser-overuse-3538647.php.

446 "Stun guns not safe for citizens, but benefit police, study finds," Michigan State University (May 1, 2012), http://news.msu.edu/story/stun-guns-not-safe-for-citizens-but-benefit-police-study-finds/.

447 Warren Richey, "Was Taser use on pregnant woman excessive force? Supreme Court declines case." *Christian Science Monitor* (May 29, 2012), http://www.csmonitor.com/USA/Justice/2012/0529/Was-Taser-use-on-pregnant-woman-excessive-force-Supreme-Court-declines-case.

448 Bill Mears, "Justices decline case of police Taser use on pregnant woman," *CNN* (May 29, 2012), http://articles.cnn.com/2012-05-29/justice/justice_scotus-taser-shocks_1_law-enforcement-officers-pregnant-woman-drive-stun?_s=PM:JUSTICE.

449 Bill Mears, "Justices decline case of police Taser use on pregnant woman," *CNN* (May 29, 2012), http://articles.cnn.com/2012-05-29/justice/justice_scotus-taser-shocks_1_law-enforcement-officers-pregnant-woman-drive-stun?_s=PM:JUSTICE.

450 Warren Richey, "Was Taser use on pregnant woman excessive force? Supreme Court declines case." *Christian Science Monitor* (May 29, 2012), http://www.csmonitor.com/USA/Justice/2012/0529/Was-Taser-use-on-pregnant-woman-excessive-force-Supreme-Court-declines-case.

451 David Morgan, "U.N.: Tasers Are a Form of Torture," *CBSNews* (Feb. 11, 2009), http://www.cbsnews.com/2100-201_162-3537803.html.

452 Amanda Goodman, "APD gets taser shotguns," *KRQE* (July 25, 2011), http://www.krqe.com/dpp/news/crime/apd-gets-taser-shotguns-.

CHAPTER TWENTY

453 Bertram Gross, *Friendly Fascism: The New Face of Power in America* (South End Press, 1980), p. 298.

454 Whitney Stewart, "Shock bracelet for airlines?" *The Washington Times* (July 10, 2008), http://www.washingtontimes.com/news/2008/jul/10/bracelet-sends-shock-waves-through-blogosphere/.

455 Arthur Gibson, "Chili Peppers—Some Like It Hot," UCLA (Jan. 19, 2010), http://www.botgard.ucla.edu/html/botanytextbooks/economicbotany/Capsicum/index.html.

456 "PepperBall Technologies Incorporated | About PepperBall." PepperBall Technologies Inc. (Feb. 2, 2010), http://www.pepperball.com/about_us.html.

457 "PepperBall Technologies Incorporated | About PepperBall." PepperBall Technologies Inc. (Feb. 2, 2010), http://www.pepperball.com/about_us.html.

458 "PepperBall Technologies Incorporated | About PepperBall." PepperBall Technologies Inc. (Feb. 2, 2010), http://www.pepperball.com/about_us.html.

459 "California campus police on leave after pepper-spraying," *CNN* (Nov. 20, 2011), http://articles.cnn.com/2011-11-20/us/us_california-occupy-pepperspray_1_pepper-spray-campus-police-unlawful-assembly-and-failure?_s=PM:US.

460 Tracy V. Wilson, "How LRAD Works," HowStuffWorks.com (March 3, 2006), http://science.howstuffworks.com/lrad.htm.

461 Tracy V. Wilson, "How LRAD Works," HowStuffWorks.com (March 3, 2006), http://science.howstuffworks.com/lrad.htm.

462 Tracy V. Wilson, "How LRAD Works," HowStuffWorks.com (March 3, 2006), http://science.howstuffworks.com/lrad.htm.

463 Tracy V. Wilson, "How LRAD Works," HowStuffWorks.com (March 3, 2006), http://science.howstuffworks.com/lrad.htm.

464 Kelly Hearn, "Rumsfeld's Ray Gun," *AlterNet* (Aug. 19, 2005), http://www.alternet.org/story/24044/?comments=view&cID=43722&pID=25941.

465 Greg Gordon, "Invisible beam tops list of nonlethal weapons," *Bee Washington Bureau* (June 1, 2004), http://dwb.sacbee.com/content/news/story/9499345p-10423294c.html.

466 "Weapons Freeze, Microwave Enemies," *Associated Press* (Aug. 2, 2004), http://www.wired.com/science/discoveries/news/2004/08/64437?currentPage=2.

467 Kelly Hearn, "Rumsfeld's Ray Gun," *AlterNet* (Aug. 19, 2005), http://www.alternet.org/story/24044/?comments=view&cID=43722&pID=25941.

468 Kelly Hearn, "Rumsfeld's Ray Gun," *AlterNet* (Aug. 19, 2005), http://www.alternet.org/story/24044/?comments=view&cID=43722&pID=25941.

469 "Tear Gas, Police Horses Deployed as MD Fans Riot after Beating Duke," *CBS News* (March 4, 2010), http://www.kens5.com/sports/Tear-gas-policehorses-deployed-as-MD-fans-riot-after-beating-Duke-86337257.html.

470 Eric Fink, "Police Speak Out About JMU Party Breakup," *NBC29* (April 11, 2010), http://www.nbc29.com/Global/story.asp?S=12290340.

471 Eric Fink, "Police Speak Out About JMU Party Breakup," *NBC29* (April 11, 2010), http://www.nbc29.com/Global/story.asp?S=12290340.

472 Sharon Weinberger, "U.S. Police Get Weapons That Shoot Around Corners," *Wired News* (Dec. 14, 2007), http://www.wired.com/dangerroom/2007/12/us-police-get-g/.

473 Sharon Weinberger, "U.S. Police Get Weapons That Shoot Around Corners," *Wired News* (Dec. 14, 2007), http://www.wired.com/dangerroom/2007/12/us-police-get-g/.

474 Robert Lamb, "How does a water cannon work?" HowStuffWorks.com (July 30, 2008), http://science.howstuffworks.com/water-cannon.htm.

475 Robert Lamb, "How does a water cannon work?" HowStuffWorks.com (July 30, 2008), http://science.howstuffworks.com/water-cannon.htm.

476 Robert Lamb, "How does a water cannon work?" HowStuffWorks.com (July 30, 2008), http://science.howstuffworks.com/water-cannon.htm.

477 Daniel Tencer, "Analysis: Taser-related deaths in US accelerating," *Raw Story* (Sept. 5, 2010), http://www.rawstory.com/rs/2010/09/05/taser-related-deaths-accelerating/.

478 Roma Khanna, "Questions grow over HPD's use of Taser guns," *Houston Chronicle* (Jan. 14, 2007), http://www.chron.com/news/houston-texas/article/Questions-grow-over-HPD-s-use-of-Taser-guns-1842941.php.

CHAPTER TWENTY-ONE

479 Richard Wheeler, "Drones Set to Invade National, State Parks," *Wired* (Feb. 28, 2011), http://www.wired.com/dangerroom/2011/02/drones-set-to-invade-u-s-national-parks/.

480 Glenn Greenwald, "The due-process-free assassination of U.S. citizens is now reality," *Salon* (Sept. 30, 2011), http://www.salon.com/2011/09/30/awlaki_6/singleton/.

481 Glenn Greenwald, "U.S. drones targeting rescuers and mourners," *Salon* (Feb. 5, 2012), http://www.salon.com/2012/02/05/u_s_drones_targeting_rescuers_and_mourners/singleton/.

482 "Obama's Budget Calls for Billions in New Spending for Drones," *Truthout* (Feb. 2, 2010), http://archive.truthout.org/obama-administrations-budget-calls-billions-dollars-new-spending-drones56588.

483 Nick Mottern, "Lobbying Report: Drones Fly Through Congress to Enter US Skies," *Truthout* (April 16, 2011), http://truth-out.org/news/item/497:lobbying-report-drones-fly-through-congress-to-enter-us-skies.

484 S. Smithson, "Drones over U.S. get OK by Congress," *The Washington Times* (Feb.7, 2012), http://www.washingtontimes.com/news/2012/feb/7/coming-to-a-sky-near-you/.

485 Jennifer Lynch, "Are Drones Watching You?" Electronic Frontier Foundation (Jan. 10, 2012), https://www.eff.org/deeplinks/2012/01/drones-are-watching-you.

486 Jennifer Lynch, "Are Drones Watching You?" Electronic Frontier Foundation (Jan. 10, 2012), https://www.eff.org/deeplinks/2012/01/drones-are-watching-you.

487 Noah Shachtman, "Army Tracking Plan: Drones That Never Forget a Face," *Wired* (Sept. 28, 2011), http://www.wired.com/dangerroom/2011/09/drones-never-forget-a-face/.

488 Peter Finn, "A future for drones: Automated killing," *The Washington Post* (Sept. 19, 2011), http://www.washingtonpost.com/national/national-security/a-future-for-drones-automated-killing/2011/09/15/gIQAVy9mgK_story.html.

489 Jo Becker and Scott Shane, "Secret 'Kill List' Proves a Test of Obama's Principles and Will," *New York Times* (May 29, 2012), http://www.nytimes.com/2012/05/29/world/obamas-leadership-in-war-on-al-qaeda.html?_r=2&hp&pagewanted=all.

490 Jo Becker and Scott Shane, "Secret 'Kill List' Proves a Test of Obama's Principles and Will," *New York Times* (May 29, 2012), http://www.nytimes.com/2012/05/29/world/obamas-leadership-in-war-on-al-qaeda.html?_r=2&hp&pagewanted=all.

491 Jo Becker and Scott Shane, "Secret 'Kill List' Proves a Test of Obama's Principles and Will," *New York Times* (May 29, 2012), http://www.nytimes.com/2012/05/29/world/obamas-leadership-in-war-on-al-qaeda.html?_r=2&hp&pagewanted=all.

492 Daniel Klaidman, "Drones: How Obama Learned to Kill," *The Daily Beast* (May 28, 2012), http://www.thedailybeast.com/newsweek/2012/05/27/drones-the-silent-killers.html.

493 Daniel Klaidman, "Drones: How Obama Learned to Kill," *The Daily Beast* (May 28, 2012), http://www.thedailybeast.com/newsweek/2012/05/27/drones-the-silent-killers.html.

494 Jo Becker and Scott Shane, "Secret 'Kill List' Proves a Test of Obama's Principles and Will," *New York Times* (May 29, 2012), http://www.nytimes.com/2012/05/29/world/obamas-leadership-in-war-on-al-qaeda.html?_r=2&hp&pagewanted=all.

495 Ibrahim Mothana, "How Drones Help Al Qaeda," *New York Times* (June 6, 2012), http://www.nytimes.com/2012/06/14/opinion/how-drones-help-al-qaeda.html?_r=1.

496 Jo Becker and Scott Shane, "Secret 'Kill List' Proves a Test of Obama's Principles and Will," *New York Times* (May 29, 2012), http://www.nytimes.com/2012/05/29/world/obamas-leadership-in-war-on-al-qaeda.html?_r=2&hp&pagewanted=all.

497 Bruce Fein and Ralph Nader, Letter to Patrick Leahy and Lamar Smith (June 11, 2012).

498 Amy Davidson, "The President's Kill List," *The New Yorker* (May 30, 2012), http://www.newyorker.com/online/blogs/comment/2012/05/the-presidents-kill-list.html.

499 David Frost, *Frost/Nixon: Behind the Scenes of the Nixon Interviews* (HarperCollins, 2007), p. 89.

500 Associated Press, "Government under pressure to open US skies to unmanned drones despite safety concerns," *FOX News* (June 14, 2010), http://www.foxnews.com/us/2010/06/14/government-pressure-open-skies-unmanned-drones-despite-safety-concerns/.

501 Richard Wheeler, "Drones Set to Invade National, State Parks," *Wired* (Feb. 28, 2011), http://www.wired.com/dangerroom/2011/02/drones-set-to-invade-u-s-national-parks/.

502 Peter Bowes, "High hopes for drone in LA skies," *BBC News* (June 6, 2006), http://news.bbc.co.uk/2/hi/americas/5051142.stm.

503 Declan McCullagh, "Drone aircraft may prowl U.S. skies," *CNET News* (March 29, 2006), http://news.cnet.com/drone-aircraft-may-prowl-u.s.-skies/2100-11746_3-6055658.html.

504 Geoff Mulvihill, "Lockheed unveils maple-seed-like drone," *Navy Times* (Aug. 11, 2011), http://www.navytimes.com/news/2011/08/ap-lockheed-unveils-maple-seed-like-drone-081111/.

505 Paul Joseph Watson, "Surveillance Drones To Zap Protesters Into Submission," *Prison Planet* (Feb. 12, 2010), http://www.prisonplanet.com/surveillance-drones-to-zap-protesters-into-submission.html.

506 Paul Joseph Watson, "Surveillance Drones To Zap Protesters Into Submission," *Prison Planet* (Feb. 12, 2010), http://www.prisonplanet.com/surveillance-drones-to-zap-protesters-into-submission.html.

507 David Hambling, "Future police: Meet the UK's armed robot drones," *Wired* (Feb. 10, 2010), http://www.wired.co.uk/news/archive/2010-02/10/future-police-meet-the-uks-armed-robot-drones?p=1.

508 Associated Press, "US drones outfitted with infrared, laser and radar targeting begin patrol on Somali pirates," *NY Daily News* (Oct. 23, 2009), http://articles.nydailynews.com/2009-10-23/news/17936654_1_international-maritime-bureau-somali-coast-drones.

509 Buck Sexton, "Aerial 'Shadowhawk' Police Drones can Now Deploy Tasers & Tear Gas," *The Blaze* (March 12, 2012), http://www.theblaze.com/stories/want-to-see-the-aerial-drone-police-could-soon-deploy-in-your-town/.

510 Congressmen Edward Markey and Joe Barton, Letter to FAA Administrator Michael P. Huerta (April 19, 2012), http://markey.house.gov/sites/markey.house.gov/files/documents/4-19-12.Letter%20FAA%20Drones%20.pdf.

511 Nick Fielding, "US draws up plans for nuclear drones," *Guardian* (April 2, 2012), http://www.guardian.co.uk/world/2012/apr/02/us-plans-nuclear-drones (accessed April 26, 2012).

512 Elisabeth Bumiller and Thom Shanker, "War Evolves With Drones, Some Tiny as Bugs," *New York Times* (June 19, 2011), http://www.nytimes.com/2011/06/20/world/20drones.html?_r=1.

513 David Zucchino, "War zone drone crashes add up," *Los Angeles Times* (July 6, 2010), http://articles.latimes.com/2010/jul/06/world/la-fg-drone-crashes-20100706.

514 Noah Shachtman, "Border Drone Flights Suspended After Comms Breakdown," *Wired* (June18, 2010), http://www.wired.com/dangerroom/2010/06/border-drone-breaks-comms-with-pilot-flights-suspended/.

515 Lolita C. Baldor, "Errant drone near DC almost met by fighter jets," *Washington Times* (Sept. 10, 2010), http://www.washingtontimes.com/news/2010/sep/10/errant-drone-near-dc-almost-met-by-fighter-jets/?page=all.

516 "Future of Policing: Unmanned Drones?" (Jan. 20, 2011), http://www.experiencedcriminallawyers.com/future-of-policing-unmanned-drones/.

517 Stephen C. Webster, "Seychelles drone crash raises more questions about security," *Raw Story* (Dec. 13, 2011), http://www.rawstory.com/rs/2011/12/13/another-u-s-drone-mysteriously-crashes-this-time-in-seychelles/.

518 Associated Press, "Surveillance drone crashes in Somali capital," *FOX News* (Feb. 3, 2012), http://www.foxnews.com/world/2012/02/03/surveillance-drone-crashes-in-somali-capital/.

519 Trevor Timm, "Drones: A deeply unsettling future," *Al-Jazeera* (Dec. 7, 2011), http://www.aljazeera.com/indepth/opinion/2011/12/201112774824829807.html.

520 Stephen C. Webster, "Mysterious virus infects America's drone aircraft," *Raw Story* (Oct. 7, 2011), http://www.rawstory.com/rs/2011/10/07/mysterious-virus-infects-americas-drone-aircraft/.

521 Nick Fielding, "US draws up plans for nuclear drones," *Guardian* (April 2, 2012), http://www.guardian.co.uk/world/2012/apr/02/us-plans-nuclear-drones.

522 Jeff Glor, "Drone use in the U.S. raises privacy concerns," *CBS News* (April 5, 2012), http://www.cbsnews.com/8301-505266_162-57409759/drone-use-in-the-u.s-raise-privacy-concerns.

Part Six: The New American Order

523 George Orwell, *1984* (Plume, 1983), p. 291.

524 George Orwell, *1984* (Penguin, 1977), p. 266.

CHAPTER TWENTY-TWO

525 Franklin D. Roosevelt, "Recommendations to the Congress to Curb Monopolies and the Concentration of Economic Power," (April 29, 1938), in *The Public Papers and Addresses of Franklin D. Roosevelt,* ed. Samuel I. Rosenman, vol. 7, (New York, MacMillan: 1941), pp. 305-315.

526 George Orwell, *1984* (Plume, 1983), p. 291.

527 William Styron, Introduction to Richard Rubenstein, *The Cunning of History: The Holocaust and the American Future* (Harper Perennial, 1987), p. xi.

528 Aldous Huxley, *Brave New World* (Harper Torchbook, 1965), p. xviii-xix.

529 Dr. Robert Gellately, *Backing Hitler: Consent and Coercion in Nazi Germany, 1933-1944* (Oxford University Press, 2002), http://www.fsu.edu/profiles/gellately/.

530 Dr. Robert Gellately, *Backing Hitler: Consent and Coercion in Nazi Germany, 1933-1944* (Oxford University Press, 2002).

CHAPTER TWENTY-THREE

531 George Will, "Blowing the whistle on the federal Leviathan," *The Washington Post* (July 27, 2012), http://www.washingtonpost.com/opinions/george-will-blowing-the-whistle-on-leviathan/2012/07/27/gJQAAsRnEX_story.html.

532 John Baker, "Revisiting the Explosive Growth of Federal Crimes," The Heritage Foundation (June 16, 2008), http://www.heritage.org/research/reports/2008/06/revisiting-the-explosive-growth-of-federal-crimes.

533 Nathan Burney, "An Illustrated Guide to Criminal Law," http://thecriminallawyer.tumblr.com/post/27956783155/work-in-progress.

534 Radley Balko, "We're All Felons, Now," *Reason* (Oct. 19, 2009), http://reason.com/archives/2009/10/19/were-all-felons-now.

535 L. Gordon Crovitz, "You Commit Three Felonies a Day," *Wall Street Journal* (Sept. 27, 2009), http://online.wsj.com/article/SB10001424052748704471504574438900830760842.html.

536 David Gumpert, "Raids are increasing on farms and private food-supply clubs — here are 5 tips for surviving one," *Grist* (July 15, 2010), http://grist.org/article/food-five-tips-for-surviving-a-raid-on-your-farm-or-food-club/full/.

537 "Criminalizing everyone," *The Washington Times* (Oct. 5, 2009), http://www.washingtontimes.com/news/2009/oct/05/criminalizing-everyone/.

538 George Will, "Blowing the whistle on the federal Leviathan," *The Washington Post* (July 27, 2012), http://www.washingtonpost.com/opinions/george-will-blowing-the-whistle-on-leviathan/2012/07/27/gJQAAsRnEX_story.html.

539 Kendra Alleyne, "Oregon Man Sentenced to 30 Days in Jail -- for Collecting Rainwater on His Property," *CNS News* (July 26, 2012), http://cnsnews.com/news/article/oregon-man-sentenced-30-days-jail-collecting-rainwater-his-property.

540 Kendra Alleyne, "Man Sentenced to 30 Days for Catching Rain Water on Own Property Enters Jail," *CNS News* (Aug. 8, 2012), http://cnsnews.com/news/article/man-sentenced-30-days-catching-rain-water-own-property-enters-jail; Kendra Alleyne, "Oregon Man Sentenced to 30 Days in Jail -- for Collecting Rainwater on His Property," *CNS News* (July 26, 2012), http://cnsnews.com/news/article/oregon-man-sentenced-30-days-jail-collecting-rainwater-his-property.

541 Mark Carlson, "Coralville Police Shutdown Several Children's Lemonade Stands," *KCRG-TV* (Aug. 2, 2011), http://www.kcrg.com/news/local/Coralville-Police-Shutdown-Several-Childrens-Lemonade-Stands-126592563.html.

542 Mark Carlson, "Coralville Police Shutdown Several Children's Lemonade Stands," *KCRG-TV* (Aug. 2, 2011), http://www.kcrg.com/news/local/Coralville-Police-Shutdown-Several-Childrens-Lemonade-Stands-126592563.html.

543 "America's 'Nanny State' Laws," *CNBC* (May 31, 2012), http://www.cnbc.com/id/47631869/America_s_Nanny_State_Laws.

544 Paul Hsieh, "The Dangerous Synergy Between The Nanny State And Universal Health Care," *Forbes* (June 18, 2012), http://www.forbes.com/sites/realspin/2012/06/18/the-dangerous-synergy-between-the-nanny-state-and-universal-health-care/.

545 Laurel J. Sweet and Chris Cassidy, "Parents: Rule's Half-baked," *Boston Herald* (May 7, 2012), http://www.bostonherald.com/news/regional/view/20220507parents_rules_half-baked_states_junk_food_ban_could_take_bite_out_of_school_fundraisers/srvc=home&position=0.

546 "Nanny State: Spoiled Milkshakes," *Richmond Times-Dispatch* (July 6, 2012), http://www2.timesdispatch.com/news/rtd-opinion/2012/jul/06/tdopin01-spoiled-milkshakes-ar-2036945/.

547 John Glaser, "'Trespass Bill' Would Violate Peaceful Assembly Rights," *Anti-War.com* (Feb. 28, 2012), http://news.antiwar.com/2012/02/28/trespass-bill-would-violate-peaceful-assembly-rights/.

548 Mike Masnick, "Chipping Away At The First Amendment: New 'Trespassing' Bill Could Be Used To Criminalize Legitimate Protests," *Tech Dirt* (March 2, 2012), http://www.techdirt.com/articles/20120301/15425317936/chipping-away-first-amendment-new-trespassing-bill-could-be-used-to-criminalize-legitimate-protests.shtml.

549 Bill Mears, "Justices reject appeal of war protester over Cheney encounter," *CNN Justice* (June 4, 2012), http://articles.cnn.com/2012-06-04/justice/justice_scotus-retaliatory-arrests-cheney_1_agents-arrest-protester?_s=PM:JUSTICE.

550 Mark Baard, "Free Speech Behind the Razor Wire," *Wired* (July 27, 2004), http://www.wired.com/politics/law/news/2004/07/64349.

551 "Judge Denies DNC Free-Speech Zone Challenge," *WCVB-TV Boston* (July 22, 2004).

552 Nathan Burney, "An Illustrated Guide to Criminal Law," http://thecriminallawyer.tumblr.com/post/27956783155/work-in-progress.

CHAPTER TWENTY-FOUR

553 Henry Giroux, "Violence, USA: The Warfare State and the Brutalizing of Everyday Life." *Truthout* (May 2, 2012), http://truth-out.org/opinion/item/8859-violence-usa-the-warfare-state-and-the-brutalizing-of-everyday-life.

554 Cevin Soling, *The War on Kids* (Spectacle Films, 2009).

555 Shaun Chaiyabhat, "Brevard County middle school student suspended for hugging girl," *WKMG Local* 6 (Nov. 3, 2011), http://www.clickorlando.com/news/Brevard-County-middle-school-student-suspended-for-hugging-girl/-/1637132/4299476/-/f0amd3z/-/index.html.

556 Laura Hibbard, "Student, 9 Years Old, Suspended For Sexual Harassment, Calling Teacher 'Cute.'" The *Huffington Post* (Dec. 5, 2011), http://www.huffingtonpost.com/2011/12/05/student-9-years-old-suspended-for-sexual-harassment_n_1129683.html.

557 Andrew Jones, "Cops arrest 6-year-old kindergartener in Georgia," *Raw Story* (April 17, 2012), http://www.rawstory.com/rs/2012/04/17/cops-arrest-6-year-old-kindergartener-in-georgia/.

558 "Hercules Family Battles Sex Assault Claim Against 6-Year-Old," *CBS San Francisco* (Jan. 27, 2012), http://sanfrancisco.cbslocal.com/2012/01/27/hercules-family-battles-playground-sex-assault-claim-against-6-year-old/.

559 Piper Weiss, "Kindergartner Charged with Battery. Why Are We Criminalizing Kids?" *Yahoo* (April 29, 2012), http://shine.yahoo.com/parenting/kindergartener-charged-battery-why-criminalizing-kids-175600847.html.

560 Stephanie Chen, "Girl's arrest for doodling raises concerns about zero tolerance," *CNN* (Feb. 18, 2010), http://articles.cnn.com/2010-02-18/justice/new.york.doodle.arrest_1_zero-tolerance-schools-police-precinct?_s=PM:CRIME.

561 "Are Zero Tolerance Policies Effective in the Schools?" American Psychological Association (Dec. 2008), http://www.apa.org/pubs/info/reports/zero-tolerance.pdf.

562 Jim Kiertzner, "4 Monroe Jefferson High School students charged in cafeteria food fight," *Click On Detroit* (March 28, 2012), http://www.clickondetroit.com/news/4-Monroe-Jefferson-High-School-students-charged-in-cafeteria-food-fight/-/1719418/9741876/-/a2v4f/-/index.html.

563 Mike Masnick, "High School Student Expelled For Tweeting Profanity; Principal Admits School Tracks All Tweets," *Techdirt* (March 26, 2012), http://www.techdirt.com/articles/20120326/04334818242/high-school-student-expelled-tweeting-profanity-principal-admits-school-tracks-all-tweets.shtml.

564 Chris McGreal, "The US schools with their own police," *Guardian* (Jan. 9, 2012), http://www.guardian.co.uk/world/2012/jan/09/texas-police-schools.

565 "In-school arrests fuel nationwide debate over when to involve police," *Detroit Free Press* (April 19, 2012), http://www.freep.com/article/20120419/NEWS07/204190543/In-school-arrests-fuel-nationwide-debate-over-when-to-involve-police.

566 Annette Fuentes, *Lockdown High: When the Schoolhouse Becomes a Jailhouse* (Verso, 2010), p. 29.

567 "Are Zero Tolerance Policies Effective in the Schools?" American Psychological Association (Dec. 2008), http://www.apa.org/pubs/info/reports/zero-tolerance.pdf.

568 Shaun Chaiyabhat, "Nurse refuses student inhaler during asthma attack," *Click Orlando* (May 21, 2012), http://www.clickorlando.com/news/Nurse-refuses-student-inhaler-during-asthma-attack/-/1637132/13560430/-/wm13uaz/-/index.html.

569 Howard Portnoy, "8-year-old ordered to remove numbered football jersey by school," *Examiner.com*, (Sept. 14, 2012), http://www.examiner.com/article/8-year-old-ordered-to-remove-numbered-football-jersey-by-school.

570 Howard Portnoy, "School disciplines 10-year-old for gun-shaped pizza slice," *Examiner.com*, (Dec. 25, 2011), http://www.examiner.com/article/school-disciplines-10-year-old-for-gun-shaped-pizza-slice-video?cid=PROD-redesign-right-next.

571 Howard Portnoy, "Deaf preschooler forbidden to sign own name because gesture resembles gun," *Examiner.com* (Aug. 28, 2012), http://www.examiner.com/article/deaf-preschooler-forbidden-to-sign-own-name-because-gesture-resembles-gun?cid=PROD-redesign-right-next.

572 Howard Portnoy, "HS valedictorian denied diploma after saying word 'hell' in graduation speech," *Examiner.com* (Aug. 23, 2012), http://www.examiner.com/article/hs-valedictorian-denied-diploma-after-saying-word-hell-graduation-speech.

573 Cevin Soling, *The War on Kids* (Spectacle Films, 2009).

574 Samreen Hooda, "Texas School ID Tracking Chips Protested By Parents And Students," *Huffington Post* (Sept. 6, 2012), http://www.huffingtonpost.com/2012/09/05/school-id-tracking-chips-_n_1861049.html.

575 David Kravets, "Tracking School Children With RFID Tags? It's All About the Benjamins," *Wired* (Sept. 7, 2012), http://www.wired.com/threatlevel/2012/09/rfid-chip-student-monitoring/.

576 Northside ISD "Smart" ID Cards: Student Locator Pilot, http://www.nisd.net/student-locator/.

577 "Texas School District Reportedly Threatening Students Who Refuse Tracking ID, Can't Vote For Homecoming," *Huffington Post* (Oct. 8, 2012), http://www.huffingtonpost.com/2012/10/08/texas-school-district-rep_n_1949415.html?utm_hp_ref=teen.

578 David Rosen, "Big Brother invades our classrooms," *Salon* (Oct. 8, 2012), http://www.salon.com/2012/10/08/big_brother_invades_our_classrooms/.

579 David Rosen, "Big Brother invades our classrooms," *Salon* (Oct. 8, 2012), http://www.salon.com/2012/10/08/big_brother_invades_our_classrooms/.

580 David Rosen, "Big Brother invades our classrooms," *Salon* (Oct. 8, 2012), http://www.salon.com/2012/10/08/big_brother_invades_our_classrooms/.

581 David Rosen, "Big Brother invades our classrooms," *Salon* (Oct. 8, 2012), http://www.salon.com/2012/10/08/big_brother_invades_our_classrooms/.

582 David Rosen, "Big Brother invades our classrooms," *Salon* (Oct. 8, 2012), http://www.salon.com/2012/10/08/big_brother_invades_our_classrooms/.

583 David Rosen, "Big Brother invades our classrooms," *Salon* (Oct. 8, 2012), http://www.salon.com/2012/10/08/big_brother_invades_our_classrooms/.

584 Bruce Levine, "Why Are Americans So Easy to Manipulate and Control?" *Alternet* (Oct. 11, 2012), http://www.alternet.org/why-are-americans-so-easy-manipulate-and-control?paging=off.

585 Hunter S. Thompson, *Kingdom of Fear: Loathsome Secrets of a Star-crossed Child in the Final Days of the American Century* (Simon & Schuster, 2003), p. xxii.

CHAPTER TWENTY-FIVE

586 Adam Gopnik, "The Caging of America," *New Yorker* (Jan. 30, 2012), http://www.newyorker.com/arts/critics/atlarge/2012/01/30/120130crat_atlarge_gopnik?currentPage=all.

587 Adam Gopnik, "The Caging of America," *New Yorker* (Jan. 30, 2012), http://www.newyorker.com/arts/critics/atlarge/2012/01/30/120130crat_atlarge_gopnik?currentPage=all.

588 Jerry Markon, "Violent crime in U.S. on the decline," *Washington Post* (May 25, 2010), http://www.washingtonpost.com/wp-dyn/content/article/2010/05/24/AR2010052402210.html.

589 Adam Gopnik, "The Caging of America," *New Yorker* (Jan. 30, 2012), http://www.newyorker.com/arts/critics/atlarge/2012/01/30/120130crat_atlarge_gopnik?currentPage=all.

590 Adam Gopnik, "The Caging of America," *New Yorker* (Jan. 30, 2012), http://www.newyorker.com/arts/critics/atlarge/2012/01/30/120130crat_atlarge_gopnik?currentPage=all.

591 "Quick Facts About the Bureau of Prisons," http://www.bop.gov/news/quick.jsp. Accessed on October 17, 2012.

592 James Ridgeway, "Locking Up Profits," *Al-Jazeera* (Nov. 28, 2011), http://readersupportednews.org/opinion2/279-82/8632-locking-up-profits.

593 Joe Weisenthal, "This Investor Presentation For A Private Prison Is One Of The Creepiest Presentations We've Ever Seen," *Business Insider* (March 12, 2012), http://www.businessinsider.com/the-private-prison-business-2012-3#-6.

594 Joe Weisenthal, "This Investor Presentation For A Private Prison Is One Of The Creepiest Presentations We've Ever Seen," *Business Insider* (March 12, 2012), http://www.businessinsider.com/the-private-prison-business-2012-3#-4.

595 Alan Prendergast, "ACLU, faith groups urge governors not to sell out to private prison giant," *Westword* (March 5, 2012), http://blogs.westword.com/latestword/2012/03/corrections_corporation_of_america_private_prisons_aclu.php.

596 Kevin Johnson, "Private purchasing of prisons locks in occupancy rates," *USA Today* (March 8, 2012), http://www.usatoday.com/news/nation/story/2012-03-01/buying-prisons-require-high-occupancy/53402894/1

597 Kevin Johnson, "Private purchasing of prisons locks in occupancy rates," *USA Today* (March 8, 2012), http://www.usatoday.com/news/nation/story/2012-03-01/buying-prisons-require-high-occupancy/53402894/1.

598 James Ridgeway, "Locking Up Profits," *Al-Jazeera* (Nov. 28, 2011), http://readersupportednews.org/opinion2/279-82/8632-locking-up-profits.

599 Michael Barajas, "ICE's 'soft' detention strategy at new immigration facility begs the question: Why do lowest-risk detainees need to be detained at all?" *San Antonio Current* (March 21, 2012), http://sacurrent.com/news/ice-39-s-39-soft-39-detention-strategy-at-new-immigration-facility-begs-the-question-why-do-lowest-risk-detainees-need-to-be-detained-at-all-1.1288365.

600 Michael Barajas, "ICE's 'soft' detention strategy at new immigration facility begs the question: Why do lowest-risk detainees need to be detained at all?" *San Antonio Current* (March 21, 2012), http://sacurrent.com/news/ice-39-s-39-soft-39-detention-strategy-at-new-immigration-facility-begs-the-question-why-do-lowest-risk-detainees-need-to-be-detained-at-all-1.1288365.

601 Joe Weisenthal, "This Investor Presentation For A Private Prison Is One Of The Creepiest Presentations We've Ever Seen," *Business Insider* (March 12, 2012), http://www.businessinsider.com/the-private-prison-business-2012-3#ixzz1pZb7JybJ.

602 Joe Weisenthal, "This Investor Presentation For A Private Prison Is One Of The Creepiest Presentations We've Ever Seen," *Business Insider* (March 12, 2012), http://www.businessinsider.com/the-private-prison-business-2012-3#-3.

603 Adam Gopnik, "The Caging of America," *New Yorker* (Jan. 30, 2012), http://www.newyorker.com/arts/critics/atlarge/2012/01/30/120130crat_atlarge_gopnik?currentPage=all.

604 Adam Gopnik, "The Caging of America," *New Yorker* (Jan. 30, 2012), http://www.newyorker.com/arts/critics/atlarge/2012/01/30/120130crat_atlarge_gopnik?currentPage=all.

605 "The Influence of the Private Prison Industry in Immigration Detention," *Detention Watch Network*, http://www.detentionwatchnetwork.org/privateprisons. Accessed March 27, 2012.

606 Justice Policy Institute (June 2011), p. 18, http://www.justicepolicy.org/uploads/justicepolicy/documents/gaming_the_system.pdf.

607 Stephanie Chen, "Pennsylvania rocked by 'jailing kids for cash' scandal," *CNN* (Feb. 23, 2009), http://articles.cnn.com/2009-02-23/justice/pennsylvania.corrupt.judges_1_detention-judges-number-of-juvenile-offenders/2?_s=PM:CRIME.

608 "Former Luzerne judge Conahan sentenced to 17.5 years," *Times-Tribune* (Sept. 23, 2011), http://thetimes-tribune.com/news/former-luzerne-judge-conahan-sentenced-to-17-5-years-1.1207994#axzz1qLJ1rNwW.

609 Michael S. Sisak, "Ex-Judge Awaits Transport in Philly," *Standard Speaker* (Aug. 13, 2011), http://standardspeaker.com/news/ex-judge-awaits-transport-in-philly-1.1188079#axzz1Uw91rqxz.

610 Adam Sorensen, "ALEC: What It Does and Why Three Major Corporations Cut Ties," *Time* (April 9, 2012), http://swampland.time.com/2012/04/09/alec-what-it-does-and-why-three-major-corporations-cut-ties/?iid=ec-main-mostpop2.

611 Adam Sorensen, "ALEC: What It Does and Why Three Major Corporations Cut Ties," *Time* (April 9, 2012), http://swampland.time.com/2012/04/09/alec-what-it-does-and-why-three-major-corporations-cut-ties/?iid=ec-main-mostpop2.

612 Adam Sorensen, "ALEC: What It Does and Why Three Major Corporations Cut Ties," *Time* (April 9, 2012), http://swampland.time.com/2012/04/09/alec-what-it-does-and-why-three-major-corporations-cut-ties/?iid=ec-main-mostpop2.

613 Salvador Rizzo, "Some of Christie's biggest bills match model legislation from D.C. group called ALEC," *New Jersey.com* (April 1, 2012), http://www.nj.com/news/index.ssf/2012/04/alec_model_bills_used_in_nj_la.html.

614 Salvador Rizzo, "Some of Christie's biggest bills match model legislation from D.C. group called ALEC," *New Jersey.com* (April 1, 2012), http://www.nj.com/news/index.ssf/2012/04/alec_model_bills_used_in_nj_la.html.

615 Salvador Rizzo, "Some of Christie's biggest bills match model legislation from D.C. group called ALEC," *New Jersey.com* (April 1, 2012), http://www.nj.com/news/index.ssf/2012/04/alec_model_bills_used_in_nj_la.html.

616 Salvador Rizzo, "Some of Christie's biggest bills match model legislation from D.C. group called ALEC," *New Jersey.com* (April 1, 2012), http://www.nj.com/news/index.ssf/2012/04/alec_model_bills_used_in_nj_la.html.

617 John Nichols, "ALEC Exposed," *The Nation* (Aug. 1-8, 2011), http://www.thenation.com/article/161978/alec-exposed.

618 Adam Sorensen, "ALEC: What It Does and Why Three Major Corporations Cut Ties," *Time* (April 9, 2012), http://swampland.time.com/2012/04/09/alec-what-it-does-and-why-three-major-corporations-cut-ties/?iid=ec-main-mostpop2.

619 Adam Sorensen, "ALEC: What It Does and Why Three Major Corporations Cut Ties," *Time* (April 9, 2012), http://swampland.time.com/2012/04/09/alec-what-it-does-and-why-three-major-corporations-cut-ties/?iid=ec-main-mostpop2.

620 Laura Sullivan, "Prison Economics Help Drive Ariz. Immigration Law," *NPR* (Feb. 22, 2012), http://www.npr.org/2010/10/28/130833741/prison-economics-help-drive-ariz-immigration-law.

621 John Nichols, "ALEC Exposed," *The Nation* (Aug. 1-8, 2011), http://www.thenation.com/article/161978/alec-exposed.

622 William Styron, Introduction to *The Cunning of History: The Holocaust and the American Future,* by Richard L. Rubenstein (New York: Harper Perennial, 1987), p. xi.

623 William Styron, Introduction to *The Cunning of History: The Holocaust and the American Future,* by Richard L. Rubenstein (New York: Harper Perennial, 1987), p. xi.

624 Richard L. Rubenstein, *The Cunning of History: The Holocaust and the American Future,* (New York: Harper Perennial, 1987), p. 54.

625 Richard L. Rubenstein, *The Cunning of History: The Holocaust and the American Future,* (New York: Harper Perennial, 1987), pp. 51-52.

626 Richard L. Rubenstein, *The Cunning of History: The Holocaust and the American Future,* (New York: Harper Perennial, 1987), p. 55.

627 "Bad Blood: The Tuskegee Syphilis Study," Claude Moore Health Sciences Library, http://www.hsl.virginia.edu/historical/medical_history/bad_blood/.

628 Richard L. Rubenstein, *The Cunning of History: The Holocaust and the American Future* (New York: Harper Perennial, 1987), p. 60.

629 Richard L. Rubenstein, *The Cunning of History: The Holocaust and the American Future* (New York: Harper Perennial, 1987), p. 83.

CHAPTER TWENTY-SIX

630 Charles T. Sprading, *Liberty and the Great Libertarians* (Ludwig von Mises Institute, 2007), p. 330.

631 A confederate is a person who is hired by the experimenter to play a subject. In reality, confederates are actors who are aware of the purpose of the experiment. In Milgram the confederates pretended to receive painful shocks, but in reality, no shocks were administered.

632 Stanley Milgram, "Behavioral Study of Obedience," *Journal of Abnormal and Social Psychology* 67, no. 4 (1963): 371-8, http://psycnet.apa.org/journals/abn/67/4/371.pdf.

633 Jerry Burger, "Replicating Milgram: Would people still obey today?," *American Psychologist* 64, no. 1 (2009): 1-11, accessed June 20, 2012, http://psycnet.apa.org/journals/amp/64/1/1.pdf.

634 Philip Zimbardo, "Stanford Prison Experiment: A Simulation Study of the Psychology of Imprisonment," (1971), www.prisonexp.org.

635 Norm Stamper, "Occupy the Police," *Nation* 293, no. 22, (2011): 6-8, http://web.ebscohost.com/ehost/pdfviewer/pdfviewer?sid=9ccce215-f1d0-4873-9c52-57192c54859c%40sessionmgr114&vid=4&hid=126.

636 Eungkyoon Lee, "Socio-Political Contexts, Identity Formation and Regulatory Compliance," *Administration and Society* 40, no. 7, (2008): 741-769, http://aas.sagepub.com/content/40/7/741.full.pdf+html.

637 Brian Lawton, "Levels of Nonlethal Force: An Examination of Individual, Situational and Contextual Factors," *Journal of Research in Crime and Delinquency* 44, no. 2, (2007): 163-184, accessed June 21, 2012, http://journals.ohiolink.edu/ejc/pdf.cgi/Lawton_Brian_A.pdf?issn=00224278&issue=v44i0002&article=163_lonfaeoisacf.

638 Adam Liptak, "A Ticket, 3 Taser Jolts and, Perhaps, a Trip to the Supreme Court," *New York Times* (May 14, 2012), http://www.nytimes.com/2012/05/15/us/police-taser-use-on-pregnant-woman-goes-before-supreme-court.html.

639 *Cockrell v. City of Cincinnati*, 468 Fed. Appx. 491 (6th Cir. 2012), http://www.ca6.uscourts.gov/opinions.pdf/12a0216n-06.pdf.

640 Jorge da Gloria, Daniele Duda, Earzaneh Pahiavan & Phillippe Bnnet, "Weapons Effect Revisited: Motor Effects of the Reception of Aversive Stimulation and Exposure to Pictures of Firearms," *Aggressive Behavior* 15, no. 4 (1989): 265-27, http://web.ebscohost.com/ehost/pdfviewer/pdfviewer?sid=4ab26126-2893-4893-918a-f6d572c7ec4f%40sessionmgr113&vid=9&hid=105.

641 Robert Johnson, "The Pentagon is Offering Free Military Hardware To Every Police Department in the U.S.," *Business Insider* (2011), http://www.businessinsider.com/program-1033-military-equipment-police-2011-12.

642 Mark Gado, "The Kitty Genovese Murder," *TruTV*, http://www.trutv.com/library/crime/serial_killers/predators/kitty_genovese/1.html.

643 P. Meyer, *Conformity and group pressure: If Hitler asked you to electrocute a stranger would you? Probably* (Free Press, 2003).

644 Phillip Zimbardo, "On 'Obedience to Authority,'" *American Psychologist* (1974): 566-567, accessed June 25, 2012, http://psycnet.apa.org/journals/amp/29/7/566b.pdf.

Part Seven: The Point of No Return?

645 http://en.wikiquote.org/wiki/Learned_Hand

646 Robert F. Kennedy, "Day of Affirmation Address," University of Capetown, South Africa (June 6, 1966), http://www.theconversation.org/archive/eulogy.html.

CHAPTER TWENTY-SEVEN

647 "Production Notes for V for Vendetta," http://en.wikipedia.org/wiki/V_for_Vendetta_(film).

648 Michael Grabell, "U.S. Government Glossed Over Cancer Concerns As It Rolled Out Airport X-Ray Scanners," *ProPublica* (Nov. 1, 2011), https://www.propublica.org/article/u.s.-government-glossed-over-cancer-concerns-as-it-rolled-out-airport-x-ray.

CHAPTER TWENTY-EIGHT

649 Robert J. Walker, *Let My People Go!: The Miracle of the Montgomery Bus Boycott* (University Press of America, 2007), p. 249.

650 Martin Luther King Jr., *Stride Toward Freedom: The Montgomery Story* (Boston: Beacon Press, 1958, 2010), p. 11.

651 Martin Luther King Jr., *Stride Toward Freedom: The Montgomery Story* (Boston: Beacon Press, 1958, 2010), p. 11.

652 Martin Luther King Jr., *Stride Toward Freedom: The Montgomery Story* (Boston: Beacon Press, 1958, 2010), p. 119.

653 Martin Luther King Jr., *Stride Toward Freedom: The Montgomery Story* (Boston: Beacon Press, 1958, 2010), p. 136.

654 Martin Luther King Jr., *Stride Toward Freedom: The Montgomery Story* (Boston: Beacon Press, 1958, 2010), p. 138.

CHAPTER TWENTY-NINE

655 Letter of Thomas Jefferson to William Stevens Smith, 1788 (*), FE 5:3.

656 Nat Hentoff, "Fierce Watchdog of the Constitution," *The Village Voice* (Aug. 5, 2003), http://www.villagevoice.com/2003-08-05/news/fierce-watchdog-of-the-constitution/.

657 *The Papers of Thomas Jefferson*. Edited by Julian P. Boyd et al. Princeton (Princeton University Press, 1950), http://press-pubs.uchicago.edu/founders/print_documents/a7s12.html.

658 James M. Washington, ed., *A Testament of Hope: The Essential Writings of Martin Luther King Jr.* (HarperSanFrancisco, 1991), p. 68.

CHAPTER THIRTY

659 James Washington, ed., *A Testament of Hope: The Essential Writings and Speeches of Martin Luther King Jr.* (HarperSanFrancisco, 1991), p. 292.

660 *As quoted in* Morris Berman, *Dark Ages America: The Final Phase of Empire* (W.W. Norton and Co., 2006), p. 282.

661 James Washington, ed., *A Testament of Hope: The Essential Writings and Speeches of Martin Luther King Jr.* (HarperSanFrancisco, 1991), p. 292.

662 Henry David Thoreau, "Resistance to Civil Government," (1849). Reprinted in *Walden, Civil Disobedience, and Other Writings*. Ed. William Rossi. (W.W. Norton 2008) p. 231.

663 Henry David Thoreau, "Resistance to Civil Government," (1849). Reprinted in *Walden, Civil Disobedience, and Other Writings*. Ed. William Rossi. (W.W. Norton 2008) p. 231.

664 Erich Fromm, *On Civil Disobedience: Why Freedom Means Saying "No" to Power* (First Harper Perennial Modern Thought, 2010), p. 5.

665 Letter of Thomas Jefferson to William Stephens Smith (1787), ME 6:373.

666 Howard Zinn, *Failure to Quit* (South End Press, 2002), p. 45.

CHAPTER THIRTY-ONE

667 James Washington, ed., *A Testament of Hope: The Essential Writings and Speeches of Martin Luther King Jr.* (HarperSanFrancisco, 1991), p. 292.

668 John W. Whitehead, *The Change Manifesto: Join the Block by Block Movement to Remake America* (Sourcebooks, 2008), pp. 225-234.

669 Carmella B'Hahn, "Be the change you wish to see: An interview with Arun Gandhi," *Reclaiming Children and Youth* [Bloomington] Vol.10, No. 1 (Spring 2001), p. 6.

Index

A

B

D

G

H

N

O

Q

R

U

V

About the Author

John Whitehead is an attorney and author who has written, debated, and practiced widely in the area of constitutional law, human rights, and popular culture. Widely recognized as one of the nation's most vocal and involved civil liberties attorneys, Whitehead's approach to civil liberties issues has earned him numerous accolades and accomplishments, including the Hungarian Medal of Freedom and the 2010 Milner S. Ball Lifetime Achievement Award for "[his] decades of difficult and important work, as well as [his] impeccable integrity in defending civil liberties for all."

As nationally syndicated columnist Nat Hentoff observed about Whitehead: "John Whitehead is not only one of the nation's most consistent and persistent civil libertarians. He is also a remarkably perceptive illustrator of our popular culture, its insights and dangers. I often believe that John Whitehead is channeling the principles of James Madison, who would be very proud of him."

Whitehead's concern for the persecuted and oppressed led him, in 1982, to establish The Rutherford Institute, a nonprofit civil liberties and human rights organization headquartered in Charlottesville, Virginia. Deeply committed to protecting the constitutional freedoms of every American and the integral human rights of all people, The Rutherford Institute has emerged as a prominent leader in the national dialogue on civil liberties and human rights and a formidable champion of the Constitution. Whitehead serves as the Institute's president and spokesperson.

Whitehead writes a weekly commentary for *The Huffington Post* and LewRockwell.com, which is also carried by daily and weekly newspapers and web publications across the country and is available on The Rutherford Institute's website (www.rutherford.org). Whitehead is the author of some twenty books, including *The Freedom Wars* (2010), *The Change Manifesto* (2008), and *Grasping for the Wind* (HarperCollins/Zondervan, 2001), the companion documentary series to the book of the same name, which also received critical acclaim. The series was awarded two Silver World Medals at the New York Film and Video Festival.

Born in 1946 in Tennessee, John W. Whitehead earned a Bachelor of Arts degree from the University of Arkansas in 1969 and a Juris Doctorate degree from the University of Arkansas School of Law in 1974. He served as an officer in the United States Army from 1969 to 1971. He lives in Charlottesville, Virginia.